CONTESTING CAPITALISM?

Published in our
centenary year
~ **2004** ~
MANCHESTER
UNIVERSITY
PRESS

CONTESTING CAPITALISM?

Left parties and European integration

RICHARD DUNPHY

Manchester University Press
Manchester and New York

distributed exclusively in the USA by Palgrave

Copyright © Richard Dunphy 2004

The right of Richard Dunphy to be identified as the author of this work has been asserted by him in accordance with the Copyright, Designs and Patents Act 1988.

Published by Manchester University Press
Oxford Road, Manchester M13 9NR, UK
and Room 400, 175 Fifth Avenue, New York, NY 10010, USA
www.manchesteruniversitypress.co.uk

Distributed exclusively in the USA by
Palgrave, 175 Fifth Avenue, New York,
NY 10010, USA

Distributed exclusively in Canada by
UBC Press, University of British Columbia, 2029 West Mall,
Vancouver, BC, Canada V6T 1Z2

British Library Cataloguing-in-Publication Data
A catalogue record for this book is available from the British Library

Library of Congress Cataloging-in-Publication Data applied for

ISBN 0 7190 6803 7 *hardback*
     0 7190 6804 5 *paperback*

First published 2004

13 12 11 10 09 08 07 06 05 04   10 9 8 7 6 5 4 3 2 1

Typeset by
D R Bungay Associates, Burghfield, Berks

Printed and bound in Great Britain
by Biddles Ltd, Kings Lynn, Norfolk

CONTENTS

Preface and acknowledgements	*page* vii
Abbreviations	x
1 Theoretical perspectives: left visions of European integration	1
2 Historical context: from Eurocommunism to the 'Euro-left'? Western European communist parties and the European Union until 1989	22
3 Case studies: European Union policy and the Left parties	72
3.1 The Italian Communist Party (PCI) and its communist successor parties (PRC and PdCI)	72
3.2 The French Communist Party (PCF)	91
3.3 The Communist Party of Greece (KKE) and the Coalition of Left and Progress (Synaspismos)	103
3.4 The Portuguese Communist Party (PCP)	113
3.5 The Communist Party of Spain/United Left (PCE/IU)	121
3.6 The Danish Socialist People's Party (SF)	131
3.7 The Finnish Left Alliance (VAS)	139
3.8 The Left Party of Sweden (V)	148
4 Comparative perspectives	156
5 Conclusion: Europe and the future of the Left parties	169
Bibliography	174
Index	193

For Paddy Gillan
and Steve Mathewson

PREFACE AND ACKNOWLEDGEMENTS

This book investigates the impact of European political and economic integration processes upon leftwing political parties that have traditionally contested the free market, neo-liberal ideas and principles that the European Union embodies. At the same time, it examines the evolution of policy and thinking on European integration within some of these parties. Historically speaking at least, these parties can be broadly described as *transformatory parties*, in the sense that they have, to varying degrees, aspired to a transformation of the liberal capitalist model of politics and economy. The extent to which they actually offer a coherent, practical and comprehensible alternative to this model of European integration is obviously a key theme that runs throughout the book.

My primary interest is in parties to the left of mainstream social democracy (which finds its embodiment in the Party of European Socialists, or PES). Whilst the choice of which parties to include is to some extent arbitrary, I have decided to concentrate on those parties that have had MEPs in the European Parliament over the past fifteen years or more (or, in the case of Sweden and Finland, since those countries joined the European Union), and whose MEPs sat during the 1999-2004 parliamentary sessions as members or associate members of the Confederal Group of the European United Left/Nordic Green Left (GUE/NGL). (An important exception is the pre-1991 Italian Communist Party, (PCI), whose inclusion I have deemed essential in setting the historical background.) This choice has the advantage of limiting the study to parties that are self-defined as being to the left of social democracy, that are of some electoral significance in their respective countries, and that engaged with the main European integration policy issues over the years, allowing us to trace the evolution of their visions of Europe. Most of the parties that belong to the GUE/NGL have their origins in the Communist or other Marxist traditions. Some, might be described as 'new left' or left-libertarian in nature (such as the Danish Socialist People's Party). Yet others, might be described as green-left, or at any rate are attempting to reinvent themselves as such. The influence of these traditions on their evolution, ideology and strategic thinking is therefore worth examining.

The extent to which the left parties are indeed *contesting capitalism* in any serious or distinctive way seems to invite comparison with what might be described as the other left-of-centre party families represented in the European Parliament, namely the Greens and the PES. In a comparative chapter, I therefore examine the visions of European integration emanating from these party groupings and pose some questions concerning points of convergence, overlap and outright disagreement with the left or *transformatory* parties.

The book is divided into five chapters. The first chapter seeks to set the scene by examining some theoretical perspectives on European integration coming from the left. Not all of the intellectuals and writers whose work is examined here are associated with the parties we will study; but the debates on the nature and future of the EU that they have engaged in, and the competing visions of European integration they have produced, form an essential back-drop to the evolution of party policy and the divergences between the various left parties that we will explore. In short, the first chapter seeks to conceptualise some of the divisions within the left and to problematise some labels that are commonly used, such as 'pro-Europeans' and 'Eurosceptics'. In terms of party politics, these divisions were reflected in the widely differing ideological and strategic thinking on national, European and international issues that, by the end of the 1970s, divided the main communist parties of Western Europe, but which also had profound resonance within the social democratic tradition. The second chapter places the debate on Europe in a historical context by examining how these divisions arose in the 1970s and 1980s, highlighting the central importance of the European issue. It also considers the fate of the Communists and Allies Group in the European Parliament – an unsuccessful experiment in transnational party co-operation that failed to survive the tumultuous end of the 1980s. Some of the issues raised by this failure on the part of the left parties to develop a strong European party federation (along the lines of the PES, for example) still have resonance today, a decade after the dissolution of the leading 'Eurocommunist' party, the PCI, and the assimilation of its majority wing to social democracy.

The third chapter consists of case studies of the European integration policies of various Left parties. In each case, I examine how the party's policy on European integration emerged, developed and/or changed during recent decades. I examine parties from eight countries: the Italian Communist Party and its communist successor parties; the French Communist Party; the Greek Communist Party and the Greek post-communist Synaspismos formation; the Portuguese Communist Party; the Communist Party of Spain and its allies in the United Left coalition; the Danish Socialist People's Party; the Left Party of Sweden; and the Finnish Left Alliance.

The fourth chapter introduces a comparative perspective by examining the visions of European integration formulated by some Green and social democratic parties and questions whether there is a distinctive 'left' view of European integration at all. Finally, some conclusions about Left parties and the challenges of European integration are drawn and I also consider the difficulties of transnational party co-operation and strategic planning that the Left parties continue to experience, partly as a result of their historical trajectories and partly as a result of ideological disagreements, focusing on the European Parliament.

In this book I try to achieve four things. First, I want to present the reader with a short, accessible summary of where the left parties stand on the 'big questions' of European integration today. Second, I am interested in examining processes of ideological and policy change within the left parties, specifically the pressures for, and obstacles to, change on the question of European integration. Third, I am interested in the extent to which the European Union itself increasingly sets the political context in which left parties – as with all other parties – must operate. This raises the issue of the potentialities and limitations of left and anti-capitalist politics after the collapse of communism and the rise of globalisation. Finally, I address the thorny problem of inter-party co-operation on the left at the supranational level.

I am indebted to colleagues and friends who have assisted me in various ways, above all to: M. Jean Marie Palayret of the Historical Archives of the European Union in Florence; Professor Luciano Bolis; Dr Serena Sordi and Dr James Newell for their hospitality in Florence; the staff of the Library of the European University Institute; and Dr Mikael Skou Andersen of the University of Aarhus. My colleague Stephen Hopkins has placed at my disposal the results of his research into dissent within the French Communist Party; and I have benefited from discussions with Hanne Coster Waldau about Danish politics. Steve Mathewson read sections of the book while it was 'work-in-progress' and gave me the benefit of his perceptive and always constructive criticism.

I am indebted also to the various MEPs and European Parliament officials who kindly provided me with photocopies of party documents and materials and willingly answered my queries about party policy, especially: Roberto Barzanti, Biagio de Giovanni, Proinsias de Rossa, Roberto Galtieri, Pedro Guerreiro, Stellan Hermansson, Steve McGiffen, Jonas Sjöstedt and Luigi Vinci. Pekka Ristelä, International Secretary of the Finnish Left Alliance, was extremely helpful, as was Anders Andersen, International Secretary of the Danish Socialist People's Party, Daniel Cirera of the International Department of the French Communist Party and Ana Serrano of the Portuguese Communist Party. I am grateful to Norrie MacQueen and Stewart Lloyd Jones for help with translating some documents from Portuguese. All translations from Italian, French and Spanish are my own.

I gratefully acknowledge the financial assistance of the European Commission and of the Nuffield Foundation, both of which have provided me with small grants that facilitated aspects of this research.

This book is dedicated to Paddy Gillan and Steve Mathewson who have long shared my interest in, and commitment to, the politics of the European left.

Richard Dunphy
Dundee

ABBREVIATIONS

CDU	Coligação Democrática Unitária (United Democratic Coalition, Portugal)
DC	Democrazia Cristiana (Christian Democratic Party, Italy)
DS	Democratici di Sinistra (Left Democrats, Italy)
GUE/NGL	Confederal Group of the European United Left/Nordic Green Left
IU	Izquierda Unida (United Left, Italy)
KKE	Kommunistiko Komma Elladas (Communist Party of Greece)
KKE-es	Kommunistiko Komma Elladas-es (Communist Party of Greece, Interior)
PASOK	Panelliniko Socialistiko Kinima (Pan-Hellenic Socialist Movement of Greece)
PCE	Partido Comunista de España (Communist Party of Spain)
PCF	Parti Communiste Français (French Communist Party)
PCI	Partito Comunista Italiano (Italian Communist Party)
PCP	Partido Comunista Português (Portuguese Communist Party)
PdCI	Partito dei Comunisti Italiani (Party of Italian Communists)
PDS	Partito Democratico della Sinistra (Democratic Party of the Left, Italy)
PRC	Partito della Rifondazione Comunista (Party of Communist Refoundation, Italy)
PS	Parti Socialiste (Socialist Party, France)
PSI	Partito Socialista Italiano (Italian Socialist Party)
PSOE	Partido Socialista Obrero Español (Spanish Socialist Workers' Party)
PSP	Partido Socialista Português (Portuguese Socialist Party)
SAP	Socialdemokraterna Arbetarepartiet (Social Democratic Workers' Party, Sweden)
SF	Socialistisk Folkeparti (Socialist People's Party, Denmark)
SPD	Sozialdemokratische Partei Deutschlands (Social Democratic Party of Germany)
V	Vänsterpartiet (Left Party, Sweden)
VAS	Vasemmistoliitto (Left Alliance, Finland)

1
THEORETICAL PERSPECTIVES:
LEFT VISIONS OF EUROPEAN INTEGRATION

Introduction

Socialist parties are unlikely to work hard at eroding national prerogatives. They too derive their legitimacy from nationally based electorates. When in opposition, lack of power may lead them to support an extension of the powers of the European Parliament. But in office, the pressures may work the other way, towards preserving the prerogatives of their own nation-states. The close collaboration between the modern democratic nation-state and the parties of the Left has profoundly marked the experience of the last hundred years. These habits will not be easily discarded. (Sassoon, 1996b, 771)

To the degree that a rule can be advanced, parties of the left opposed intergovernmental decision-making – and most importantly the European Community – for longer and more vehemently than those of the right. They were apt to see in EC aspirations to a common market the seeds of a new international capital. With the same qualification as to generalisation, the reverse tendency now holds. Socialists and social democrats – especially party leaders and activists – tend to view the Union as a vehicle for interventionist trade, labour and environmental policy, while their opponents on the right are more likely to bemoan the loss of national sovereignty this role entails. (Butler, 1995, 111–12).

It is a well-known and widely recognised fact that parties of the West European left tended, in the main, to view the creation of the EEC in 1957 with intense suspicion, if not downright hostility. Social democratic parties – what we might call the parties of the Second International – had, since the debacle of 1914–18, nailed their colours to the mast of the 'modern democratic nation-state' and to policies of national Keynesianism. Most continued to do so, at least until the 1980s. Communist parties – the parties of the Third International – tended towards their own Soviet-influenced version of 'national roads to socialism'. Sassoon, in his epic history of the West European left during the twentieth century, quoted above, analyses the processes by which almost all social democratic parties and a minority of communist parties in Western Europe came during the 1970s and 1980s to accept the reality of the European Union and even, as Butler implies, to celebrate its progressive potential. Yet the fact is that the 1980s in particular was a decade of profound regression for the left in general, and the shift in attitudes towards the EU may not reflect a profound change in the nature and direction of European integration so much as a profound loss of faith in national Keynesianism and in the power of the nation-state as an agent of change on the part of many left and social democratic parties. These were the years, after all, that witnessed the rise of so-called New Right neo-liberalism with its attacks on the powers of trade unions, programmes of privatisations and reductions in workers' rights under the banner of 'labour market flexibility'; the rise of a culture of consumerism with negative implications for the left's traditions of solidarity and community; the apparent electoral triumph of a politics that seemed to place individual greed before redistribution of wealth and social justice; and a disastrous fragmentation and decline of the traditional working-class. The 1980s opened with high hopes generated by the election of a reformist Mitterrand government in France in 1981 on an ambitious platform of reflation and redistribution and closed with the apparent headlong embrace of privatisation policies by the French Socialists – tempered only by the hope that maybe Jacques Delors (a social Catholic, as much as a Socialist) might rescue something of the faded dream with the European Social Charter of (very basic) workers' rights. The 1990s opened with the hope that the removal of the deathly shadow cast by Stalinism in Eastern Europe, the end of the Cold War between the USSR and the USA, and the reunification of Germany might herald the renaissance of the European left and closed with social democratic parties seemingly more on the defensive than ever before and communist and left parties throughout the EU countries further reduced in political influence and size.

It is therefore perhaps timely to consider whether the hopes and fears that left-of-centre parties have expressed about European integration have so far proven well founded – whether the EU as a (quasi-)state actor has emerged as an agent of progressive political change or has increased, deepened and accelerated processes of capitalist exploitation. And whether left-of-centre parties have articulated a vision of European integration that amounts to a credible alternative programme or have either retreated into an oppositional laager or been simply swept along by events.

The present study will concentrate on what I have called transformatory parties – parties to the left of social democracy that have historically called for a transcendence of the capitalist economic system and that still voice such aspirations. Having said that, the European visions of social democratic and Green parties will also be considered in order to give the study a comparative dimension and to allow the reader to interrogate whether left parties' European integration policies possess a unique or distinctive aspect – what an early 1980s Berlinguerian in Italy might have described as the quality of *diversità*.

What is beyond dispute is that questions of European policy are now central to the politics of the left – and indeed the right – as never before. Many of the dilemmas that confront any left or social democratic party – economic and social restructuring; the impact of globalisation; political dealignment and realignment; the debate over 'Fortress Europe', immigration and racism; issues of workers' rights; environmental degradation; the apparent decline in the efficacy of democratic politics; to name but a few – can only be addressed at a European, and indeed global, level. The 1990s, of course, saw a marked acceleration of European integration with the ratification of the Maastricht and Amsterdam Treaties, the establishment of the European Central Bank, the advent of the euro, and the gathering momentum behind the expansion of the EU towards the east. The 'pick-up' really began in the mid-1980s when the European Parliament's 1984 ratification of a Draft Treaty on European Union, followed a few years later by the signing of the Single European Act, effectively ended a period of relative stagnation in EU affairs. All of these events have had a profound impact on the left parties that we will examine, often changing the political context in which they operate in ways that have been unsettling and even undermining.

The collapse of the USSR and the political systems of East European countries where communist parties held absolute power also contributed to a rising feeling, in the 1990s, that there was no feasible alternative to neo-liberalism. Even left parties that were sincerely critical of the Stalinist model of socialism have experienced the negative fall-out: utopian visions of Europe that were developed during the Cold War years suddenly look very dated. Calls for 'real' European unity as opposed to the 'little Europe' of the EC/EU have to cope with the reality that the countries of post-communist Europe are queuing up to join the EU – and their admission to membership may well exacerbate unequal development, and undermine further the influence and appeal of radical left parties. Slogans that sounded pretty convincing in the 1970s and 1980s – about the need for a Europe that is neither pro-Soviet nor pro-American ('neither Moscow now Washington but the European working-class') – now struggle, in the post-Soviet era, to fend off charges of anti-Americanism. In short, we need to bear in mind at all times not only how left parties propose to change (or challenge) the EU, but how the politics of European integration and the wider political context of European reunification have challenged, at times changed and at times profoundly unsettled the left parties.

In this chapter, I examine some differing approaches to European integration that have been adopted on the left in recent years. There is a considerable variety of positions and emphases, reflecting the clashing traditions of the European left as well as differing national and regional contexts in which left politics has developed. An exploration of the logic inherent in some of these approaches will help set the scene for an examination of the different left parties later in the book. Finally, in this chapter, I consider the question of the dynamics of party change, concentrating of course on the issue of European policy.

(At least four) approaches to European integration

According to Luciana Castellina, writing towards the end of the 1980s, most left-wing parties initially opposed the EEC for three main reasons (Castellina, 1988, 26–7). First, they saw it as having emerged out of a Cold War division of Europe and as having the logic of consolidating the 'the Atlantic system capitalist structures' – in short, as being, more or less, the economic arm of NATO. Second, there was a widespread concern that the USA would use the institutions of the EEC to establish its economic and political control, once and for all, over Western Europe, eliminating the potential for West European autonomy. Given the fact that the USA had used Marshall Aid to force the Communists out of post-war coalition governments in a number of countries in 1947–48, this was perhaps a not unreasonable worry. Third, and this is a factor that influenced many social democratic as well as communist parties, the left parties tended to distrust a Treaty of Rome that was written largely by right-of-centre governing elites in Western Europe and that seemed inspired by free market capitalist principles.

For Castellina, the left in general was slow to move beyond these positions. Many communist parties continued their hostility to the EEC, largely unchanged; many social democratic parties came to accept the reality of the EEC but largely ignored it, focusing their strategic efforts at the level of the nation-state. A profound rethink really only came about within part of the West European left during the 1980s (although the seeds of this were of course present in some parties much earlier). A position emerged that saw the EEC as 'a positive ground for a socialist alternative' (Castellina, 1988, 27).

In actual fact, by the mid-1980s at any rate, it is probably possible to speak of at least four discernible strands of thought on the West European left. Admittedly, some of these tend to shade into one another and the question of when a political party or formation has crossed the line from one to another is a matter of political judgment. The first and most distinctive position is that which sees the EEC/EU as an agent of multinational capitalist exploitation and of German or American hegemony, pure and simple. It threatens workers' rights, national welfare standards, and national democracy and sovereignty. It promotes and sustains gross economic inequalities and unsustainable development. It stands in a relationship of exploitation with countries of the developing world and indeed with would-be member states from Eastern Europe. It threatens to become a new capitalist military superpower and/or (the emphasis sometimes changes) underpins US militarism. It is diametrically and fundamentally incompatible with a socialist, or even mildly progressive, programme and indeed many of the developments of the past fifteen years within the EU have the effect of making such a programme illegal. For all these reasons, left parties should oppose membership of the EU in the first place, or continue to campaign for withdrawal from membership once their countries have joined. Sometimes this conclusion is implicit rather than explicit. It is perhaps most explicit in the analyses of the Greek Communist Party (KKE), the leftist adherents of the Danish anti-EU movements, such as the June Movement, and indeed it used to characterise most of the Nordic Green/Left parties, but these are no longer as decisively 'pro-withdrawal' as they once were.

A second position would agree with most of the foregoing analysis as a description of how the EU is currently constituted, and of how it has historically developed, but nevertheless argue that a campaign for withdrawal from membership of the EU, or for the immediate dissolution of the EU, is unrealistic and perhaps even undesirable. Influenced perhaps by Marxist economic determinism to some extent, its advocates would argue that one cannot turn back the clock or ignore the extent to which the EU has contributed to the development of productive forces. One must move forward. Thus, it is accepted (sometimes reluctantly and pragmatically) that a retreat to all-out national protectionism is not 'really on'. Moreover, the fact that campaigns for withdrawal from EU membership would place the left in an uncomfortable alliance with extremist right wing, xenophobic and racist elements is a further incentive to back away from the 'withdrawal' position. Instead, what is advocated is a root-and-branch restructuring of the EU, turning its hitherto priorities upside down, and challenging the free market, capitalist logic inherent in the Single Act, the Maastricht Treaty, the Common Agricultural Policy, the operations of the European Central Bank, etc. How this is to be achieved is of course a moot point – and a central question that will be raised later in this book. For now, we may note that this position tends to be characteristic of most of the Nordic Green/Left parties and of the French Communist Party, for example, since the late 1980s. In practical terms, it may lead these parties to reject capitalist aspects of the EU that they find unpalatable – they may campaign against the Maastricht Treaty or the Euro, for example – yet to laud and support calls for stronger EU environmental legislation or stronger protection for vulnerable workers.

A third position is also critical of the limited and restrictive nature of the EU as it has developed to date but much more enthusiastic about the prospects for a strong reformism at the EU level. To a much greater extent than the advocates of the second position, its proponents see the EU as a potential agent of social and political change – indeed of a regeneration of the European left. They tend to argue the cause for more European integration, sometimes in the direction of a political federation, seeing in the development of strong democratic political institutions – a European Parliament that can legislate and elect the European Commission, for example – the key to providing the EU with the mechanism it needs (but currently lacks) to stand up to the powerful multinational corporations and to expand the 'democratic space'. Such a position is strongly reformist and also, of course, strongly idealist. Accepting that the nation-state can no longer deliver the traditional goals of the left – a point painfully underlined by the failures of the Mitterrand and Papandreou governments in the 1980s, for example – it posits a reinvention of a strong and interventionist social democracy at the EU level as a way forward. Such a position was characteristic of the Italian Communist Party during the 1970s and 1980s and is still characteristic today of many Italian and Spanish communists, sizable constituencies within some of the Nordic left parties, and many on the leftwing of the social democratic parties (one thinks of Oskar Lafontaine, within the SPD). Indeed, it is on the terrain of this 'strong reformism', as I would call it, that pro-integrationists within the ranks of new left parties, communist and ex-communist parties and social democratic parties effectively find common ground. This is perhaps the terrain of that elusive 'Euro-left' that Enrico Berlinguer and the Italian communists dreamed of in their search for a 'new internationalism' during the traumatic years after the Soviet invasion of Afghanistan and the imposition of martial law in Poland.

Advocates of this strong reformism tend to be critically supportive of policies such as the ratification of Maastricht, the introduction of the euro, etc. They condemn the rampant neo-liberalism and weak regulation associated with such policies – they would advocate, for example, democratic control over the European Central Bank and the prioritising of the fight against mass unemployment – but nevertheless argue that their ratification, even if in an unsatisfactory way, is a first and necessary step towards longer-term goals. Of course, a position of strong reformism – of critical support – is a difficult balancing act to maintain with credibility, especially when the parties in question are fairly small and unable to exercise much influence over events. There is always the risk of being blown off course and seeming to support policies that are inimical to the interests of one's natural supporters. There is the constant danger that the inevitable search for political allies – in order to exercise some influence over the progress of events – will lead to a fatal erosion of political identity. There is the difficulty of sustaining a credible 'yes, but ...' position and explaining it to supporters and potential voters when the political climate is dominated by media sound bites, the decline in traditional party allegiances and the voting public displays a growing cynicism. Some would argue that the fate of the Italian Communist Party from the mid-1980s onwards illustrates all of these dangers and difficulties only too clearly.

There is the danger, in short, of crossing the line that separates strong reformism from the fourth strand of thought on EU policy. This, for want of a better description, I will call 'weak reformism'. (In the Italian political lexicon during the 1980s, the politics of the Craxi government were often referred to as a 'reformism without reforms'.) Another, if no more elegant, way of putting this would be to contrast critical with uncritical pro-integrationism. By this I mean that the pursuit of more and deeper European integration can appear to become, at a certain point, an end in itself for some on the left. The building of a United States of Europe (however this is expressed) becomes the primary project of the left, 'Europe' being seen as a panacea, an all-powerful magical invocation to be produced when faced with seemingly insurmountable or incomprehensible problems. To sustain this, a historic compromise at the European level between 'pro-European' political forces of centre-left and centre-right is urged. Thus, by eliding European socialist idealism and European federalist idealism – both sometimes presented as the one-and-the-same expression of anti-fascist European progressive thought, the repository of the best of the European Enlightenment – the difficult task of *imagining socialism* is sidestepped. The net outcome tends to be a more or less uncritical support for 'the European project' under the guise of 'modernisation'. This approach to Europe arguably came to characterise some social democratic parties in power in southern Europe in the 1980s, elements of New Labour in Britain in the late 1990s, and several social democratic parties elsewhere. None of the parties in the Confederal Group of the European United Left/Nordic Green Left (GUE/NGL) group in the European Parliament that I examine can be accused of adopting this position. But the Italian Communist Party was certainly open to the charge of having strayed over the line from strong reformism to weak reformism towards the end of its life, and it must be admitted that the temptation is always present for reasons that I hope will become clear.

This brief (and somewhat schematic) presentation of some of the possible responses to European integration from within the left parties should, I hope, succeed in drawing the reader's attention to the fact that attitudes and responses are often complex and nuanced, sometimes shade into one another, and always reflect both tactical and strategic, pragmatic and ideological considerations. For these reasons, I reject as too simplistic the tendency to divide the world into rival and mutually exclusive camps of 'Eurosceptics' and 'pro-Europeans'. Of course, sometimes *it is possible* to describe a party's position as straightforwardly anti- or pro-EU. More often, however, we are dealing with shades and degrees of enthusiasm for, and criticism of, integrationism.

Taggart (1998, 365–6), in his attempt to measure 'Euroscepticism' within Western European party systems, admits that 'opposition to and support for the EU are rarely either binary or absolute' and that the category of 'Euroscepticism' includes a variety of positions. Yet attachment to the concept seems inevitably to lead him into a potage of contradictions. For example, 'Euroscepticism' is defined as 'an encompassing term [that] expresses the idea of contingent or qualified opposition, as well as incorporating outright and unqualified opposition to the process of European integration'. Thus, he allows that 'not all sceptics are opponents [of the EU]' and that one may reject certain aspects of integration without rejecting it altogether. However, when he takes attitudes for or against the Maastricht Treaty as being indicative of degrees of 'Euroscepticism', he illustrates the problem with deploying this concept. For it is perfectly possible to oppose the Maastricht Treaty on the grounds that it was *not sufficiently integrationist* – that it didn't go far enough. It is difficult to see how useful it can be to dub such a position as 'Eurosceptic', especially as the label is overwhelmingly understood in popular parlance, and indeed in the academic literature, to denote one who is (to some degree) sceptical about the *desirability* of integration, and not merely the management or speed of that process. For example, it is logically possible to be a convinced European federalist on the left, who strongly supports the single European currency but bemoans the fact that it is to be managed by an undemocratic European Central Bank without any strong commitment to full employment, and then to face a *difficult tactical choice* as to whether one votes for or against the Maastricht Treaty or joining the Euro-zone. Parties and individuals, starting from the same general attitude, might well end up on different sides of the 'yes/no' debate for tactical reasons. Terms such as 'Eurosceptic' and 'Europhile' are highly problematic; even worse are blatantly polemical labels such as 'pro-European' and 'anti-European'. In what follows, I will endeavour not to lose sight of the fact that we are examining degrees of pro- and anti-integrationism – support for or opposition to 'the further integration of European economy and society' (McGiffen, 2001, 144).

Before we move on to examine the evolution of the policies of the left parties themselves, it may be useful to cast further light on the range of different perspectives on European integration to be found on the left and left-of-centre by examining briefly some writings on the subject by leading left and left-of-centre commentators. I am not implying that these intellectuals are in any sense 'mouthpieces' for the parties, or indeed the political traditions, that we will later examine; rather, some of their writings may give us a taste of the intellectual and political debates that have helped to shape the context in which processes of policy formation and policy change within left parties have taken place.

Writing just before the fall of the Berlin Wall and the sweeping transformations in European political and economic life that followed in its wake, Patrick Camiller saw the single market project that is so central to the European integration process as 'rest[ing] on essential aspects of the neo-liberal agenda of the 1980s'. These included increasing the profit levels of private capital by eroding trade union rights and bargaining positions, and segmenting the labour force, and reducing the capacity for state regulation:

> Whatever elements of indicative planning it may originally have contained, the programme of European integration has been progressively stripped down to a core idea that the removal of national barriers to capital movement and economic activity will clear the path to dynamic renewal of the European economy. It would be fundamentally wrong to imagine that the dense networks of institutions and norms which, in the post-war Fordist boom years, regulated the national markets of Western Europe are about to be replaced by a similar EC structure organized from Brussels. The task of the EU institutions ... will be to ensure that nothing stands in the way of the consolidation of giant trans-European blocs of capital operating within the broad internal market – and, above all, to ensure that the labour movement is not free to exert effective pressure on its national government or on EC institutions to block the multifarious corporate strategies for breaking down and flexibly circumventing positions of labour strength. (Camiller, 1989, 7–8)

Yet Camiller also argues that the lessons of Mitterrand's retreat in France in the early 1980s, and of the failure of the Soviet experiment, are that 'it is neither possible nor desirable to withdraw from the immensely complex and productive international division of labour'; rather, the left must think in terms of a programme for a pan-European recovery that seeks to provide an alternative model for economic development. In terms of political strategy, this involves seeking to mobilise support behind full employment policies and democratisation of economic policy-making (Camiller, 1989, 11–13). Much of this remains tantalisingly vague. Should the EU itself form the principal terrain upon which the left agitates and mobilises – should left parties campaign for democratisation of the EU institutions – or should they seek an alternative to the EU? The former would appear to be a more realistic implication perhaps. Other writers (Marquand, 1995, Milward, 1996, Wilde, 1994) are much more explicit in arguing for the necessity of a democratisation and development of the EU. For example, Marquand argues that, in the absence of stronger EU institutions able to exercise democratic control over policy, the social democratic project will remain utopian because 'the nation states of the Union will already have surrendered too much power to supranational institutions to implement it on the national level, while the institutions of the Union will continue to be too weak to implement it on the supranational level' (Marquand, 1995, 221). Wilde (1994, 181) even argues that the Maastricht Treaty, for all its flaws, 'probably offers the best chance for the Left to push for developing the strongest possible United States of Europe with full powers to the European Parliament and effective regional decentralisation to give citizens a variety of arenas in which to counter the dominant economic powers'. He recognises that much work needs to be done; the left suffers from major disadvantages in terms of organisation. 'The representatives of capital have put far greater resources into the lobbying process, and they represent interests which are consciously international. The nation-state remains the focus for labour movement activity, and there have been few examples of international industrial action.' Nevertheless, the Europeanisation and internationalisation of the left's political and economic programmes – both on the part of trade unions and political parties – is a logical and necessary step to take. The dream that Wilde holds out is a familiar one to leftwing advocates of integrationism – 'a strong European state with a Red-Green political leadership' challenging US economic hegemony (the euro versus the dollar), writing off the debts of the poorest countries in the world, and advocating a more interventionist approach and a more progressive management of trade policies. Wilde recognises that obstacles to such a future scenario are many, and include the danger of a 'Fortress Europe' institutionalising new forms of racism and marginalisation, and the 'world market logic' thwarting this new interventionist politics at the pan-European level. His basic conclusion, however, is that there is little possibility of any other strategy for the left having any chance of success (Wilde, 1994, 181–6). Indeed, such views gained even greater cogency following the Anglo-American war on Iraq in March–April 2003.

Opposition to that war was of course overwhelming on the European left (and not just the left), where it was seen as a war of imperialist aggression designed to secure the natural resources of Iraq for American strategic interests. The war raised important questions about the future direction of the EU. Would the USA succeed in dividing the EU and robbing it of momentum, playing off against each other what US Defense Secretary Donald Rumsfeld referred to as 'Old Europe' and 'New Europe' (the latter including the soon-to-be new member states)? Would UK subservience to American interests, even under a Labour Government, utterly defeat the dreams and hopes of the left pro-integrationists? Is the EU destined now to play 'second fiddle' to US imperialism regardless of the wishes of its citizens? The lesson that the British anti-capitalist writer and activist George Monbiot drew from the war is that it is more important than ever for the left to rally to the cause of European integration. Announcing his conversion to the cause of the euro, Monbiot argued that its success represents the only realistic check on US power globally: 'That we have a moral duty to contest the developing power of the US is surely evident. That we can contest it by no other means is equally obvious. Those of us who are concerned about American power must abandon our opposition to the Euro' (Monbiot, 2003).

One of the most cogent arguments for deeper and fuller integration as a necessary precondition of a successful relaunch of the European left has been developed by Jurgen Habermas in a series of articles in the *New Left Review* (Habermas, 1998,

1999 and 2001). Habermas outlines the process by which globalisation has reduced a state's 'autonomy, capacity for action and democratic substance' and argues that 'today, it is rather states which are embedded within markets than national economies which are embedded within the boundaries of states' (1999, 48). Nation-states are no longer able to protect citizens from global problems such as pollution nuclear waste, drugs, arms trafficking, etc. Democracy itself is undermined, as those involved in democratic decision-making are not the same as those affected. Within the EU intra-state agreements increase this democratic deficit. We live in an era in which markets have supplanted politics, capital flows undermine governments, and international stock exchanges have taken over the function of assessing national economic policies (1999, 49–50). Habermas, however, is extremely critical of those who think that a politics of territoriality can offer an adequate form of defence of those who are adversely affected by globalisation. Reminding us that protectionist rhetoric is 'grist for the mill of ethnocentric rejection of diversity, xenophobic rejection of the other, and antimodernist rejection of complex social conditions', he points out that it stands no chance of success as an anti-globalisation strategy (although it can of course do enormous damage to democratic society); protectionism will inevitably meet with sanctions.

Habermas introduces a distinction between what he terms 'defensive' and 'offensive' versions of the search for a 'third way'. In some respects, this approximates the distinction I drew earlier between weak and strong reformism within the ranks of pro-integrationists. Habermas summarises what he calls 'defensive' third-way thinking as involving an acceptance of the ethos of neo-liberalism, reducing equality to equal opportunities, and arguing that the forces of global capitalism can be cushioned at the national level by the state providing citizens with the skills they need to compete. (There are clear echoes here of the position of the Blair government in the UK.) By contrast, 'offensive' third-way thinking stresses the need for transformative power at the supranational level. Politics takes precedence over the logic of the market. 'The politics that sets up markets is self-referential, to the extent that every step toward market deregulation entails a simultaneous disqualification or self-restriction of political authority *qua* medium for enacting binding collective decisions. A "catch-up" politics inverts this process; it is reflexive politics in its positive rather than negative version' (Habermas, 1999, 54–5). As regards the evolution of the EU to date, Habermas sees this as flawed by weak political regulation. With the introduction of the euro, new contradictions and pressures between the member states are likely to emerge. The only way to avoid a downward spiral is through the development of a political federation, but Habermas detects a 'tacit alliance' of 'market Europeans' and Blairites against this; both have a vested interest in defending the 'free market' against the removal of any restrictions on state power (1999, 56). By contrast, a strong reformism would involve not only an extension in the EU's 'capacity for political action' but also 'a broadening of the base for its legitimation' (1999, 57). Those who share this vision need to fight not only for stronger political institutions and a European constitution, but also for a growth in a shared European political culture.

In a later article, in which he compares favourably the European policies of the then French prime minister, Lionel Jospin, with the weaker and more neo-liberal line of Tony Blair and German Chancellor Schroeder, Habermas argues that 'a European constitution would enhance the capacity of the member states of the Union to act jointly, without prejudicing the particular course and content of what policies it might adopt. It would constitute a necessary, not a sufficient condition, for the kind of policies some of us are inclined to advocate' (Habermas, 2001, 12). The case for a positive co-ordination of policies is increased in an era of monetary union in which nation-states have ceded to the European Central Bank control over key aspects of economic policy yet respond to similar problems on the basis of a wide variety of national legal systems and social security and taxation systems. Moreover, equipping the Union with the means to intervene in a co-ordinated way against the undesirable effects of globalisation would enable it to rally the support of those who are adversely affected or alienated. Habermas argues that there is a clear connection between increasing the democratic legitimacy of the Union and building a shared 'European public space' (2001, 17), and ultimately a European civic nation, based on solidarity from below, that strengthens civil society. The view of civil society inherent in this is not, of course, the neo-liberal scenario in which competitive individuals reject political regulation that is intended to 'right the wrongs' of the market economy, but rather a vision of a strongly democratic Europe in which politics is put back in the driving seat and new solidarities are forged across national boundaries.

As should be clear by now, many of the pro-integrationist theorists and writers of the left see the development of strong and democratic European political institutions, capable of exerting political control in the face of rampant neo-liberal globalisation, as the *sine qua non*, not only of a revival of the fortunes of the left, but of the future of European democracy itself. But other writers – including some who are not necessarily anti-integrationist by any means – have pointed out that there are formidable obstacles in the way of this goal.

Butler, for example, warns of the tendency that some on the left have to see in the process of integration a means to 'reassert the politics of unitary agency but at a larger scale'. From a point of view clearly influenced by post-modernism, he lambasts the temptation that some socialists may fall prey to to use the end-goal of a powerful EU state as a way of avoiding confronting the limitations of their statism head-on. He warns of the complex nature of identities and the uncertain possible outcomes inherent in efforts to create a new European 'national identity'. And he argues that 'enthusiasts for a centralised European state falsely expect a change of scale to bring a change of fortune', whereas 'an equally plausible scenario is one of degradation' (Butler, 1995, 125–7 and 141–8). This last point is indeed well taken and emphasises the problematic nature of some of the assertions made by pro-integrationists. For example, Habermas's hopes for a written constitution for the EU have to be tempered by the distinct possibility that such a constitution might actually be used by supporters of the nation-state to *place limitations* upon integrationism and to *restrict* the extent to which the EU can acquire new powers. Indeed,

UK Foreign Secretary Jack Straw's announcement, in August 2002, of support for an EU constitution was accompanied by public claims of this nature. And pro-integrationists on the left can only have watched in horror in March 1999 as Oskar Lafontaine was forced out of the German Finance Ministry after a combined campaign against his economic policies by the European Central Bank and German big business. This was perhaps the most vivid illustration to date that the European Central Bank as established by the Maastricht Treaty (unelected and beyond effective democratic control) has acquired considerable ability to undermine and defeat elected politicians from the left who are *pro-integrationist* and who argue for a more social and democratic EU.

Eric Hobsbawm (2000, 88–93) draws attention to the formidable practical obstacles in the path of deeper integration. He argues that there are likely to be 'severe limitations' to the extent to which many EU governments are likely to wish to go down the path of political federalism. EU enlargement may well make it less likely than before that countries such as the UK or France will be willing to agree to ever-increasing surrender of the national veto; they risk being outvoted by a coalition of smaller member states on a range of issues they deem vital to their interests:

> Sooner or later, Europe [sic] will find itself in the situation of the United Nations Security Council, where the countries that are really capable of making decisions will simply not want to give up their power to majorities ...This is why Europe will grind to a halt on the really important issues. It is extremely difficult to determine a common foreign and defense policy, and this proves that there aren't the necessary conditions for an effective and total political integration, whereas there are for social and economic matters. The enlargement of the European Union will make the situation even more difficult: above all, you will increase the number of irresponsible votes. A majority made up of Slovenia, Estonia, Latvia and a few other states of this kind could never be considered an adequate majority to be respected by Germany, France, Britain, or even Italy.
> (Hobsbawm, 2000, 90–1)

And, of course, it is precisely the case that the 'big powers' succeeded in the Nice Treaty (which faced ratification difficulties following its initial rejection in a referendum in Ireland), in strengthening their voting rights and, in consequence, their immunity from a possible coalition of smaller states. This perhaps bodes ill for the speed and progress of integrationism, as Hobsbawm argues.

Other obstacles he points to include: the practical impossibility of extending to the impoverished farmers of East and Central Europe the benefits that West European farmers have derived from the Common Agricultural Policy, until now – thus necessitating drastic reform of the CAP; and the difficulty involved in accelerating the process of integration by strengthening the powers of the European Parliament. Hobsbawm argues that, with the exception of Italy, it is unlikely that member states will allow the European Parliament to become a full legislature; and, moreover, that low electoral turnouts at European Parliamentary elections and lack of interest in its proceedings fatally undermine its democratic legitimacy. His argument here is not anti-integrationist – he argues that 'obviously, it's a good thing that the European Parliament is given greater powers'; rather, that 'for many Europeans, Europe is still a technical term, and not something to which they feel tied by any bond of loyalty. The question that people pose in relation to Europe is still always formulated in instrumental and domestic policy terms: how useful will it be?' (Hobsbawm, 2000, 92). Writers such as Habermas are clearly well aware of this problem – which is why Habermas argues so forcefully for the necessity of forging a new European consciousness if a fully integrated European democracy is to be constructed. Hobsbawm's position would seem to be sceptical of the likelihood of success, at least in the short term. And here we come back to the dilemma that so often faces leftwing pro-integrationists: what to do when the dream of progress towards a democratic and social United States of Europe comes unstuck. Are a few slices of bread better than no loaf at all? Or do they amount to little more than crumbs of comfort from the rich man's table – and a renunciation of an autonomous socialist vision of the future?

Of course, the debate between 'maximalists' and 'minimalists', 'reformists' and 'revolutionaries' (though all these terms are immensely problematic), is one of those perennial disputes that is as familiar to anyone who has ever been involved in leftwing politics as their favourite old woolly jumper. And, in an obvious sense, this is one way in which left arguments over European integration can be conceptualised.

An eloquent statement of a pro-integrationist left position, that wishes to maintain the necessity for a 'strong reformism' whilst accepting that 'half a loaf is better than no loaf' is a sensible point of departure, is offered by Aaronovitch and Grahl (1997), two economists who were close to the 'Eurocommunist' wing of the old Communist Party of Great Britain. The authors strongly criticise the 'narrow and dogmatic' nature of the Maastricht Treaty's insistence upon monetary stabilisation, which they see as damaging Europe by aggravating unemployment, social exclusion and loss of popular faith in the integration process (and in the EU itself). However, they argue that there is no point in dreaming of beautiful but unrealistic scenarios; the left has to deal with existing realities and aim at a 'precise strategic orientation within a very narrow space' (Aaronovitch and Grahl, 1997, 178). Although it is proceeding on a basis that the left dislikes intensely in many ways, monetary union is nevertheless a desirable goal in itself. Its failure would leave the EU in a vacuum 'in which it would be impossible to formulate a constructive strategy'. In such a vacuum, with the growth of nationalistic forces and the implosion of the wider integration project, the EU might well be reduced to a mere free-trade zone.

> Nor would the disabling of central political structures permit a larger choice of strategies at national level. On the contrary, constraints on national economic policy would be tightened by uncontrolled competition to attract investment and economic activity from one territory to another. The pressures on state budgets arising from the Maastricht convergence process would be perpetuated by efforts to advance national competitiveness in a Dutch auction of welfare cuts, deregulation and tax give-backs. (Aaronovitch and Grahl, 1997, 179)

Although rejection of Maastricht and of the euro leads to a 'strategic dead-end', uncritical acceptance Maastricht also disarms the left altogether. The only positive strategic orientation, therefore, is one that accepts monetary union and tries to make a success of it while emphasising the 'dysfunctionality' of the Maastricht Treaty in certain key respects – the narrow emphasis on fighting inflation (but not unemployment), the excessive constraints imposed on governments, the failure to place the European Central Bank under democratic control, the failure to advance the cause of supranational democracy, etc.

> This is the narrow space in which strategic intervention must be considered: between a rejection which would strike, effectively or otherwise, at integration as such; and the endorsement of a programme so narrow and dogmatically conceived that it has already begun to disorganise the political and economic life of the Union. The only feasible approach is to attempt initiatives inserted into the Maastricht agenda itself – into its incoherences [sic], its lacunae, its limitations – with the aim of *strengthening* the advance to EMU, securing the political and economic basis of a common currency, rationalizing the process by which it is pursued and enhancing the further objectives of the unified currency area. (Aaronovitch and Grahl, 1997, 179-80)

Although globalisation is 'an unavoidable and irreversible process, full of dangers for the European populations', a strengthened and democratised EU can influence globalisation in two ways: 'internally, by organizing economic life to improve adaptation to external constraints and by redistributing some of the gains and losses that occur. But it can also act externally to modify the constraints themselves, using its immense political, commercial and, tomorrow, monetary powers to obtain advantageous reforms in the global economy itself through compromises with the other principal actors'. In other words, monetary union can strengthen the EU, and a democratised and more socially just EU could act as force for good on the world stage, ameliorating the effects of globalisation and exercising 'social control over the terms and methods which govern the insertion of the European economies into the global economy'. Such an EU, led from the left, could have profoundly positive implications too for the developing countries and for social justice on a global scale. From this perspective, even though the current direction and perspective of the integration process and its lynchpin – monetary union – may be narrowed and warped by the straitjacket of monetarism into which they have been forced, that process itself has much broader potential: it has the potential, if freed from monetarism's constraints, to rescue democratic politics – to reintroduce the possibility of exercising a measure of democratic political control over the faceless and dehumanising processes of economic globalisation. The alternative to deeper and fuller integration would be to 'throw European peoples back on national state structures that are increasingly unable to exert decisive leverage over external conditions'. It therefore follows that the 'least bad strategy' for the left is to accept Maastricht and seek to build upon it by introducing gradual reforms, however piecemeal. 'This strategic orientation has to recognize multiple political, financial and economic limits that cannot as yet be overcome', but can take comfort in the fact that ultimately

Maastricht is unworkable. Finally, the authors conclude that 'the modesty of the immediate goals which can be formulated in this way should not be confused with a lack of ambition as regards ultimate objectives' (Aaronovitch and Grahl, 1997, 199–200).

This is perhaps one of the clearest statements of the strategic and tactical orientation towards EU integration of those intellectuals on the left who, thinking dialectically, have tried to develop a strong reformism at the pan-EU level; and it is all the more interesting for being formulated by two writers whose intellectual and political roots lie within the communist tradition.

Writers such as the late Ralph Miliband and Alex Callinicos take a much more critical line on European integration altogether. Miliband stops short of calling for withdrawal from EU membership but is highly critical of the integration process. He comes close to the political positions favoured by the French Communist Party (and like-minded parties) for many years. In his last book, *Socialism for a Sceptical Age*, he concedes that it is possible that the EU might move beyond its neo-liberal limitations but thinks this is highly unlikely. Moreover, arguments for an increase in the powers of the European Parliament are countered with the claim that 'it is extremely doubtful whether that body could come to exercise a strong control over the European Commission or the Council of Ministers, and to exercise it for left purposes' (Miliband, 1994, 180). Although he agrees that left parties 'cannot retreat into a national bunker', Miliband argues that the correct strategy for a socialist government that came to power in an EU member state would be to

> loosen integration in favour, at most, of arrangements which would leave a socialist government with the greatest possible degree of autonomous decision-making in economic and all other fields of policy ... It will be time enough to consider closer connections when socialist governments exist in many countries: until this happens, the Left cannot accept integration into a 'union' whose members are actively opposed to the kind of fundamental transformation which it is the purpose of a left government to achieve. This is not to underestimate in any way the importance of the globalization of capital or the internationalization of economic life. It is simply to say that socialists cannot accept a parallel political internationalization which, for the present and the immediate future, is bound to place intolerable constraints on the purposes they seek to advance. (Miliband, 1994, 180)

But critics would of course respond that this is *precisely* to under-estimate the 'importance of the globalization of capital [and] the internationalization of economic life'. What such a hypothetical socialist government would do, faced with the inevitable flight of capital and of employment, is nowhere very clear. The position that Miliband adopts is always open to the criticism from pro-integrationists that it is not so much a strategy for transformation of society as a principled 'last stand' of the old left.

Callinicos (2001, 99) sees the downfall of Lafontaine in Germany as proof that the hopes for a revival of a strong reformist left through an acceleration of the EU integration process that leftwing social democrats such as Habermas and

Lafontaine himself have expressed are misguided. (Coming from a broadly Trotskyist background, Callinicos tends to describe all those he regards as 'reformists' as social democrats – including many whose political roots and traditions are not only *on the left* of social democracy but *to the left* of social democracy. In other words, many within the left parties I examine in this book would doubtless merit the label, in his view.) He argues that the Lafontaine incident 'should serve as a warning that international institutions do not necessarily promote greater democratic control, and indeed may work with rather than against markets'. Against Habermas, he argues that the EU (and other international institutions) as presently constituted works in the interests of the USA and other Western capitalist powers. In the rhetoric of the so-called 'third way', neo-liberalism has found a convenient mask to cover its essentially exploitative nature. Allegedly centre-left governments in the EU in recent years, especially those most seduced by the 'third way', have done nothing to challenge or change the capitalist and exploitative nature of the EU; rather, they have intensified it: 'the claims made on behalf of Third Way governments that they represent new ways of regulating capitalism have thus proven false. They have in fact embraced and in certain respects radicalized the neo-liberal policies of their predecessors' (Callinicos, 2001, 107). For all their criticisms of Blairism, left integrationists are guilty of falling into the trap of believing that the alternative to the Anglo-American model of capitalism is 'another, more humane and democratic form of capitalism ... what is sometimes called the Rhineland model of regulated capitalism ...' Left integrationists, in fact, 'seem to advocate an international version of Rhineland capitalism, in which the European Union provides the regulation that the nation-state can no longer supply'. Against this, he advocates an anti-capitalist strategy that draws inspiration from the current anti-capitalist movement in several countries and that challenges head-on the 'logic of capital accumulation'. Callinicos admits that 'bringing such a society into existence will be an arduous task. It will mean a revolution ...' (Callinicos, 2001, 119–20). This is stirring stuff, redolent of what many communists would once have described as 'leftist maximalism'; but as is so often the case with Marxist analyses it is more convincing as a critique of what is wrong than as a practical guide on how to go about changing existing realities. Apart from support for mass demonstrations against capitalism (which many of those dubbed 'reformists' would have no problem in going along with), there is little indication of how left parties should formulate their EU policies, though the general thrust is obviously anti-reformist and the logic is that they should oppose further political and economic integration.

Two of the most trenchant anti-integration statements to come from the left in recent years are those offered by Carchedi (2001) and McGiffen (2001). The former is a Marxist economist; the latter is an official with the Confederal Group in the European Parliament (GUE/NGL) with many years of working within the EU institutions. Both writers arrive at broadly similar conclusions about the EU: that it is imperialist and exploitative in nature, thoroughly undemocratic in its workings, wasteful, environmentally damaging and socially regressive. Carchedi emphasises the extent to which the EEC was a response on the part of European capitalism to a particular conjuncture in post-war history, above all 'the realisation that European nations were no longer large enough to hold their own in world markets'. Thus, it came to embody the power of European capital over European labour and, indeed, the dominance of European capital over developing nations and economies. 'Given the imperialist past and nature of the countries founding the European Economic Community, the body emerging from their integration could not but contain the same seeds and develop into the same weed' (Carchedi, 2001, 9). As part of the imperialist core, the EU imposes deteriorating trade terms on the dominated periphery, enjoys permanent and self-reinforcing processes of technological and efficiency advantages over the periphery, and thus fosters dependent development which has consequences for wage levels in the periphery and affects the structure of dependent economies. The Common Agricultural Policy (CAP) imposes dependent development on weaker agricultural economies outside the EU (Carchedi, 2001, 117). McGiffen sees the CAP as 'certainly the biggest single cause of environmental degradation in Western Europe since the war' (McGiffen, 2001, 135).

Carchedi is keen to emphasise the 'symbiotic relationship between big business and EU institutions, especially the Commission'. He argues that 'even within the confines of parliamentary democracy, the democratic deficit is much more than Parliament's extremely limited legislative power. It is also oligopoly capital's ability to tailor the Commission's proposals to its interests, thus inscribing those interests into the decisions taken by the Council, with or without Parliament's co-decision before those decisions are taken' (Carchedi, 2001, 34); although, he is also keen to stress that such institutions are not merely spokespersons for big business but have the role of mediating between class interests. McGiffen emphasises the corrupt and elitist nature of the Union's main institutions. The lobbying by big business of MEPs is so blatant that 'some would get marks for honesty if, like footballers, they wore the names of their corporate sponsors on their shirts'. The European Parliament is so remote from the peoples of Europe, and so unaccountable to ordinary voters, that like the other main EU institutions, it expresses no will other than its own. And the fundamental nature of the EU reflects the fact that it 'is a technocratic project. That is to say that it is based on the premise that politicians can no longer be trusted with macro-economic policy. Neither they, nor we, the people who elect them, understand it well enough. It must be left to specialists, to bankers, whom we are expected to believe are above the sectional interests that motivate the rest of us' (McGiffen, 2001, 23, and 134–5).

For Carchedi, the great integrationist project of our times – monetary union – has it roots in the needs of German oligarchic interests. German dominance in the high technology sector was accepted by other European countries by the 1980s, but the price was paid by labour as wages were forced down in the name of competition. The non-inflationary monetary policy pursued by the European Central Bank, and which underlies the Maastricht Treaty and the monetary union project, is far from neutral: it disproportionately benefits German capital over others who no longer have the option to devalue, and of course leads to rising unemployment (Carchedi, 2001, 123, and 139–42). McGiffen adds that the Maastricht convergence criteria 'are designed to reduce the choices available to member-state governments, so that whatever goals they wish to pursue must be achieved within the confines of a highly liberalised market economy. The real arguments for the euro are the same, then, as the arguments for such an economy, but they are rarely, at least for broad public consumption, presented as such.' The siren calls for 'increased labour market flexibility' that usually accompany pro-euro statements are detrimental to European workers: 'For working people who value the stability provided by reliable contracts, decent wages, a functioning system of social security and welfare, and some recognition of their humanity, the benefits of such "reform" may be hard to fathom' (McGiffen, 2001, 60–1).

For Carchedi, the only rational and sensible strategy for the European left is one of total opposition to the EU. The left must seek to turn 'the Europe of the industrial and financial multinationals not into a vague "Europe of the Citizens", but into the Europe of labour, into a Europe based on equality and solidarity' (Carchedi, 2001, 35). McGiffen stresses that there is nothing inevitable about the European Union; it is not the only available answer to the problems we face at the start of the new century. He claims that 'try as I might, I have been unable to identify a single policy area in which the Treaty of Rome has had a beneficial effect. Everything the EU does is either undesirable or could have been better achieved by other means.' Expansion of EU membership to the countries of Eastern and Central Europe is merely a means of copper-fastening the new neo-liberal order in those countries and denying their peoples the means of challenging this. The Union's employment and social policies have failed entirely to reduce unemployment or social inequality. Much of the Amsterdam Treaty is about new forms of internal repression and increased border policing, in a Union in which racism and fascism are on the rise. McGiffen is keen to emphasise his total rejection, as a socialist, of nationalism, including '"European" nationalism, as promoted by the self-styled "pro-Europeans"'. And he adds:

> Simply because we need an international approach to the problems facing humanity in the twenty-first century does not mean that *this* international approach, this European Union, a single currency based on extreme and discredited monetarist principles, a political system which seems almost designed to maximise corruption and the hegemony of wealthy elites, is the only or best form of international co-operation on offer.

His conclusion is to argue for a dissolution of the existing EU. His experience of working inside the institutions of the EU on behalf of the GUE/NGL group has rendered him 'an opponent of this European Union' (McGiffen, 2001, 134–43).

As is clear by now, left writers and intellectuals have responded in a wide range of ways to key questions about the nature, direction and desirability of the sort of integration that the EU embodies. Their advice on what tactics and strategies should influence the EU policies of left parties, trade unions and other progressive movements is equally diverse. It is to be hoped that this brief discussion of some of these views will help the reader place in an intellectual context the party debates and divisions on the 'European question' which we will examine in subsequent chapters. Before we do so, it might be helpful also to reflect upon some of the factors that can influence processes of policy change within parties. Clearly, political parties, including parties of the left, are influenced and motivated by many factors and considerations other than intellectual debates.

Europe and the dynamics of party change

Policy formation and policy change within political parties is influenced by numerous factors. These can be as diverse as: the impact of the electoral system that a polity possesses; the need for strategic alliances with other parties; the pull of political opportunism; the party's assessment of the international situation; and the internal balance of forces within a party. The first point might be illustrated by pointing out that the workings of the British electoral system (although a form of PR was introduced for European Parliamentary elections in 1999) might account for the absence of an electorally significant left party in the UK that we could include within the scope of this book. The second point might explain the French Communist Party's marked moderation of its anti-EU language after its decision, in the mid-1990s, to pursue an alliance with the Socialist Party, and its participation in coalition government during the years 1997–2002; years that saw that French government take the country into the single currency and sign both the Amsterdam and Nice Treaties. No doubt the charge of political opportunism might be levelled at the French Communist Party (PCF); but it might apply also to those parties (perhaps in some Nordic countries) that have seen in anti-integrationism a popular vote-winner and a way of widening their appeal. The assessment of the international situation is particularly important for left parties, above all the communist and ex-communist parties, after the fall of the USSR and its allies. Finally, the evolution of policy may be affected by, and in turn lead to changes in, the party's internal balance of forces, as opponents of change and defeated advocates of unsuccessful change (or 'renewal') leave or slide into political apathy. It is necessary to keep of these factors in mind when examining the left parties.

Featherstone, in his late 1980s study of social democratic parties and European integration, placed the factors affecting their responses to the European Union into three categories: internal influences from within the parties, influences from the wider political system, and the impact of external events (Featherstone, 1988). More recently, Johansson and Raunio (2001), in their study of Finnish and Swedish parties, have produced a very useful checklist of seven sets of factors that help us understand how parties perceptions of European integration change and evolve.

The first of these is *basic ideology*. In the case of the left parties this involves understanding how these parties differ in their interpretations of socialism and how their assessment of the possibilities for socialist transformation have changed over the years. Some of these parties come from a communist tradition in which 'national roads to socialism' was clearly entrenched. Other, new left and non-communist parties may have very different experiences. Likewise, green and social democratic parties may display different ideological influences. Ideological change – which cannot be separated from organisational (and perhaps generational) change – is therefore at the heart of our survey.

The second factor Johansson and Raunio mention is *public opinion*. Put simply, 'political parties are ill-advised to ignore the degree of support for, and opposition to, European integration ... parties are particularly tentative for respect to their core supporters and to various interest groups associated with them' (Johansson and Raunio, 2001, 228). Thus, it is important to bear in mind how left parties judge the public mood – and how they interpret evidence of the disposition of their members and supporters towards European integration. To give a (perhaps rather) obvious example, there may be much less political leeway for a left party espousing anti-integration policies in a country such as Italy than in one such as Norway. The issue of whether left parties are linked or not to powerful interest groups such as trade unions, environmental groups, feminist movements, etc., which may see threats or opportunities in further integration, is also important.

A third factor is *party factionalism*. Internal dissent and factionalism may be caused by disagreements over EU policy. Alternatively, there may be a history of factionalism, schisms and splits that the leadership is anxious to avoid repeating at all costs. This inhibition – with the possibility of electoral annihilation for small left parties if they fail to contain factionalism; witness the terrible travails of the Spanish communists during the 1980s, when degeneration into more than twenty separate communist parties by 1988 led to a huge loss in support and influence – may have important effects. The leadership may feel that policy change or renewal has to move more slowly than it would like. Or a leadership committed to policy change may feel that 'legitimising' internal disagreements over European policy is the only feasible option. This latter course is arguably what happened with the Danish Socialist People's Party and the Finnish Left Alliance during the 1990s.

Leadership influence is indeed the fourth factor. Johansson and Raunio (2001, 229) argue that the leadership of a party may have particular leeway in formulating policy changes on an issue such as European integration, where the knowledge or interest of rank-and-file members and supporters may not be great. Whether this applies to radical left parties, whose members and voters tend to be either strongly ideologically driven or motivated by a desire to protest against the status quo, remains to be established.

Party competition, the fifth factor, refers to the prevalence of domestic political considerations. The authors claim that green and communist parties have tended to temper or moderate their opposition to European integration in order to be taken seriously as potential or actual parties of government, as responsible coalition partners. Certainly, this is true of several of these parties. However, a number of radical left parties may not, of course, see any possibility at all of their entering government in the short or medium term. They may instead see effective party competition residing in vigorous defence of those most marginalised by European integration, or by mobilising the 'protest vote'. Although, on the terrain of European integration policy, they may face stiff competition for this vote from far-right parties, this in turn can lead to very different responses – from backing off in horror at any possibility of 'contamination' by association with the far right to campaigning more vigorously to ensure that disillusioned anti-EU voters do not 'fall into the hands' of the far right. Some parties may, indeed, critically reassess their failures in government as due to their inadequate mobilisation of the disaffected. Such a reassessment may well be underway within the PCF after the failure of the Jospin government to gain re-election in 2002, and may lead to a further turn in EU policy on the part of that party.

Transnational links is a factor that arguably figures larger in the consideration of the social democratic and Christian democratic parties than it does in the case of the left parties. In the case of the former, their respective European party federations – the Party of European Socialists and the European People's Party – now publish common European Parliamentary elections manifestoes, and operate (albeit in a very incomplete way) as transnational party federations. The same is true of the Greens. The left parties have yet to evolve anything like such a transnational structure, notwithstanding the various left groups in the European Parliament since the 1970s or initiatives such as the New European Left Forum (NELF), a network launched in the 1990s to facilitate exchanges of ideas and policy initiatives between EU and non-EU left parties. The next chapter examines many of the reasons for this, and I will return to the question of transnational party links in the Conclusion.

The final factor Johansson and Raunio refer to is the development of integration. This refers to the very important fact that 'no single party or family of parties can determine EU policy' and very often parties are forced to adapt to changes within the EU. Global changes also lead to changes in perception. As I hope will become clear throughout the book, this is a very important consideration where the left parties are concerned. The EU has had, at times, at least as large a role in challenging and changing the left parties as the left parties have had in challenging and changing the EU.

2
HISTORICAL CONTEXT: FROM EUROCOMMUNISM TO THE 'EURO-LEFT'? WESTERN EUROPEAN COMMUNIST PARTIES AND THE EUROPEAN UNION UNTIL 1989

Introduction

The late 1980s and early 1990s marked the end of an era in the history of the European left. The path followed by a significant part of the socialist movement in the European continent since the October Revolution was proven to have been a cul-de-sac; and an ideology and culture that fired the idealism and raised the hopes of millions of adherents had collapsed. As the communist regimes in the eastern part of the continent fell, the question of what shape and form the political architecture of the new Europe should take was thrust to the forefront of politics. The main Left parties of the EU, whether their origins lay in the communist or 'new left' traditions, would struggle to produce convincing answers to a new range of questions, as indeed would the social democratic parties of the centre-left. The 1990s may have opened with hopes in some quarters of the European left of a new flowering of socialist ideas, freed at last from the dead weight of Stalinism. But the decade would end with little sign of any renaissance, as neo-liberal ideas about Europe's future continued a seemingly inexorable advance under the banner of 'globalisation'. Even some centre-left governments – most notably, the 'new Labour' government in the UK – would appear less interested in reshaping the direction of European integration from the left than in joining with Berlusconi, Aznar and the forces of the right in chanting the mantra of privatisation, 'labour flexibility' and pro-Americanism.

In a real sense, the collapse of the Stalinist regimes in eastern and central Europe and the ex-USSR would call into question not merely the 'distortions' of socialism that took place under Stalin, but the very feasibility of any socialist project – in the sense of a qualitative rupture with the existing capitalist economic model. Not only that, but the profound ideological, organisational and electoral crisis of the Western communist parties, which long predates the events of 1989–90 of course, would undermine their capacity to act as political organs of those social classes and strata most adversely affected by neo-liberal economic transformations. As political scientists would put it, their capacity to attract the protest vote and to act as conduits for profound political and social discontent was impaired. This, in turn, would help to 'free up' voters traditionally associated with the left in general, and radical Left parties in particular – for example, amongst the young, the working-class and even, in some countries, public sector white collar employees – for 'poaching' by populist and often openly racist parties of the radical right. These parties, sometimes preaching a message of xenophobia and authoritarianism, would seek to position themselves as offering the only truly 'radical' alternative to the dominant neo-liberal model of European integration. The communist and Left parties would face another challenge in the 1990s and beyond: their capacity to offer an *effective* critique of neo-liberalism would be challenged by a wave of street demonstrations and popular anti-globalisation (or at least anti-*neo-liberal* globalisation) social movements, which seemed to underline the despair that many on the left felt with the paralysis of traditional political parties.

In short, the question of the European Union and the model of economic, political and social development that it embodies would become both crucial and central to left politics and to the future prospects of Left parties. It is my contention in this book that policies and attitudes towards European integration have increasingly become the terrain upon which battles over the future of democratic politics, social justice, environmental protection and capitalist economic development are fought. 'Europe' and European policy are becoming increasingly important in the struggle to define a distinctly left or anti-capitalist politics, notwithstanding the fact that profound divisions over questions of the future development of the EU run through both left and right parties, leading to confusion and bewilderment for many voters.

The strategic importance of the nature and development of the EU in the formulation of any feasible and convincing 'transformatory' political project for the European left is not something new, although communist and Left parties have differed widely in both the urgency with which they have recognised this fact and the policies they have elaborated in response to it.

For many years before 1989, the question of these parties' reaction to the processes of European integration was recognised as touching on every aspect of their strategic and conceptual orientations. It raised the issue of the possibilities or limitations of 'socialism in one country' (however one defines socialism), so central to left thinking, despite the rhetoric of proletarian internationalism, since the 1920s. It posited centre-stage the problem of how (supposedly) Marxist parties should react to the process of capitalist modernisation and internationalisation – to resist or to adapt? It went to the heart of the parties' political culture, forcing a response to the question of where they should stand in an increasingly multipolar world. In the bipolar world order which emerged after 1945, and which was strengthened of course by the Cold War, the response was relatively straightforward: all communist parties, even the most revisionist such as the PCI, tended to stand with the Soviet Union against Western (and chiefly US) imperialism. Indeed, many other (non-communist) Left parties took a similar stand, certainly where issues such as the war in Vietnam or the Cuban revolution were concerned. By the 1970s, and especially after the Soviet invasion of Czechoslovakia in 1968, the picture became much more complicated. Some West European communist and 'new left' parties argued that their task was to seek to defuse international confrontation and polarisation between the Soviet and American superpowers, which threatened global conflict on a catastrophic scale at worst, and political rigidity at best, and to work for democratisation and progressive change in both camps. How could this be accomplished? By alignment with the 'socialist camp' against the 'imperialist'? Or by forging a new Europe which was neither pro- nor anti-soviet, neither pro- nor anti-American?

If such a Europe was possible, how might it come about? What would it look like? Above all, how would it relate to the existing European Community? Could that body, which came into existence with the Treaty of Rome in 1957, be reformed from within so that it acted as a catalyst of progressive and democratic change throughout the continent, and as an alternative model to both rampant American-style market capitalism and Soviet-style authoritarian socialism; or was it merely the economic arm of American- and German-led multinational capitalism and as such an instrument of exploitation?

Questions such as these would become central to the divisions within and between communist and Left parties in Western Europe long before the collapse of the Soviet Union. Our first task is to place in historical context the question of how Europe emerged to such prominence in the thinking of communist and Left parties, and of how and why political parties that sprung from similar origins nevertheless arrived at diametrically opposed conclusions about virtually all the major questions concerning the nature and future of the EU.

Europe, transnationalism and the crisis in communist strategy, 1968–89

This is not the place to sketch a history of the phenomenon of 'Eurocommunism'. The 1970s and early 1980s saw the appearance of a vast academic literature on that subject (and some of the outstanding examples are cited in the bibliography). Rather, what concerns me here is the extent to which Eurocommunism was an attempt by the major communist parties of Western Europe – above all, the Italian, French and Spanish, but not the Portuguese or the majority of Greek communists – to articulate a common strategy for the attainment of certain goals; the reasons behind the failure of that attempt; and the subsequent qualitative change both in the international policies of the parties and in the balance of relations between them.

What came to be known as Eurocommunism emerged in the aftermath of the Soviet invasion of Czechoslovakia in August 1968. Although differences between the substance and style of those parties that embraced Eurocommunism were apparent from the outset, a number of common points of departure can be listed.

First, all of those parties that became known as Eurocommunist had condemned the Soviet invasion of Czechoslovakia and expressed sympathy, in varying degrees, with the regime of Alexander Dubcek. Thus, from the outset a key component of Eurocommunism was the assertion of the right of every communist party to follow its own path to socialism, free from interference or intervention from the Soviet Union. Allied to this was the view that the communist movement had long entered a phase of polycentrism and that the notion of a leading role being assigned to any one party (the Soviet party) was unacceptable. This was true not only of the Italian and Spanish parties which condemned the invasion in the most outspoken terms, but also of the French Communist Party and of the Eurocommunist formation which emerged in Greece – the so-called Greek Communist Party-interior – which broke away from the pro-Soviet Greek Communist Party precisely over the question of Soviet domination.

Second, all of the Eurocommunist parties expressed the conviction that socialism and democracy were indivisible, and the road to socialism to be followed in the advanced capitalist democracies of Western Europe would have to embrace liberal democratic institutions including parliamentary democracy. Of course, there were considerable differences in emphasis between the parties and in the credibility with which their declarations were greeted. The Italian Communist Party (PCI), for example, with its proposed 'historic compromise' with the Italian Christian Democrats in 1975–79, effectively abandoned the transition to socialism as its short-term or even medium-term aim, seeking a West German-style Grand Coalition to save the institutions of (bourgeois) parliamentary democracy and regenerate Italian society through a 'moral *risorgimento*'. Arguably, this orientation was to have profound implications for the evolution of its policy on European integration, a point well understood by leading European federalist and member of the European Commission, Altiero Spinelli, who embraced the historic compromise wholeheartedly. Sensing that the historic compromise was a fundamental strategic commitment on the part of the PCI to the consolidation of liberal democracy in Italy, and that the party leadership could be convinced that European integration was the terrain upon which this consolidation might be achieved, Spinelli sought election to the European Parliament as an independent candidate on the PCI's electoral lists; his subsequent role in both the formulation of a future strategy for the European Community, and the conversion of the PCI to both European federalism and social democracy, was to be considerable. By contrast with the PCI, the French Communist Party (PCF) repeatedly called into question the sincerity of its 'democratic conversion' and highlighted the ambiguities in its approach by adding ominous qualifications – such as when party leader Georges Marchais cited East Germany and other Soviet bloc states as examples of multi-party democracy.

Third, with varying degrees of emphasis again – and probably with varying sincerity also – the Eurocommunist parties condemned abuses of human rights in the Soviet Union and Eastern Europe, assuming a critical autonomy which, to the observer of communist politics, would have been unthinkable in the old days when the world was said to be divided into two camps – imperialism and 'actually existing socialism'. The Communist Party of Spain (PCE) was probably the most outspoken at first, with its General Secretary Santiago Carrillo openly calling into question in public for the first time the socialist nature of the USSR (Carrillo, 1977). This book brought a stinging rebuke from the Soviet side, accusing Carrillo of playing into the hands of 'imperialism'.

Fourth, the parties sought during the early and mid-1970s to give expression to their apparent autonomy from Moscow by articulating a vision of a world no longer divided between two superpowers. The key international task of the communists was identified as being to strive for peace and disarmament and a weakening of 'reactionary' and 'imperialist' forces in a world context characterised by increasing multipolarity. In fact, the existence of détente and the struggle against the rigidity of the Yalta settlement – however these aims may have been interpreted differently by, for example, the PCI and the PCF – were seen as central to the realisation of the governmental vocation of the communist parties.

Fifth, it seemed during the 1970s that this meant in effect striving to effect a programmatic convergence between the main Western European communist parties so as to enable them to articulate a common vision of a Europe, no longer dominated by either of the two superpowers and led from the left. This was very much the mood in which the Eurocommunist summit meeting in Madrid in March 1977 – when the Italian and French parties rallied in support of their emergent (and not yet formally legalised) Spanish comrades – was greeted both in communist circles and in the corridors of power in Western Europe. The March 1977 summit, according to one authoritative commentator, 'had seemed to signal an evolving formation by the three major Western European Communist parties of a dynamic unified bloc aimed at strengthening Communist influence on the policies of the European Community, and possibly at undermining the community over time' (Timmermann, 1979, 31).

This seeming emergence of a common front had been preceded by a number of significant meetings between the three main Eurocommunist parties: the bilateral PCI–PCE meeting in Livorno in July 1975, the PCI–PCF summit in Rome in the summer of 1976, and the common approach to Soviet assertions of hegemony adopted at the Berlin Conference of European Communist and Workers' Parties in 1976 (when the Eurocommunists successfully established, at least in theory, Soviet acquiescence with the principle of non-interference in other parties' affairs). It was at such inter-party summits and bilateral meetings that the Eurocommunist vision of the road ahead was spelt out.

The articulation by the Eurocommunist parties of a vision of socialism that claimed to offer a 'third way' between Stalinism and social democracy, transcending the limits of a classical social democracy that confined itself to managing the affairs of capitalism rather than seeking to qualitatively change capitalist society, and avoiding the atrophy which had robbed the Soviet model of much of its attractiveness for Western workers and intellectuals, both inspired hopes for socialist change within the ranks of the left, and caused considerable alarm within ruling circles on both sides of the Atlantic. Eurocommunism was widely perceived amongst the latter as a threat to the fundamental interests of the West, a 'Trojan horse' by which Moscow would subvert Western intelligence, disrupt Western unity and destabilise Europe. Indeed, the electoral growth of the PCI and PCF during the early and mid-1970s, and the uncertain prospects of post-Franco Spain, produced a flurry of official studies designed to inform US and West

European governmental policy in the event of the Communists entering the Governments of France and Italy.

And yet, by the end of the 1970s, the Eurocommunist challenge was visibly receding, not only in terms of the failure of the leading Eurocommunist parties to realise their electoral goals, but significantly in terms of the ability of those parties to agree upon any transnational strategy for socialist or even democratic transformation. The ensuing crisis of ideology, of strategy and of programmatic content was to lead some of those parties – most notably the PCI, but also the PCE – to redefine their agenda, shifting the emphasis to the need to create a new European left or 'Euro-left', whilst others – most notably the PCF – were to retrench on the terrain of 'socialism in one country'. By the early 1980s, commentators were already able to speak of Eurocommunism as a political strategy that had ended in failure (Sodaro, 1984; Steinkühler, 1985). One of the most perceptive analysts of Eurocommunism was even to call into question the extent to which Eurocommunism could ever have been more than a transitional platform, and to suggest that its meaning might ultimately be unravelled only in the light of the transmutation of parties such as the Italian, as they picked their steps towards a redefinition of the Euro-left (Hassner, 1980–81, 461–3).

Before we can fully understand the circumstances in which the communist parties of Western Europe diverged fundamentally in their search for a response to the processes of internationalisation and European integration we need, therefore, to reflect upon the collapse of the Eurocommunist attempt to posit a co-ordinated approach to economic and political transformation. Why is it that the dream of a more or less simultaneous ascent to governmental office by the communist parties of Italy, France and Spain, in coalition with other progressive political forces, ended so disastrously? What happened to the hopes of challenging the hegemony of monopoly capitalism and leading a gradual, democratic advance towards socialism, changing the nature of the European Union and transforming the international order?

Much commentary has focused upon the declining domestic electoral fortunes of the communist parties concerned, suggesting that in order to understand the failure of the Eurocommunist project we need to study the domestic strategy of each party and its failure to overcome relative isolation within the domestic polity. While this is certainly important I wish to suggest that the domestic difficulties and setbacks encountered by the communist parties cannot be fully or properly understood within the domestic context alone. I wish to emphasise here the extent to which the limitations of Eurocommunism (1) reflected common problems that the parties experienced in attempting to transform, modernise or adapt communist culture and identity; and (2) inhibited the ability of the communist movement in Western Europe as a whole to articulate a transnational strategy which might have addressed the key question of the era: internationalisation of both politics and economy.

Perhaps this is best approached if we focus our minds again on those concepts which I suggested earlier formed a common point of departure for the

Eurocommunist parties: the independence of parties; the necessary relationship between democracy and socialism; an insistence upon autonomy from, and a critical stance towards, the countries of 'actually existing socialism'; the search for a new international order; the search for a new conception of Europe.

The early phase in the development of Eurocommunism saw the main Western European communist parties struggle to assert their right to chart their own paths towards socialism, free from interference from Moscow; and, importantly, to force from the Soviet side an explicit acceptance of this fact. That the Western communist parties still had a fight on their hands to end outside interference in their internal affairs, despite Khrushchev's acceptance of the notion of 'national roads to socialism' and subsequent Soviet rhetoric to this effect, was underlined by the Soviet response to Western communist criticism of the invasion of Czechoslovakia, when Moscow attempted to use its influence with pro-Soviet leadership elements to the full – seeking, for example, to block the election of Enrico Berlinguer as General Secretary of the Italian party. The principle of independence of communist parties – their right to determine their own course – thus became an important goal, and a jealously guarded acquisition.

This very advance for the Western communist parties was also to prove an obstacle to transnational party co-operation. For in enshrining the concept of the independence and sovereignty of each communist party and elevating it to a sacred principle of inter-party relation, the Eurocommunists were inadvertently beaching their parties on the rocks of 'socialism in one country'. Whilst freeing themselves from the false internationalism of Soviet domination was certainly a step forward, the concept of national roads to socialism was a highly dubious point of departure in an era characterised above all by internationalisation. This was recognised by Altiero Spinelli as far back as 1956. Writing in the journal *Europa Federata* on 10 April, he declared:

> Oggi il problema fondamentale per l'umanità è la costruzione di comunità più ampie di quelle nazionali, di comunità di dimensoni continentali fra popoli di civiltà affine. In modi diversi queste strutture sono oggi possedute degli Stati Uniti, dall'URSS, dall'India, dalla Cina. L'Europa ne è priva grazie alla resistenza dei suoi vari nazionalismi. I comunisti hanno dato a credere di avere una riposta a questo problema. Oggi essi mostrano di essere invece anch'essi prigionieri del nazionalismo, di non avere che 'una via nazionale al socialismo', di essere cioè uno degli elementi della reazione nazionale.

> (Today the fundamental problem for humanity is the construction of communities that are broader than those of nations, of communities of continental dimensions between peoples of similar political cultures. In different ways, these structures are possessed today by the United States, the USSR, India and China. Europe lacks them, thanks to the resistance of its various nationalisms. The communists led us to believe that they had an answer to this problem. Instead, they show themselves also to be prisoners of nationalism, of having nothing beyond a 'national road to socialism', and thus of being one of the elements of national reaction.) (Spinelli Archives, cartella 17)

The point is not merely that the notion of the independence and sovereignty of each party mirrored the concept of the independence and sovereignty of the nation-state, which the PCI and others were recognising throughout the 1970s as anachronistic, but, moreover, that the sacred principle of 'non-interference' could be used, and was used, to inhibit relations between the Western parties moving beyond the purely formal level to embrace a pooling of ideological and strategic perspectives. Not merely were attempts by communist parties to engage in dialogue with intellectuals or leading members of other parties outside of official channels likely to be branded as interference, but even mild criticism of the policy positions of other parties, or attempts to contribute to the policy debates underway in other parties, was likely to be frozen out in the name of party sovereignty. This is particularly true of relations between the French and Italian parties. The Western communist parties, having won – in varying degrees of course – their independence from Moscow, were to prove much more reluctant then the socialists, liberals or conservatives to sacrifice party autonomy in the interests of inter-party exchange. The legacy of this was to bedevil attempts at transnational party co-operation within the various communist and Left groupings inside the European Parliament, for example.

An early example concerned the reactions of the Italian, French and Spanish parties towards the Greek Eurocommunist splinter group, the Communist Party of Greek-Interior (KKE-es), which emerged as a result of a split in the hardline Communist Party of Greece (KKE) in February 1968. (As we will see, the KKE-es would later transmogrify into the Coalition of Left and Progress, or Synaspismos, one of the parties we consider in the next chapter.) Although the subsequent evolution of the KKE-es during the 1970s and 1980s was to mirror, in many ways, the evolution of the Italian Communist Party, the PCI was most reluctant to extent formal recognition to the new party at first. Eventually the PCI resolved its dilemma by recognising both Greek communist parties – the contradictions in this position being eased by the fact that both parties were to sit together inside the Communists and Allies Group of the European Parliament after Greece's membership of the European Community in 1981. The French Communist Party preferred to refuse any recognition to the KKE-es during the 1970s, dealing exclusively with the KKE. The Spanish communists were most sympathetic to the new Greek Eurocommunist formation, but both the PCE and the PCI sought to avoid anything that smacked of favouritism in their dealings with the KKE-es. Kapetanyannis (1979, 458–9) suggests that relations were complicated by a desire to see the Greek communist movement reunited and by nervousness at upsetting Moscow. An additional and important factor was probably a desire not to transgress against the principle of non-interference that meant that support for Eurocommunist minorities within more hardline parties – or even for splinter groups – had to be discreet and indirect.

This unwillingness on the part of the PCI and PCE to be seen to be advocating convergence with their policy positions by supporting sympathetic minorities within the Greek or French communist movements obviously reflected the fears of these parties too at outside interference in their affairs. The PCE was to allege repeatedly throughout the 1980s that Moscow's hand (on occasions with the blessing of the Portuguese Communist Party, the PCP) was at work in fomenting dissent and schism within the Spanish communist ranks; by the late 1980s, after countless splits and schisms, there were more than twenty communist parties in Spain! And the PCI was always sensitive to relations between the Soviet embassy in Rome and the small pro-Soviet group within the PCI leadership around Armando Cossutta.

In practice, this served to inhibit transnational party exchanges of ideas and advances in policy and strategy for all such exchanges had to be conducted through carefully respected official bilateral channels to avoid the charge of manipulation of another party's internal disputes.

We can see this most clearly, perhaps, if we consider relations between the PCI and the PCF during the 1970s and 1980s. The traditionally suspicious and tense relations between the two parties had seemed, to many commentators, to give way to a new departure in the era of Eurocommunism, based on equality and mutual cooperation. Macleod (1980, 169) was to dub this new relationship one of 'fraternal diplomacy' and to date it from the Berlinguer–Marchais summit at Bologna in May 1973.

Whilst it was certainly true that the dawn of the new diplomacy involved the creation of channels of communication between the two parties, no longer so mediated by Moscow or the international communist movement, it was also the case (as Macleod points out) that the PCF was unwilling to engage in any pooling of decision-making power with the PCI or other Western European parties. Indeed, the PCF insisted throughout the period of Eurocommunism upon a formalistic interpretation of relations between the communist parties. This manifested itself in a number of ways.

First, the PCF saw no reason why divergences in policy or even fundamental strategy should lead to either open criticism of each other's position or to any rupture in relations. So long as the rites and rituals of the international communist movement were observed, relations between the parties could proceed on a 'correct' basis. This contrasted greatly with the evolving position of the PCI and PCE, which regarded the principle of non-interference as in no way inhibiting their right to pass comment on other parties' positions and increasingly saw common European problems as demanding not merely common solutions but an erosion of the formalism and rigid demarcations which characterised relations both between the communist parties and between the communists and other traditions. By the end of the 1980s, the PCI certainly had concluded that the concept of an 'international communist movement' was redundant, and that the challenges facing Europe demanded the immersion of the party in a much broader European left.

Second, the PCI and PCE interpretation of the exigencies of the evolving political situation in Europe led to a fundamental imbalance in relations between the parties. The PCI and PCE increasingly gave freer rein to their intellectuals and commentators to analyse in the party press developments within the PCF, whilst the latter stuck to the line of supporting the PCI line on all things Italian, reserving its criticisms for divergences in respect to the international communist movement. There is no doubt that this imbalance greatly facilitated the efforts of the PCI, in particular, to both deepen its critique of the PCF's half-hearted stance on the Soviet question, its unconvincing European commitment and its domestic sectarianism (and at the same time send a message to those within the PCI who might have been shared some of these positions), and to take its distance from the PCF when this was deemed politic. Macleod (1980, 180–3) gives a fairly detailed analysis of PCI criticisms of the PCF's relations with the socialists in France during the 1970s. Other examples include the detailed analysis by Augusto Pancaldi of a summit meeting between Berlinguer and Mitterrand and Jospin in Paris in 1982, which marked a further and perhaps decisive step down the road to the 'Euro-left' (reported in the PCI monthly paper, *Rinascita*, 2 April 1982), and the PCI's willingness to accord space in its press to the Spanish socialist leader Joaquin Leguina to expound his views on the crisis of the PCE (*Rinascita*, 5 November 1982). But the situation also gave rise to a noticeable resentment on the part of the PCF leadership towards the Italians, perceived as arrogant, interfering and undisciplined.

Perhaps where this resentment made itself felt most was in the PCF's suspicion of PCI involvement in promoting, or at any rate supporting, dissident groups within the PCF. This was especially so during the mid- and late-1980s, when the PCF leadership finally gave vent to its fury at the PCI – apparently no longer seeing that party as a true communist party. Following the launch of the *Mouvement des Rénovateurs Communistes* in 1988 – a group of PCF dissidents and former members who made explicit reference to the experience of the PCI (Hopkins, 1990, 25) – PCF criticism of the PCI grew shrill. This culminated in late 1989 and early 1990 when the two parties, by now at odds on every major issue and no longer even seated together in the European Parliament, came to blows over the PCI's decision to withdraw from a 30-year agreement under which Italian communists resident in France had been encouraged to join the PCF. The PCI moved to organise its own sections in France amongst Italian immigrants there.

The ensuing polemic was of unprecedented frankness and bitterness, marking the demise of the PCF's attempt to maintain formal relations on the old lines. The PCF denounced the PCI initiative as 'an act deeply contrary to communist morals' and expressed the conviction that the appeal to PCF members 'of Italian origin' to 'leave their communist party ... in order to adhere to a party whose future characteristics are not known and whose choices regard Italian political life' would fall on deaf ears. The PCF went further, lodging 'an angry protest' because a representative of the PCI had attended a conference of PCF dissidents (so-called *reconstructeurs*) and had thus 'not only brought his support to these few French communists fighting against their own party' but was guilty of 'an open aggression against the French communists' (all quotes are from *The Italian Communists*, October–December, 1989). The 'break' could not have been more explicit, ringing with resonance of earlier splits within the international communist movement.

But the fact is that by the end of the 1980s, the PCI no longer considered itself part of any communist movement, or bound to any other political party by sentiment. Its evolution had led it to seek programmatic convergence with other left forces, not based on ideological prejudgment. The yawning gulf between the PCF's letter to the PCI and the latter's response illustrates the point. The PCI, in rejecting 'this unfounded attack', reasserted 'its right to participate in any debate, organised by whoever' and pointed out that 'it would be quite strange if it were to reject [Italian immigrants'] membership applications or, worse, if it were to force them to join the PCF, from which deep differences in ideals and political views on essential questions separate us, unfortunately not only from today' (quoted in *The Italian Communists*, October–December 1989).

The point here is that the dramatic decline in PCI–PCF relations throughout the period, ending in rupture, is not simply notable for the policy differences or even ideological divergence which lies behind it; but also for the fact that the obvious hurt and sense of betrayal of the PCF and the impatience and barely concealed contempt of the PCI reflect the fact that the two parties had long ceased to speak a common language. Ultimately, the ritualism and rigid formalism that characterised relations between most of the Western communist parties contributed to the decline of dialogue and understanding between them. Whilst Eurocommunism equalled national communism, Eurocommunism was doomed to die of its own contradictions.

It is generally agreed that Eurocommunism involved an attempt by the parties concerned to address in a new way the question of the relationship between socialism and democracy – going beyond the worst aspects of the communist tradition which stigmatise 'bourgeois democracy' and human rights as purely formal and of secondary importance. But the search to reconcile the communist tradition with Western-style multi-party parliamentary democracy – based upon acceptance of political pluralism, diversity of social and political interests, the principle that a party may be ejected from office by the electorate in the same way that it is elected to office, a separation between party and state, and a clear delineation of the powers of state and rights of the individual – opened a Pandora's box of contradictions for the communist parties.

By the late 1980s it had become clear that the communist parties of Western Europe meant very different things when they spoke of their commitment to combining socialism and democracy. This was hardly surprising. The Eurocommunist commitment to pluralist parliamentary democracy called into question the very basis of the communist – i.e. Leninist – tradition. Although it was not initially obvious, the contradiction between accepting Western political democracy and adhering to Leninist concepts such as the democratic centralist model of party organisation and the notion of the special mission of the communist parties as 'vanguard' parties became steadily more acute as Eurocommunism staggered towards the exhaustion of its potential.

Considering the case of the PCE at the end of the 1970s, Diaz Lopez (1979, 351–2) wrote that the Eurocommunists could either attempt to renounce Leninism but retain allegiance to Marxism, seeking to reconstruct a third way or neo-communist course between social democracy and Soviet-style communism, or they could 'relativise' Leninism, effectively reducing it to a sentimental attachment to the symbols of the Bolshevik Revolution. The problem they faced is that a complete renunciation of Leninism 'would mean complete rejection of the socialist character of the October Revolution ... and consequently would force them to recognise their historical error and to accept the socialist thesis, critical of Stalin's misinterpretation of a state economy as true socialism and endangering, in this way, their separate identity'.

Such a course would also provoke internal dissent, lead to a profound crisis of identity and call into question any linkage to a world communist movement comprising in the main of ruling parties that were no longer defined as 'socialist' and non-ruling parties which, in the main, supported the positions of the Soviet Union and its allies. This is, in essence, the course adopted by the PCE under the leadership of Santiago Carrillo in the late 1970s and such a profound rejection of the communist tradition, whilst intellectually coherent and in keeping with the PCE's allegiance to the new Spanish democracy, contributed to the effective collapse of the party between 1979 and 1988 into warring factions. This is also the course followed by the PCI from the late 1980s onwards. And regardless of whether they retain the label 'communist' or not, virtually all of the parties we examine continue today to grapple with the fundamental existential questions implicit in Diaz Lopez's comments: if they are 'communist' then what does this mean after the collapse of the USSR? If they are no longer 'communist', then presumably their continuing existence as parties that are separate and distinct from mainstream social democracy reflects their adherence to a 'socialism' that has been betrayed or renounced by the social democrats. In this case, the question immediately arises as to whether – as Left parties, Green Leftists, or left-social democrats – they are capable of 'contesting' capitalism in any distinctive way.

In the 1970s, the PCI still sought to avoid such profound questions by following a more cautious strategy, stressing its fidelity to the communist tradition whilst, at the same time, pushing ahead with a dismantling of democratic centralist power structures, a profound rewriting of the content of socialist internationalism and a strengthening of its presence within, and contribution to, the institutions of both Italian and European parliamentary democracy. Critics might argue that whilst such a gradualist strategy helped preserve continuity – until the dramatic upheavals of 1989 – it also forestalled necessary debate and ultimately contributed to a profound loss of ideological clarity and political direction.

The Italian, Spanish and French communist parties, in particular, were to struggle unsuccessfully throughout the 1970s and 1980s to resolve the contradictions between their declared democratic vocation and their communist identity – contradictions rooted in communist tradition and ideology. The glaring contradiction between a commitment to social and political pluralism and a pledge to uphold human rights and individual freedoms, on the one hand, and democratic centralism, on the other, for example, was to haunt all three parties. In the case of the PCE, the allegedly authoritarian style of leadership of Santiago Carrillo – accused of implementing Eurocommunist reform by force – led to widespread dissatisfaction within the party and ultimately to the downfall of Carrillo himself in 1982. His successor, Gerardo Iglesias, was to struggle with the dilemma of leading a party whose hierarchical structures were so obviously at odds with its professed ideological renewal for the next six years (Mujal-León, 1983 and 1986). Only with the final transcendence of democratic centralism and the acceptance of internal pluralism – a development greatly facilitated by the birth of the Izquierda Unida electoral coalition in 1987 – was the PCE's identity crisis able to reach some sort of resolution. The birth of Izquierda Unida can be seen as an acknowledgement that the potential for further growth, whilst remaining within the communist tradition, was exhausted; for whilst Izquierda Unida did involve the beginning of a process of unification with some hard-line communists who had previously left the party, it also involved a decisive opening to the Green, feminist and pacifist movements. Most significantly, it permitted the PCE, whilst remaining in existence as a party in its own right, to effectively bury the legacy of Carrillo's hyper-centralism and to experiment in practice with the political pluralism that its theoretical positions had embraced. But by then its political and electoral weight in Spain had suffered enormous damage. The transcendence of democratic centralism and the adoption of an organisational model more familiar to non-communist leftwing parties was finally completed in 1990 when the PCE voted to permit the formation of currents within the party.

In the case of the PCF, the leadership of George Marchais was to reject all attempts to modify democratic centralism, driving wave after wave of critical leaders and intellectuals out of the party, and critically undermining public confidence in the sincerity of the PCF's professed acceptance of political democracy in the process (Hopkins, 1990).

The PCI, by the end of the 1980s, had come to the realisation that democratic centralism could no longer be sustained. Faced with growing internal opposition from both the left and the right of the party, the leadership of Alessandro Natta and later Achille Occhetto chose to legitimise internal diversity rather than take a step backwards by attempting to impose the authority of the centre by force. The period 1988-91 saw a significant and real transformation of the PCI's internal power structures with the acceptance of the rights of minority and majority to state their case openly, the election of delegates to the party's leadership bodies on the basis of differing platforms and the publication of divisions within the party central committee. When the PCI daily, *l'Unità*, carried the front-page headline '*Battaglia politica nel comitato centrale*' ('Political battle in the central committee') in its report of 27 June 1987, it was obvious that a fundamental break with communist organisational tradition has been made.

The abandonment of democratic centralist practices by the PCI had already been anticipated during the 1970s by the Greek Eurocommunist formation, the KKE-es. According to Kapetanyannis (in Featherstone and Katsoudas, 1987, 56), the KKE-es had evolved, since the transition to democracy in Greece, as a much looser and more liberal party than the KKE:

Discussions are free – there are no 'unanimous' decisions any more – and there is a statutory obligation to publish minority opinions, which has been standard practice in recent years. Respect for democratic values and procedures, party and media pluralism and the 'democratic road to Greek socialism' by popular voting consensus constitute fundamental party principles which are basically adhered to in political practice.

The KKE-es, then, had almost from its inception – certainly from its emergence into the democratic light following the overthrown of the Greek colonels' dictatorship in 1974 – broken significantly with an important part of the communist tradition and cleared the way for its participation in the search for a new alignment of the left. Indeed, the decision of this party in 1986 to rename itself Greek Left (EA) represented more than just a change of name; it marked the decisive move of the party into the post-communist phase, thereby anticipating the PCI by some four years. The new Greek Left was to be a party of the broad democratic socialist left, holding out against the Pan-Hellenic Socialist Movement's (PASOK's) drift to the political right in economic terms and attacking PASOK's alleged involvement in political corruption and the old practices of clientelism, but essentially not differing in principle from a socialist perspective. Its subsequent absorption into an even more post-communist formation, the Coalition of Left and Progress (Synaspismos) would complete the transition.

But perhaps of even more significance than the debate over democratic centralism has been the Western communist parties' efforts to grapple with another aspect of their inheritance which casts doubt on the compatibility of communism with democracy: the concept of the communist party as the vanguard party. For this old Leninist concept implied that, even when a communist party entered into alliances with other socialist or social democratic parties or movements, the cause of socialism could only be advanced if the communist party – the holder of the scientific truths – was entrusted with the leadership of such alliances.

Vanguardism undoubtedly served to undermine the communist parties' capacity to engage in genuine political co-operation with other political forces and led to a barrier of suspicion and distrust isolating the communists from other political forces. Whilst the communists clung to the notion that they were qualitatively different from other political forces – superior – they could scarcely expect to be taken seriously as potential coalition partners by non-communist parties, which were all too aware of what had happened in Eastern Europe in the name of vanguardism during the late 1940s and early 1950s.

The political culture of vanguardism expresses perhaps most clearly the limitations of communist strategy. Whilst the vanguardist legacy might well serve to reinforce the party's unity and effectiveness in conditions of underground struggle, it lacks all logic when a party is competing electorally with other political forces in conditions of pluralist democracy. Given that none of the communist parties of Western Europe has ever stood the slightest realistic chance of winning an absolute majority of the electorate to its side, the question of alliances becomes central to communist thinking. The search for socio-political alliances capable of carrying forward a radical transformation of capitalist society has, however, been frustrated time and time again by the fact that potential allies have, for good reason, been wary of association with a movement which has long instrumentalised other peoples' struggles. The variety of communist responses to this dilemma underlines the contradictions of Eurocommunism: the fact that Eurocommunism, by its nature, could indeed only ever have been of a transitional nature.

For the French, Portuguese and Greek communist parties, vanguardism remained an untouchable concept – without which the very existence of the communist parties as independent political forces could be called into question. (Ironically, the belated abandonment of the concept by the PCF in recent years coincides with a calamitous decline in that party's electoral fortunes that has, indeed, called its existence as an independent force into question; likewise, in Portugal, the PCP's painful efforts in the 1990s to edge away from past dogmas reflect a real crisis in terms of membership and electoral support.) These parties sought therefore to place a higher premium on their self-proclaimed leadership roles than on the success of their alliance strategies. In the mid-1980s, as in the late 1970s, the PCF, faced not merely with electoral losses but, arguably of greater importance, with an erosion of its ability to control and direct the 'Union of the Left' in France, would prefer a complete rupture of relations with the socialists and a re-ghettoisation to an acceptance of the loss of its vanguard role within the left. The PCF, during the 1980s, would speak of the need to create a new '*rassemblement des forces de la gauche*' to oppose the 'revisionism' of the Mitterrand presidency and the Socialist Party. The critical point here is that such a front, unlike the old 'Union of the Left', would be under PCF leadership and guidance. This attempt to solve the problem of the party's isolation and the collapse of its alliances strategy came to nothing and by the end of the 1980s the PCF seemed more ghettoised than ever. From the mid-1990s, a new leader, Robert Hue, would once again tie the party's fortunes to the Socialist Party's coat tails, though without any clearly discernible strategy in mind and without any end to the haemorrhaging of members and voters.

The PCP, ever since its attempt to ride to power on the back of the Armed Forces Movement (MFA) in Portugal in 1975, has found itself likewise isolated – perhaps not surprisingly, given its insistence upon clinging to the notion that '... only the communist parties and no other political force can show the workers and the peoples of their countries how to resolve their pressing problems' (Cunhal, 1988, 7). And the KKE has, with little success, sought to protect its 'leading role' by building a popular front from the bottom up with disillusioned PASOK activists (Loulis, 1986).

By contrast, the Spanish and Italian parties had effectively abandoned vanguardism by the end of the 1980s, though not without problems and contradictions in the process. The PCE under Carrillo was forced to reconsider its ambitions to become the hegemonic party of the Spanish left, faced with electoral setbacks and internal disarray. It is only in the late 1980s, with the advent of the Izquierda Unida experiment, that the party seems to have abandoned the notion of a 'working-class party armed with the correct Marxist method' in favour of a looser and more amorphous political formation. The PCI illustrates most strikingly the agonies of a communist party seeking to transcend this central aspect of its tradition without destroying its own legitimacy and perhaps even *raison d'être* in the process (a struggle it would ultimately lose, of course). During the 1970s the party conceded that it no longer possessed a monopoly of the political truth with party leader Enrico Berlinguer, in his famous exchange of letters with Bishop Luigi Bettazzi, stressing the non-dogmatic nature of the PCI's politics and political commitment (Swidler and Grace, 1988). And yet, Berlinguer's very insistence upon the 'moral superiority' of the PCI to other political forces, which he accused of having degenerated, was to both obstruct the party's search to construct a 'new historic bloc' and lead to a sharp exchange of views within the party at the beginning of the 1980s, with many arguing against what they saw as vanguardism in a new guise. (For a discussion of the exchange of polemics on this point between Berlinguer and the leader of the PCI's social democratic wing, Giorgio Napolitano, see Ruscoe, 1982.)

During the course of the 1980s, the PCI was to effectively jettison the Gramscian view of the party as the 'organic intellectual of the working-class' in favour of a more modest ambition – the rebirth of the party in 1991 as a Democratic Party of the Left, beyond the communist tradition. This decision would seem to reflect, in the eyes of the party majority, the impossibility of achieving a programmatic and theoretical integration of communism and Western pluralism.

The inability of the communist parties either to consummate the marriage between socialism and democracy or to articulate any transnational strategy without moving beyond the communist inheritance is also illustrated by the fact that Eurocommunism masked some very different, indeed opposing, views as to the content of democracy. Whereas the Italian and Spanish parties, together with their allies elsewhere, generally came to see democracy as a process whereby power is disseminated and civil society strengthened at the expense of the state, the French and Portuguese and Greek parties continued to speak of democracy as the exercise of power by a state machine controlled by the party of the working-class. Whereas the Italians and the Spanish essentially accepted the absolute (not relative) value and importance of formal rights, such as freedom of speech and association, representation of interests and protection of minorities, the Portuguese and Greek parties continued to dismiss 'bourgeois democratic' rights as at best something to be instrumentalised and at worst an illusion to be shattered. The PCF, too, during the Eurocommunist phase, consistently revealed its ambiguities in two ways: (1) by insisting on the regional nature of Eurocommunism – i.e., the innovations of Eurocommunism in the field of democratic theory were to be understood as a response to the conditions of advanced capitalist societies and did not imply that other (more traditional) communist paths could not be trodden elsewhere (as in Cuba, for example); and (2) by, on occasion, invoking the 'peoples' democracies' of Eastern Europe as examples of multi-party systems.

The fact that Eurocommunism, despite the rhetorical eloquence of the joint communiqués issued by the PCI, PCF and PCE, clothed a variety of incompatible positions on the question of democracy was evident from the response of the various parties to the role of the Portuguese Communist Party's attempt to seize power in 1975, following the Portuguese anti-fascist revolution. The Portuguese events of 1974-76 confronted the three principal Eurocommunist parties with a dangerous situation, for here was an unashamedly pro-Soviet communist party openly 'pouring scorn on bourgeois democracy' (Gallagher, 1979, 211) and declaring itself ready to take advantage of a revolutionary situation. The PCI and PCE reacted to the Portuguese party's adventurism with alarm and great hostility – condemning the attempt to seize power as authoritarian and demanding protection for the Portuguese Socialist Party (PSP), which felt most threatened by the PCP's behaviour.

Indeed, an early convergence here with the social democratic camp can be noted. The Italian and Spanish communists, fearing that the imposition of a pro-Soviet single-party dictatorship in Portugal would do irreparable damage to the cause of Eurocommunism in Western Europe, effectively closed ranks with the party of Mario Soares (strongly supported by the West German SPD) in demanding a reversal of the PCP's strategy in the summer of 1975. In particular, the PCI and PCE condemned the PCP for abandoning the parliamentary road to socialism. By contrast, the PCF defended the PCP's actions and 'upbraided the Italians for openly attacking a brother party in its hour of difficulty' (Macleod, 1983, 300). The sharp divergence in the parties' reactions to the Portuguese events can be seen as highlighting a number of fundamental differences in the meaning that they attached to Eurocommunism.

First, it is clear that the Italians and Spanish had by now committed themselves firmly to Western pluralist and democratic political institutions and to Western democratic values – accepted now in good faith and no longer in a tactical sense – and that they had come to regard the political terrain upon which the Eurocommunist parties operated as being very firmly located in the 'Western camp', whilst hoping, of course, for an eventual withering away of the blocs in Europe. The PCF by contrast was in a much more ambiguous position, both in terms of its attitude towards the international role of the Soviet Union and in its inability to transcend a dual-track approach to democracy: playing according to the rules of the game, but seeing no contradiction between this and 'seizing the revolutionary opportunity' should one arise. (Although when a revolutionary opportunity arguably did arise, in May 1968, the PCF, ever the most conservative of political animals, helped to stabilise the situation.)

Second, the Italian and Spanish communists were already evolving a very different approach to the socialist and social democratic parties of Western Europe. Although it would be 1979 before the PCI would formally embrace the 'new internationalism' as its official policy, it was already moving closer to the main social democratic parties and beginning to conceive of Eurocommunism as more than just a common front adopted by the Western European communist parties; rather, as a step towards a more profound realignment of the European left forces prepared to engage in a search for a third way between classical social democracy and the traditions of the communist movement. In this, the PCI could count upon the support of the PCE (although both parties were, in the 1980s, to experience major problems in their relations with their domestic socialist competitors) which had, as early as its Eighth Congress in 1972, outlined a vision of a Europe between the superpowers where 'Communists, Socialists and other forces' worked together (Mujal-León, 1983, 119). (The real differences between the PCI and the PCE would arise years later. With the failure of the envisaged 'third way', the PCI would reconceptualise Eurocommunism as a transition towards full immersion in European social democracy, setting itself the goal of transmogrification into Italy's main social democratic formation, with or without Bettino Craxi's corrupt and discredited smaller party. The PCE, faced with the larger and immensely more successful Spanish Socialist Workers' Party of Felipe Gonzalez, could never contemplate that leap without fatally undermining its own existence. It would have to struggle to maintain a political space to the left of social democracy.) The PCI and PCE had no intention of allowing the PCP to interfere with their search for such a realignment and were particularly concerned with PCP attacks on the Portuguese socialists in consequence. The PCF, by contrast, was locked in struggle with the French Socialist Party (PS) for leadership of the French left.

Third, once again, the parties were clearly displaying very different understandings of the ground rules supposed to govern relations between communist parties, with the PCI and PCE insisting on their right to offer criticism of the policies of another party they considered to be engaging in fundamentally mistaken behaviour, and the PCF once more insisting on a literal and formalistic interpretation of 'non-interference'.

The irreconcilable divergence between the new internationalism of the PCI and the PCE and the PCF's inability to turn its face westwards marked the final demise of Eurocommunism in the period 1979-81. This period was marked both by electoral setbacks that the PCI, PCF and PCE all shared in common and by the Soviet invasion of Afghanistan and the imposition of martial law in Poland, events that demanded from the three parties a clear and painful 'choice of camp'. In other words, the early project of Eurocommunism – the search for a common understanding between the major communist parties of Western Europe which would enable them to play a major role (for some, *the* major role) along with other progressive and socialist forces in building a newly autonomous Europe – was crucially bound to the possibility of détente and the gradual dismantling of the two blocs in Europe. The onset of the new cold war posed a major and ultimately fatal dilemma: to push ahead with democratic reformism, even at the risk of a break with the international communist movement, or to rally to the defence of the USSR as during the original Cold War. The PCI and PCE opted (not without internal strain and even anguish) for the first course; the PCF retrenched on terrain never vacated by the Portuguese and Greek communist parties. (For the text of the main PCI resolution on the events in Poland, and for extracts from the debate in the PCI central committee, see Berlinguer, 1982.) It is fair to say that the PCI, although its room for manoeuvre was greatly contracted by the cold war, sought consistently to act as a mediator between East and West, opposing in no uncertain terms the Soviet actions and declaring that the imposition of martial law in Poland was 'a blow to the cause of socialism' and marked the exhaustion of the potential of the communist model rooted in October 1917. At the same time, it stressed its support for liberation movements in the Third World such as the ANC and the PLO, and refused to engage in a cold war campaign of sanctions and boycotts against the USSR. In the PCI's view, such a campaign could only contribute to the weakening of Europe as a whole. However, such a consistent espousal of the need for transcendence of the Yalta division of Europe was lost on the chorus of journalists and commentators for whom 'proof' of the party's commitment to Western-style democracy necessitated uncritical acceptance of Western-style capitalism.

The 1980s thus opened with the Eurocommunist project effectively abandoned, although it was to be some time before this to be become apparent. From the beginning of the decade, the vague and nebulous concept of a 'Euro-left' began to figure prominently in the propaganda of the PCI especially, effectively replacing the notion of Eurocommunism (although vagueness allowed the two terms to appear compatible at first). In fact, the Italians had begun their search for allies capable of giving expression to the transnational European left programme which they believed essential if the future of the European Community was not to be left in the hands of conservative forces. It was ultimately the European question that was to prove decisive in bringing the PCI and its allies to assist in the creation of a new Western European left, from one perspective; or in contributing to the social democratisation of these parties, from another.

The Soviet invasion of Afghanistan in the winter of 1979, which accelerated the onset of the new cold war, can be seen in retrospect as drawing a line beneath the experience of Eurocommunism. It is from this point on that the realignment of the European left (of which the PCI and others had spoken) begins – although, ultimately, the institutional forms which that realignment was to take would, to the chagrin of many within the PCI and the PCE, suggest not so much a convergence of Eurocommunism and social democracy on some 'third way' as a mutation of the former into a variant of the latter. But this did not become clear until the end of the 1980s, and even then the leadership of the PCI would insist that the Europeanisation of the social democratic parties had made possible the realignment by pointing towards the supersession of the limitations of traditional social democratic strategy (as well as the limitations of the communist tradition). Moreover, there remained those who disputed that the creation of a new 'Euro-left' was in fact best served by entrance into the Socialist International and who continued to hope that the 'third way' might yet lead in a different direction.

The PCF reacted to the Soviet invasion of Afghanistan by supporting the Soviet version of events; the PCI by condemning the invasion in strong terms. Indeed, the incident saw communist Members of the European Parliament on opposite sides of the political divide when the European Parliament debated the issue. Again, the imposition of martial law in Poland saw a clear divide between those parties, such as the PCI, PCE and the KKE-es, which unreservedly condemned the Polish coup, and those, such as the PCP and KKE, which supported it. The PCF, expressing 'concern' at events in Poland, effectively moved to normalise relations with the Polish military regime, implying full acceptance of events in that country.

In actual fact, the PCF was reacting to the rupture of its relations with the French PS and to electoral setbacks imposed upon it by the socialists by seeking to retrench in at least three ways. First, it sought to emphasise once again those characteristics that distinguish a communist party from a 'revisionist' party such as the PS, which could only be expected to betray the working-class. This led the PCF leadership both to assail any tendency towards a 'Euro-left' which blurred the distinctions between the communist and socialist traditions (deemed tantamount to undermining the former's identity) and to insist upon an appeal to the core elements of the communist sub-culture: vanguardism, democratic centralism, party discipline, ideological unity, etc. Second, the PCF, in attempting to maintain the unifying force of the communist sub-culture, sought to give its militants 'the feeling that in world terms they are on the winning side' (Hassner, 1980–81, 459). This necessitated yet another of the PCF's swings back toward the USSR. The 1980s opened with the party 'facing eastward' and with some socialist commentators even speculating that the party was banking on a strengthening in Soviet power world-wide by the end of the decade to compensate for electoral losses which it was prepared to accept rather than abandon its exclusivity (PS leader Jean Poperen, quoted in Friend, 1980, 42). Third, the PCF sought to overcome the dilemma of breaking out of its isolation whilst simultaneously resisting all osmosis by aggressively projecting itself as the defender of French national interests against the dual threat of American imperialism and the European Community.

This retrenchment on the terrain of nationalism – wrapping itself in the flag of France – was fully in keeping with the tradition of 'socialism in one country' so central to the PCF, as to many other communist parties. The psychological and political connection between pro-sovietism and the national communism of non-ruling communist parties such as the PCF, PCP and KKE – both rooted in the concept of 'socialism in one country', both reflecting nationalistic arrogance and appealing to patriotic sentiment, both involving an essentially statist vision of socialism that prioritises the role and potential of the nation-state, and both accepting, and indeed, taking strength from a simple bipolar, bloc-against-bloc view of the modern world – is often overlooked by commentators who focus on the contradictions between Soviet demands and the electoral interests of the Western European communist parties in power. In reality, the source of friction and tension between a party such as the PCF and the USSR from time to time was not to be found in the fact that it is pursuing a 'national road to socialism' per se, but in other factors such as the search for tactical and strategic advantage through alliance strategies which might necessitate a distancing from Moscow.

The fact that the PCF should, with the Polish party, convene a Paris Conference of European communist and workers' parties in May 1980 to launch a (blatantly pro-Soviet) campaign against NATO missiles (nothing being said against Warsaw Pact missiles), at the same time as asserting its nationalism once again, should not therefore surprise us.

For the PCI, however, the recourse to a leftwing variant of nationalism was not a viable option. Whilst the coupling of nationalism and revolution had a long tradition in France, the Italian situation was quite different. For one thing, as Altiero Spinelli has pointed out (Urban, 1978, 15), the relative weakness of the Italian nation-state and of Italian nationalist ideology in general, meant that an Italy led by the PCI that detached itself from the rest of the European Community risked suffering chronic political instability. Such a course, argued Spinelli, 'would have put Italy in the company of half-developed countries nursing their grievances without much hope of putting them right. This might have been an acceptable prospect for a certain type of atavistic fascism, but not for a modern and progressive party'. Much the same might be said of Spain, given the weakness of that country's democratic institutions that weighed on the minds of the Spanish communists. The PCE would increasingly share with the Spanish Socialist Workers' Party (PSOE), especially after an attempted rightwing coup in the early 1980s, the view that Spain's anchorage inside the European Community would help to consolidate democracy.

Having rejected the Soviet model and asserted their independence of Moscow, then, the Italian communists 'had no choice but to adopt European unification as the central plank in their new foreign policy' (Urban, 1978, 15) – and, it might be added, having witnessed the failure of the main communist parties of Western Europe to articulate a common strategy for the attainment of a united Europe led from the left, they had no choice but to look beyond the communist tradition for allies in their struggle for European unification.

In moving beyond the parameters of the communist movement to embrace the socialist and social democratic parties of Europe as partners in the search for a European model of democratic socialism capable of articulating a reformist strategy at the level of the European Community, the PCI could also count upon the support of the Greek Communist Party-interior. The KKE-es had long established working relations with a number of Western European socialist parties, including the French Socialist Party (Kapetanyannis, 1979, 459). The Communist Party of Spain – in fundamental agreement with the PCI on most ideological and strategic issues, and differing fundamentally with the PCP over the latter's behaviour during the Portuguese revolution, and with the PCF over that party's opposition to Spain's membership of the European Community – also had an interest in extending its horizons further beyond the communist tradition. Indeed, from the mid-1970s, the PCE under Carrillo was attempting to strengthen its ties to socialist and social democratic parties (Mujal-León, 1986, 4).

Not surprisingly, the PCI was joined by the KKE-es and the PCE (despite strong internal opposition by critics of Carrillo) in boycotting the May 1980 Paris Conference of communist parties called by George Marchais with East European support. The conference, attended by the PCP and KKE amongst others, marked the PCF's final break with the PCI in terms of any possible attempt to articulate a transnational Western European communist strategy and its retrenchment on the grounds of communist tradition. Indeed, the May 1980 conference may be seen as an attempt by the PCF to respond to the problem of its growing isolation both within France and within the ambit of the Western communist forces represented in the European Parliament by proposing the reconstitution of the 'international communist movement'. PCI and PCE non-attendance was explained by those parties precisely in terms of their refusal to countenance any such resurrection of an internationalism that was confined to the communist parties and might serve to prevent them from extending their horizons to embrace other political traditions. From 1980, the PCF consistently sought to lend its support to Soviet initiatives that aimed at convening a world conference of communist parties, only to be resisted by the PCI and PCE and their allies. At the PCF congress in December 1990, George Marchais again returned to this theme, calling for a regrouping of communist forces in defence of Cuba and Vietnam, *inter alia*.

The early 1980s also saw the beginning of direct and formal contacts between the PCI and PCE and the main socialist and social democratic parties of Western Europe. In March 1980 Berlinguer met with Willi Brandt to discuss Afghanistan and he returned to the theme two months later when he met Mitterrand in Strasbourg (Macleod, 1980, 195). In so doing he violated, in the PCF's eyes, the sacred principle of non-interference – for this was clearly understood by the PCF to rule out not merely interference in the internal affairs of another communist party, but (unauthorised) contact with other political forces in that party's country or even commentary on a country's affairs that did not follow the party line of the domestic communist party. In effect what the PCI and PCE were moving towards, and what the PCF was anxious to prevent, was the development of a 'Euro-left' strategy that would liquidate the vanguard role of the communist parties (Macleod, 1980, 195).

So what exactly was meant by the term 'Euro-left' as it was developed by the PCI especially during the 1980s? And how did it relate to the so-called new internationalism of that party and its allies? Although many contemporary writers tended towards the view that the 'Euro-left' was primarily a device by which the PCI hoped to free itself of embarrassing association with other (less reputable) communist parties, shake off its isolation, and so increase its attractiveness to the Italian electorate, it can also be argued that the new departure was rooted in the logic of the party's European policy and that, moreover, this was the decisive factor in bringing about the party's eventual break with the communist tradition altogether. It was also suggested that, in courting the friendship of powerful social democratic parties such as the German SPD and the French PS, the PCI leadership was also hoping to put pressure on Bettino Craxi's Italian Socialist Party and to break down opposition from within the Second International to the PCI's entrance into the government of Italy (Macleod, 1980, 196). The point is that the PCI's innovation in terms of a 'Euro-left' was widely seen as determined by domestic political and tactical consideration. I would argue, however, that the 'Euro-left' must be understood as a transitional device enabling the PCI to relocate itself within the European political spectrum – a relocation necessitated by strategic concerns: principally the inability of the communist movement to give effective expression to any transnational and supranational reformatory programme. In fact, the leadership of the PCI and PCE had arrived at a conclusion hinted at by Donald Sassoon in 1979:

> if Eurocommunism is to develop at all it can only be to the extent to which it enters into a fruitful dialogue with the rest of the European Left. There is thus little point in continuing the discussion on Eurocommunism without having as a general perspective the whole of the European labour movement and the distinct contribution which each party (whether communist or socialist) can give to the elaboration of common policies. (Sassoon, 1979, 88)

The 'new internationalism' as defined by Berlinguer, in the wake of the Soviet invasion of Afghanistan and the imposition of martial law in Poland, was clearly related to the search for a 'third way' between social democracy and Stalinism (or Soviet-style Marxism-Leninism). At this stage, Berlinguer was at pains to point out that this did not involve any acceptance of capitalism, but rather was a radical transformatory project necessitated by the new requirements of the era and fully in keeping with the PCI's dialectical and Marxist analytical tradition:

> Obviously we are not trying to find a middle road halfway between socialism and capitalism – but we point this out once more because there are still some misunderstandings. The matter at issue is how to overcome capitalism at the stage it has reached for us here, in the industrialised and developed West, and to overcome it by building a socialism which is achieved by guaranteeing protection of the democratic liberties which have already been won and by extending them. (Berlinguer, 1982, 40)

These 'new requirements of the era' were essentially three-fold. First, Berlinguer mentioned the total exhaustion of the economic, political and moral potential of the Soviet model and of a communist tradition that remained trapped within the parameters of Third Internationalism, and the corresponding failure of classical social democracy (as practised in the countries of northern Europe, for example) to achieve any real transformation of capitalist production relations or to escape from American tutelage. Second, he spoke of the increasingly grave problems of the era – the onset of a new cold war with a renewed arms race, consuming precious resources; the widening gap between the north and the south of the world, with the danger that a united Europe could become simply a new exploitative superpower; and the increasing incidence of uneven economic development within Europe, with mounting sectoral unemployment and discrimination against weak and marginalised groups. Third, there was the inability of the nation-state to address such problems as the internationalisation of the economy (with growing concentration of power and influence upon governments in the hands of the multinationals and the monopolies), the environmental crisis, the need to master new technology, etc.

In a reflective article published in 1989, the PCI foreign affairs spokesperson, Antonio Rubbi, was to explain the motivation behind the new internationalism as a growing realisation that the fundamental and immediate task facing the left was not so much the achievement of socialism – but the struggle to preserve the planet from catastrophe through wars, environmental pollution, waste of resources and international anarchy:

> The Communists [previously] saw the struggle for socialism as their urgent and immediate task and naturally oriented their work on the forces that had a direct stake in socialism – first and foremost the working-class and its closest allies, national and international working-class unity and close co-operation among communist parties. All this was reflected in the concept of 'proletarian internationalism'. But it was becoming increasingly clear to us that reality and the practical aspects of social struggle highlighted the flaws in a formula that only emphasised the unity of proletarian, communist forces.
>
> Priority shifted to the preservation of peace, human survival, closing the gap between developed and underdeveloped countries, the population explosion, the spread of hunger, environmental protection, etc. – away from socialism as the immediate objective. (Rubbi, 1989, 64)

In other words, an internationalism which confined itself to the reconstitution of an international communist movement, assuming the prioritisation of the class struggle for example (and by extension the struggle between the blocs), was not merely deemed undesirable but was seen as positively harmful and contrary to the struggle for a progressive resolution of humankind's problems. Such views did not merely reflect Gorbachev's 'new thinking' in Moscow in the late 1980s: they long preceded, and may well have strongly influenced, Gorbachev's evolving philosophy. Of course, the new internationalism can be read in a number of ways. Those sympathetic to the PCI leadership will see a genuine and inspired attempt to come to terms, dialectically, with the new contradictions of the epoch, and to make the strategic and ideological adjustments necessary to address these contradictions – an undertaking worthy of any Marxist party deserving of the name. Those less sympathetic – or swayed by hindsight – will see an attempt to provide an ideological justification for the extension to the international arena of the party's domestic strategy of the historic compromise, rooted in the party's increasingly desperate search for acceptance and legitimacy, not merely with the Italian voters, but in Washington, Bonn and elsewhere; and leading to a progressive loss of the party's identity. The PCI was in consequence to struggle against any initiative designed to encourage an international gathering of communist parties, insisting on the presence of social democratic parties and other progressive forces (for example, Christian forces) on an equal footing.

Berlinguer, in the early 1980s, saw ferment and new thinking within a number of the social democratic and socialist parties of northern Europe, where self-criticism and questioning had been provoked by the electoral stagnation afflicting such parties in the late 1970s and 1980s and by the crisis of the welfare state. New thinking could especially be seen within the German SPD, which seemed to be moving away from the positions of the Bad Godesburg programme towards a dialogue with the peace movement and the Greens, a renewed analysis of the processes of production and consumption, and above all a profound Europeanisation of its programme during the early 1980s. But the PCI's new internationalism was, in theory at least, not supposed to be confined to relations with creative elements within the social democratic and socialist parties; also of importance was a new relationship with the social movements: the peace, environmental and women's movements, for example, which had arisen in response to the failure of the traditional left to come to grips with new challenges. The notion of a 'Euro-left', then, at this stage in the PCI's thinking certainly, was not simply (or not yet) a camouflage behind which the party could quietly assimilate to prevailing social democratic practice and theory. It involved a genuine attempt to articulate a new transformatory strategy for the left in Europe that both went beyond the existing communist and socialist traditions and embraced new issues that these traditions had both ignored.

The role of the PCI in helping to create such a 'Euro-left' was seen as pivotal. The party should, according to Berlinguer's view, act as a go-between and a mediator between those socialist or social democratic parties engaged in the search for new answers to problems and those communist parties prepared likewise to question old assumptions. For this reason, there could be no question of breaking off relations with any communist party in Europe (such as the French or the Portuguese) that did not conform to the PCI's policy stance. Such a break would merely unbalance the PCI's delicate attempt to create something new. Likewise, the party should seek to preserve those characteristics which distinguished it from other social democratic *and* communist parties: it should refuse to either retreat into dogmatism or to become a mere electoral machine but should remain a mass party, responsive to changes in society.

The three concepts – third way, new internationalism and 'Euro-left' – can thus be seen to be interrelated. The third way between social democracy and Marxism-Leninism represented the strategic direction which the forces of a radical and transformatory left should take, not merely converging on some point midway between the traditions of the Second and Third Internationals but going beyond both. The 'Euro-left' indicated the conglomeration of forces capable of embarking on such an adventure – drawn from within both communist and socialist traditions and from other progressive traditions including feminism, ecology and the Catholic (and other denominational) peace movements. The term had the double advantage of both indicating the centrality of the transnational or supranational aspect to the new strategic thinking – 'Euro-left' forces shared a common determination to change the nature of the European Community from within and to redress relations between Eastern and Western Europe and between Europe and the Third World – and of being sufficiently vague as to allow other communist and socialist parties and social movements to be 'won over' later. Finally, the new internationalism referred in essence to the secularisation, or de-ideologisation, of relations between the PCI and other communist and socialist parties, permitting a programmatic (and ultimately, ideological) convergence between forces unhindered by old dichotomies now deemed obsolete. Of course, all of this depended, for its success, on the willingness and ability of other parties to change their thinking and move their positions; from the outset, the success or failure of the 'Euro-left' project was beyond the PCI's control. This was to prove crucial, and fatal. After 1989, the rapidly accelerating speed of events and the failure of any significant leftwing party outside of the social democratic mainstream to converge with the PCI's strategic thinking on the future of Europe and of the left, would ultimately lead the PCI to abandon the search for a 'third way' in favour of assimilation to social democracy. By the time the phrase, 'third way', would resurface in the late 1990s, it would be far removed from its Berlinguerian usage – reflecting, instead, the desire of some within the Italian Left Democrats (DS) to wholeheartedly embrace Blairism.

In the early 1980s, Berlinguer's thinking – to which the PCI's European commitment was central – had very broad support within the PCI, from the radical Marxist left led by Pietro Ingrao to the social democratic right led by Giorgio Napolitano. By the end of that decade – Berlinguer died in 1984 and the PCI suffered electoral setbacks (apart from a sympathy vote in the 1984 European Parliament elections) and a growing sense of isolation and crisis thereafter – little remained apart from the enthusiasm for European integration. For many Italians, and not just those supporting the PCI, 'Europe' had come to exercise an almost talismanic power – the universal solution to the corrupt, paralysed, blocked and delegitimised Italian political system. The support for European federalism would if anything grow in intensity, but the PCI's principal successor-party would rapidly abandon any serious transformatory project that pointed towards the transcendence of capitalism, as the changing domestic and international situation demolished the fragile edifice upon which Berlinguer's key concepts rested. The collapse of the Soviet Union and the discrediting of communism in general, the retreat of the PCF and the refusal of the PCP or KKE to engage in the search for a new European left, the virtual disintegration of the PCE during the 1980s, a considerable weakening in the presence and influence of the new social movements, and an uncertain and defensive response by some of the main social democratic parties to events after 1989 – all forced the PCI to play the part not so much of a mediator between the communist and social democratic components of the traditional European left but rather a supplicant knocking on the door of social democracy.

When it first entered the European Parliament the PCI had explained its role there as involving not just the defence of Italian workers' interests but also the representation of the interests of the other communist parties in the Community, which were either too weak electorally to merit representation or (like the French) were still excluded by their national governments on prejudicial grounds. During the course of the 1980s it was to conduct a privileged dialogue with the social democrats aiming at a redefinition of the European left, whilst effectively speaking on behalf of, or representing, those communist parties which broadly shared its positions but were too small (the KKE-es, later EA) or too troubled internally (the PCE) to play a full part in the process. At the same time, it refused to 'burn its bridges' with other communist parties and sought to extend the dialogue to non-traditional progressive forces such as the German Greens.

Eventually, however, it was the PCI's growing dialogue with the French socialists and the West German social democrats in particular that was to lead to much speculation as to the direction in which the PCI was evolving. From one point of view – perhaps the most widely shared – the 1980s can be seen as the decade in which the social democratisation of the PCI is completed. Eurocommunism, the argument goes, was implicitly social democratic in the first place, at least in its Italian and Spanish versions; however before parties such as the PCI and the PCE could carry the promise of Eurocommunism to its logical conclusion – assimilation to social democracy – they first had to resolve important contradictions rooted in their ideological, organisational and historical experience. The evidence cited in support of such an argument is well-known: the increasing bilateral contacts between the PCI and the French PS and the Social Democratic Party of Germany (SPD); the presence of representatives of the major social democratic parties at the Seventeenth Congress of the PCI in 1986 for the first time; the growing programmatic convergence, symbolised by joint conventions and increasing exchanges, and culminating in the adoption of very similar policies for the 1989 European elections (although PCI General Secretary Alessandro Natta's goal of a common 'Euro-left' manifesto was not realised); the self-redefinition of the PCI in 1986 as 'an integral part of the European left' – by which, Natta quickly made clear, was meant the democratic West European left; and finally the decision in 1989-90 to seek affiliation to the Socialist International, paving the way for an abandonment of the Eurocommunist Group for a Unitary European Left in the European Parliament in favour of membership of the Socialist Group.

However, to simply characterise this process as a return of the PCI to the fold of European socialists (Baker, 1986) is to risk a superficial and unidimensional interpretation of the changes which are taking place, not just in the PCI but in the socialist and social democratic parties.

The fact is that the PCI had come, already by the end of the 1970s but with greater urgency throughout the 1980s, to regard the failure of the left *as a whole* to produce an adequate programmatic response to Europeanisation and internationalisation as the fundamental source of its weakness and retreats in government (the social democrats) and its inability to rise decisively above the culture of protest in opposition (the communists). From this point of view, the key lesson to be drawn was that a model and culture of the left rooted in nation-statism, common to both the communist and social democratic traditions, had entered into terminal crisis; and that both those traditions needed to return to the internationalism and European federalism of earlier socialist thinkers, enriched by interaction with the best in the liberal democratic, Christian and humanist traditions. At the 1986 Party Congress, Alessandro Natta recalled with pride and emphasis that Enrico Berlinguer had once spoken of a world government, adding that if this was utopian, then it was the sort of utopianism that the left had need of. Of course, ideas of European federalism and of a United States of Europe had had resonance in both the Second and Third Internationals. This, precisely, was the ideological, cultural and moral patrimony of such a profoundly European figure as Altiero Spinelli, to which he continually and successfully recalled Amendola, Berlinguer, Guido Fanti, Gian Carlo Pajetta, Eugenio Peggio and other PCI leaders.

It was precisely here that the PCI was to hail developments in many of the social democratic parties of Western Europe as proof of positive movement. For example, the PCI regarded as positive the fact that the lesson which the French socialists drew from the failure of the left in the early years of the Mitterrand presidency to pursue classical expansionist and interventionist policies was that 'social democracy in one country' was no longer a viable strategic option. The PCI press was to hail the 'svolta europea di Mitterrand' (Mitterrand's U-turn on Europe) in 1984 – when the French president pronounced in favour of the Spinelli project – as a major step forward. (Needless to say the PCF drew the exact opposite conclusion.) And the Europeanisation of the SPD programme, culminating in the emphasis given to both the Europeanisation of the German question and the need for a transnational economic strategy in the SPD's November 1984 programmatic declaration, was seen as converging with the 'fundamental European choice' of the PCI. Indeed, the mid-1980s saw the PCI's publishing company, Editori Riuniti, make the SPD's documents and major policy statements available to Italian readers (Glotz, 1985 and SPD, 1986).

The publication of SPD National Secretary Peter Glotz's book on the future of the European left was hailed especially by the Italian communists as representing an immensely important step forward. Glotz's programme contained little that could be considered unacceptable by the PCI leadership. His vision of a social democracy that could meet the challenges of the future was one that embraced:

1 A policy of détente created by and for Europe with the goal of radically reducing the costs of armaments in both Eastern and Western Europe.
2 Institutional reform of the European Community by strengthening the powers of the European Parliament, particularly by enlarging its legislative competence and establishing majority rule in the Cabinet.
3 Industrial and structural policies that are co-ordinated and goal-directed.
4 A unified European currency.
5 Control over investment and speculative capital; increased yield on invested European capital.
6 A co-ordinated policy for reducing the working week to 30 hours.
7 Ecological modernisation by means of thoughtful, systematic augmentation of the environmental demands, when necessary, on the part of both producers and consumers.
8 Equal rights for women, by affirmative action and quotas if necessary.
9 A campaign against the domestic colonisation of Europe, if necessary by measures protecting Europe's culture and media.
10 Europe as a partner of the Third World – out of self-interest, not philanthropy. (From Glotz, 1986, 337–8).

It is hard to see any significant wing of the PCI disagreeing with any of this – not least because of its essential vagueness. And yet agreement on the need for a transnational European strategy, and even significant programmatic convergence, still left open two critical questions: the institutional form which the new European left would take, and the ideological basis of such a left. Karsten Voight, of the SPD directorate, could well tell the Eighteenth congress of the PCI in 1989 that:

> Una sinistra europea che voul cambiare l'Europa deve essere pronta a cambiare se stessa. Noi siamo pronti, e impariamo anche da altri partiti. E ció non significa dover abbandonare la propia identità: imparare da altri partiti, lavorare insieme ad altri partiti non significa tradire le proprie idee, ma é invece un modo di esprimere la propria forza. E io penso che noi, in Europa, dobbiamo imparare a guardare oltre i confini classici tra i partiti, altrimenti non possiamo creare l'Europa.

> (A European left that wants to change Europe must be ready to change itself. We are ready, and we are learning also from other parties. And this doesn't mean having to abandon one's own identity: to learn from other parties, to work together with other parties doesn't mean betraying one's own ideas, but on the contrary is a way of augmenting their real force. And I think that we, in Europe, must learn to look beyond the classic barriers between parties, otherwise we cannot create the Europe [we desire].) (Italian Communist Party (PCI), 1989b)

His tone was doubtless helpful to the PCI leadership in their struggle to win the party to the difficult decision that many felt by now was necessary. For the leading group within the party had come to the conclusion that the pursuit of a common European strategy required, to be effective, an institutional basis to relations between the major left parties which had been engaged in that project. The hope that programmatic convergence might lead to organisational and institutional innovations – with either the merger of communist and socialist parties in each of the major European countries to form new left parties, or the merger of the communist and socialist groups inside the European Parliament into a new European Left Group – was frustrated in a number of ways. In Italy, Craxi's virulent anti-communism made any hope of unity into a single left party (of which Amendola had dreamt as far back as the 1960s) unrealistic. In Germany, there was no communist party as such with which the SPD could, or would, merge. In France and Portugal the communists had clearly identified the socialists as enemies and rivals. In Greece, not only the hard-line KKE, but even the PCI's allies in the Greek Left, were locked in a struggle against the corruption of the PASOK regime, under the banner of *katharsis*. In Spain, the PCE-led Izquierda Unida was likewise faced with a socialist government which was tainted with scandal and which had adopted neo-Thatcherite free market policies. And inside the European Parliament, although the PCI and its allies had launched the Group for a Unitary European Left in 1989, and although co-operation between this Group and the Socialist Group was at a high level, in the wake of the fall of the regimes in Eastern Europe and the host of new problems that events in the East had produced, a firmer and rapid realignment was deemed necessary to give the PCI's European vocation a solidity and concreteness that it seemed to lack. Hence the decision, taken in 1990 and ratified at the Twentieth congress of the PCI in February 1991, to apply for membership of the Socialist International and to prepare for admission to the Socialist Group in the European Parliament.

The decisions were controversial. To many, they seemed to represent a loss of the PCI's uniqueness – of the special contribution that it could make to the redefinition of the European left, only if it remained true to its own ideological and moral patrimony. To others, they were simply recognition of reality and a necessary step if the party's European choice was to go beyond mere aspirations and unfulfilled hopes.

But at root was another dilemma: what exactly would be the ideological basis and the political mode of operation of the European left? Would it involve, as the PCI's own leftwing demanded, a clear commitment to a politics of empowerment which sought to mobilise people in mass struggle for political change, carrying forward the characteristics of the old PCI deemed of lasting value – the mass party, the culture of extra-parliamentary as well as parliamentary struggle, the emphasis on an 'organic' link with all marginalised social classes and strata? Or would it, as the right of the party preferred, involve an acceptance of the methods and culture of the social democratic parties, albeit with a Europeanised programme – i.e., concentration on electoral politics, on the formation of a 'culture of government', on moderation and responsibility?

The PCI – and the PCE – had for years insisted on the primacy of 'universal values' such as democracy, progressively extended to all spheres of life, and human rights and liberties, over class-specific doctrines. These universal values had been proclaimed to form the basis of the parties' conception of socialism. In this respect, the PCI and PCE had anticipated by years Gorbachev's 'new thinking'. But the question facing the parties at the start of the 1990s was how such universal values might translate into a programme for a new social democracy of which the PCI certainly was by now in essence a part. Many points remained unclear, not least the commitment of many of the parties of the Socialist International to the transformation of the European Community from a market dominated by the power of monopoly capital to a federal and strongly social democratic Europe.

Problems also dogged the relationship of the PCI to its old partners, first in the Eurocommunist movement and then in the grouping it launched within the European Parliament in 1989. The PCE has shared the PCI's search for a new 'Euro-left', and indeed the launch of Izquierda Unida marked an important step beyond the parameters of the communist tradition. The same can be said of the transformation of the KKE-es into the Greek Left (EA) and later into Synaspismos. And of course the Danish Socialist People's Party (SF), linked to the PCI inside the European Parliament, was a post-communist party from its inception. And yet a clear contradiction existed between the PCI's perception of the urgency with which the institutional and organisational unification of the European left must be completed and the problems which its smaller allies faced in maintaining their *raison d'être* following any entrance into the Socialist International, or the Socialist Group in the European Parliament.

The fact is that the PCI was able to approach the changes that it deemed necessary in the post-communist phase of the European left from a position of relative strength: it was still the leading party of the Italian left, and hoped that its transformation into the Democratic Party of the Left (PDS) would enable it to assert this with renewed conviction. But its Spanish, Danish and Greek allies were all relatively small organisations forced to define themselves in opposition to social democratic parties that were associated with unpopular 'rightwing' policies in government. At its December 1990 Congress, the Izquierda Unida rejected a merger with the PSOE, not on ideological grounds but on the grounds on policy disagreement and opposition to corruption in the government. This left open the question of realignment should events within the PSOE take a different course. The Greek Left, opposed to the corruption associated with the 1980s PASOK government, remained open to the possibility of a realignment of the left in Greece on radical and pro-EU grounds. Support for the PCI position also came from groups of dissidents within the PCF, following a visit to the French capital by Pietro Folena (member of the PCI leadership and an MEP) in June 1990. Present at a convention at the invitation of the PCF's *Rénovateurs* and *Reconstructeurs*, Folena outlined the PCI's appeal for a single European left, and its pursuit of new relations with the socialist and social democratic parties as well as Greens and Catholic movements, defending the decision to adhere to the Socialist International as a step in this direction (*The Italian Communists*, April–June, 1990).

However, practical problems stood in the way of the realignments across Europe that the PCI sought. Many of its smaller allies would feel uneasy, even resentful, about the prospect of the Italians 'going it alone' and leaving them isolated. For example, the presence of both Achille Occhetto and Giorgio Napolitano at the Madrid launch of the new socialist magazine *El Socialismo del Futuro* – a forum for the principal socialist and social democratic parties of Western Europe and left-of-centre forces from Eastern Europe – in March 1990 brought press reports of nervousness on the part of the PCE at the good relations between the PCI and the PSOE, with PCE General Secretary Julio Anguita reported in *l'Unità* as being displeased at being excluded from the debate. (According to the PCI, a 'cordial meeting [between Occhetto and Anguita] cleared the field of the misunderstandings fostered by the local press' (*The Italian Communists*, January–March, 1990).)

By the time of the dissolution of the PCI and the birth of the Democratic Party of the Left (PDS) in 1991, it might at one level be said that both Eurocommunism and the 'Euro-left' had failed, leaving the biggest and the only electorally significant Eurocommunist party firmly anchored within moderate social democracy, and its smaller allies 'floating free' – and to some extent in danger of regressing as they sought to define themselves in opposition to social democratic parties and found themselves forced into an alignment inside the European Parliament with parties whose international outlook was very different from that which they had elaborated over the years. However, that is only part of the story. The long search by communist and Left parties had led to ideological and policy change and realignment, and would continue to do so. Central to that search was the terrain of European policy. The PCI and its allies had prioritised the search for a strongly reformist transnational strategy, which aimed at a peaceful and gradual evolution beyond the existing economic and political configuration in Europe through the transformation of the European Union into a socially and politically united power capable of exerting control over economic processes, breaking with the logic of the EU conceived merely as a free market, and emerging autonomous on the world stage. Other Left parties would argue that such a vision was based on illusions about the true nature of the European Union.

The failure of transnational party co-operation: the Communists inside the European Parliament, 1973–89

For reasons that should by now be abundantly clear, the formation of a Communists and Allies Group in the European Parliament during the 1970s failed to transcend the dramatic divergence in European policy between the main actors. The breakdown of that Group in the summer of 1989 took few observers by surprise.

The first communist MEPs took their seats on 12 March 1969 when seven PCI members and two left-wing independents (or 'allies') who chose to sit with the PCI finally overcame years of exclusion on grounds of anticommunist prejudice. Although commanding the support of one quarter of the Italian electorate, the PCI had been black-listed by the governing parties in Italy on grounds that were of dubious democratic credibility: namely that, as the party had originally opposed the Treaty of Rome, it should be excluded from the delegation of politicians nominated by the Italian national parliament to the Strasbourg assembly regardless of its electoral strength. The PCI, consistent with its argument that changes in the nature of the Community should be fought for by the working-class conquering positions of strength within the Community's institutions, and with its drive to overcome its political isolation within Italy, had fought against such exclusion. When Giorgio Amendola led his group into the European Parliament chamber, it was therefore perceived as a considerable democratic victory for the party.

By contrast, the PCF still maintained that its opposition to the existence of the Community was incompatible with participation in the Community's institutions. One French leftwinger, elected from the French national assembly, did, however, sit with the PCI delegation (Leich, 1971, 275).

The fact that the Parliament's rules required a recognised political group to have at least fourteen members meant, however, that the PCI delegation did not as yet constitute a formal grouping and were instead categorised as 'non-aligned'. The PCI's presence inside the Community's assembly thus began with the communists suffering certain disadvantages, as a result of the absence of their French comrades. These were the lack of secretarial back-up, a group office and participation in deciding procedure and the selection of parliamentary officers.

In 1973 the PCF, reversing its previous position, gained admittance to the parliament and the presence of its four representatives permitted the launch of a Communists and Allies Group in October 1973 under the presidency of Giorgio Amendola. From the outset, however, it was clear that fundamental divergences between the positions of the parties on Europe, together with the unwillingness of the French in particular to accept any infringement upon the principle of the right of each communist party to choose its own 'path to socialism', would inhibit the capacity of the Communists and Allies Group as an institutional actor upon the European stage. In fact, the group was to be characterised throughout its existence by ineffectiveness and disunity – later rationalised by group secretary Gérard Laprat as 'unity in diversity' (Laprat, 1985b). The group never managed to agree upon any common platform and, unlike the Socialist Group, for example, was never to reach the stage of issuing a joint manifesto for the European parliamentary elections. It continued in existence as a curious anachronism, a gesture towards the common ideological and organisational roots of the member parties and a token in the direction of communist internationalism, until its final and logical dissolution in 1989.

Nevertheless, there were times – for example, during the mid-1970s, when the PCF for largely tactical reasons seemed to modify its position on Europe – when the communist parties of Western Europe appeared superficially to be converging on common European positions and such episodes tended to lend the Communists and Allies Group a logic which in reality it always lacked. Indeed the entrance of the PCF into the European Parliament had been welcomed in 1973 by no less a committed European than Altiero Spinelli – several years before he was to join the Communists and Allies Group himself. In May 1973 Spinelli claimed that 'the creation of an "international" communist group cannot but increase the role of all the forces of the left in the European debate'. Moreover, he added,

> the French communists have themselves affirmed in recent days the importance of a democratic and social transformation of the European Community. The democratisation of the institutions must move towards greater powers for the European Parliament. And the communists, wanting to maintain the commitments already made, will certainly give a positive contribution to this battle. (*Corriere della Sera*, 30 May 1973)

Berlinguer, too, had welcomed the presence of the PCF at Strasbourg with enthusiasm at first. In a meeting with Spinelli in January 1974 he had emphasised that the PCF appeared to have made important steps forward, renouncing their traditional intransigence towards the EEC and accepting the idea that the communists should work for a democratisation of the Community's institutions (Spinelli Archives cartella 31). However, within months of the formation of the new transnational communist grouping at Strasbourg the fundamental differences between the positions of the constituent parties – which were to grow progressively more striking – were surfacing again.

At a meeting of Western European communist parties, which the PCI promoted at Brussels in January 1974, both Berlinguer and Giorgio Amendola spelt out the line that the Italians were to pursue within the European Parliament. First, the PCI signalled its acceptance of Spinelli's proposal that the European Parliament should receive constituent powers for the institutional revision of the Treaty of Rome, as a first step towards the formation of a European government. And second, the Italian leaders postulated that a convergence between various political forces – communists, socialists and Christian Democrats, for example – on the need for a democratic transformation of the community was both possible and desirable. In other words, the strategy of the historic compromise should be extended to the European level where, if anything, the prize – attainment of a united Europe led by democratic and progressive forces – was even greater and the urgency more pressing than at the national level. These views, most clearly associated with Spinelli and with Giorgio Amendola, also enjoyed the backing of Enrico Berlinguer and of a majority within the PCI leadership. From the outset, the political line on Europe articulated by the PCI was to have four important consequences for the Communists and Allies Group at Strasbourg.

First, it would pave the way for realignment between Altiero Spinelli and the PCI, from which he had been expelled as a young man in the 1930s. Italy's leading exponent of European federalism in the post-war period, and the co-author of the federalist manifesto of Ventotene, Spinelli had gravitated towards the pro-Western Italian Social Democratic Party (PSDI) in the late 1940s and early 1950s, only entering the political orbit of Pietro Nenni's Italian Socialist Party (PSI) after it broke with the communists in 1956 (interview with Spinelli's former aide, Luciano Bolis, Florence, September 1989). It was on Nenni's suggestion that he was appointed as one of Italy's European Commissioners in the late 1960s. However, throughout the late 1960s and early 1970s he had participated in the reformulation of the PCI's European policy and had drawn closer to the party. His formal endorsement of the PCI was both to help legitimise it within Italy and Western Europe, and to draw the PCI into what was almost a relationship of moral and intellectual dependence upon Spinelli in all matters European. Spinelli was to enter the European Parliament on the PCI's electoral lists in 1976, having wrought from the party firm guarantees of his absolute independence of action, and was to conduct his tenacious battle for a United States of Europe with characteristic single-mindedness – some would say ruthlessness. Spinelli was not in the least bit concerned with the corporate interests of the Communists and Allies Group as such. According to his friend and fellow federalist, Luciano Bolis, he did not even bother to attend regular meetings of the group at which the French communists were present, preferring the quite separate meetings of the Italian component, or bilateral meetings with Berlinguer and Amendola. But he did not hesitate to use whatever forum the Group offered, and the prestige which his own election as vice-president of the Group afforded, to press forward his most cherished initiatives such as the creation of a commission on institutional affairs and the elaboration of the Draft Treaty on Political Union, or the formation of the so-called Crocodile Club of European Parliamentarians to press for European union. Indeed, one can speak of an intellectual and political hegemony that Spinelli exercised with respect to the PCI's European policy, which means that it is impossible to discuss the Communists and Allies Group at Strasbourg without constant reference to him.

Second, it would mean that, superficial appearances to the contrary, there would be in reality an ever-diminishing possibility of the French and Italian Group components converging or agreeing. In fact, the Group was shortly to give up even the hope of attaining such agreement and instead to attempt to make a virtue out of the 'agreement to disagree'.

Third, the Italian numerical weight throughout much of the Group's history meant that in reality initiatives undertaken in the name of the Communists and Allies Group were those which had PCI support – leaving the PCF and its allies to dissent. This created an anomalous situation that was to become increasingly irritating to the Group's two main member parties.

Fourth, PCI representatives at Strasbourg, consistent with the strategy outlined in January 1974, and ever under the influence of Spinelli, were to consistently go beyond the logic of the Communists and Allies Group, seeking allies within other political groupings of both the left and, indeed, the centre-right who supported the European project. This aspect of the PCI MEPs' orientation was to predispose them towards the transcendence of a Communist Group, within the confines of which they felt trapped by the late 1980s, and the creation of a new explicitly pro-EU left grouping.

The 1970s were of course years of economic crisis throughout the capitalist countries of Western Europe, and years of apparent stalemate and stagnation as far as moves towards European union were concerned. The differing analyses of the communist parties of these phenomena further prevented the Strasbourg Group from attaining any clear identity. The PCI at Strasbourg, with Amendola to the fore, would insist that Italy's economic problems were in large part caused by Europe's failure to achieve a co-ordinated economic policy in industrial, regional, credit, monetary and energy spheres; and that Italian political and institutional renewal could also be facilitated by renewal at the European level. Thus the PCI attacked the allegedly nationalistic and regressive postulations of the German and French governments as threatening the democratic development of the Community. The PCI also faced the pressing need to counter both propaganda from conservative forces inside Italy that the party's growing electoral success during the mid-1970s would lead to Italy's isolation from the rest of Europe, and threats from American statesmen such as Henry Kissinger that the PCI, which Kissinger chose to define as 'antidemocratic', would destabilise Italy's good relations with the USA. Thus by anchoring Italian renewal within the broader necessity of European renewal, and insisting upon the need for a Europe which was autonomous from both Washington and Moscow whilst enjoying good relations with both, the PCI hoped to circumnavigate a major obstacle to its advance.

The PCF, by contrast, emphasised the need to struggle for economic and political renewal at the national level first, and to seek a convergence between 'working-class forces' in Europe as a consequence of this struggle.

The important point here is that the differing analyses of the two parties inevitably implied differing degrees of importance attached to their European Parliamentary groupings, and differing views as to the role and function of the MEPs within the two parties' overall strategies. For the PCF, the main focus of parliamentary activity would remain very definitely the French National Assembly. The PCI, by contrast, would send a succession of top party figures to Strasbourg, not merely to lend their names to the party's European electoral lists, but to play a key part in the workings of the European Parliament and its various committees. Berlinguer himself, for example, would choose an address to the European Parliament to outline his party's condemnation of the Soviet intervention in Afghanistan. (On 16 January 1980, the PCI supported a socialist resolution condemning the Soviet intervention in Afghanistan, but at the same time refusing to back a centre-right motion calling for punitive sanctions against the USSR. The PCF, along with the French Gaullists, abstained – allegedly because they contested the right of the European Parliament to pronounce on matters of foreign policy which ought to be the prerogative of national governments. The convergence between the PCI and the Socialist Group on a foreign policy issue involving a position of autonomy from both Washington and Moscow was regarded by some commentators as the most important event of the first year of the new European Parliament.) This difference in fundamental approach inevitably facilitated Italian pre-eminence within the Communists and Allies Group.

Three major issues were to require a response from the Communists and Allies Group at Strasbourg during the fifteen years of its existence: (1) The nature of the Community's economic and social policies; (2) the question of the enlargement of the Community's membership; (3) and the institutional development of the Community. Perhaps a useful way of surveying the efficacy of the Group as a transnational political actor within the European Parliament would be to consider its responses to each of these dimensions of the European Community in turn. In addition, we might then add a fourth issue: attitudes towards the role and function of the Communists and Allies group itself.

Economic and social policy matters

The PCI, and later its Spanish and Greek allies, was to see the struggle for a new Communitarian economic and social policy as essential to the development of Europe. The Italian component of the Communists and Allies Group fought consistently for an increase in the Community budget, which, it added, should be used to strengthen the regional policy. The party opposed the Council of Ministers' attempts to reduce regional spending during the mid 1970s and demanded instead a reform of the Common Agricultural Policy to reduce the two-thirds of the budget spent on price support, thus releasing more monies for structural policy. In truth, it was in fighting for economic and social reforms – a redirection of funds away from 'big farmers' and 'rich countries' towards peripheral areas and sectors, and an increase in spending on social and regional policies – that the positions of the communist parties belonging to the Group most converged. In 1977, for example, the communists united in voting against the approval of the budget by the European Parliament. But whilst the parties were sometimes able to present a facade of unity in opposing economic policies which were clearly detrimental to the interests of the peripheral areas or the working-class or other marginalised strata, problems arose when it came to actually articulating what the parties stood for. Within the Group, the PCI and its allies were to consistently link the struggle for progressive economic and social policies with the struggle for the development of the Community itself into a genuine peoples' union. The PCE's approach to reformist gains was much more tactical and devoid of the conviction that from such reforms could spring a fundamental qualitative change in the nature of the Community. Thus, the PCI related its opposition to ratification of the Commission's budget proposals, for example, to the struggle to redress the respective weights within the decision-making process of the Council of Ministers, the Commission and the European Parliament, upon which was said to rest the democratic legitimacy of the Community. And indeed PCI MEPs consistently linked their critique of the capitalist common market aspect of the Community precisely to the lack of comprehensive Community economic and social policies, which, in turn, was linked to the failure to develop a truly politically united and socially integrated European Community. The PCF, by contrast, saw the role of its parliamentarians at Strasbourg as being to struggle against the evolution of any Community economic and social policies that might restrict the powers of the French state; and to fight for broader representation of the trade unions and other working-class organisations within the Community institutions so as to redirect the existing budget resources towards working-class interest, as it perceived them. The economic face of the Community which the PCF insisted upon was essentially that of a zone of trade and co-operation between nation-states, led by leftwing governments, which are committed to strong anti-multinational and anti-capitalist policies – nationally determined but made effective, of course, through mutually beneficial co-operation.

Within the Group, then, two quite different conceptualisations of the economic and social nature of the Community emerged. The PCI, PCE and KKE-interior came to favour the development of strong Community initiatives in the economic and social fields – entirely consistent with their views on the internationalisation of capitalism and the nature of interdependence, the need for political and social integration if the democratic deficit was to be redressed and control over economic direction exercised by 'the people', and the urgency of relaunching a new radical reformism of the left at a continental level. The PCF, PCP and KKE, consistent with their view of the potential of the nation-state led from the left, advocated a Community which, in economic and social matters, was severely curtailed. They urged their MEPs to wage a strategic battle against any move in the direction of a strong common Community policy on economic or social matters. Against this background, the ability of the Group to formulate any common approach to the economic and social dimension of the European question was paralysed.

Enlargement of the Community

The debate surrounding the extension of Community membership to Greece, and later to Spain and Portugal, provided ample evidence of the deep divisions existing within the Communists and Allies Group. Obviously the question of the enlargement of the Community raised more fundamental issues of the nature of the Community and its future direction. Was Community membership a means by which German and American capital sought to further penetrate and dominate the economies of the peripheral countries, ensuring that their anti-fascist revolts did not take a socialist turn? From this point of view, of course, the 'internationalist' duty of the communists was to resist the proposed enlargement. Or was the Community, if not exactly a model of socialist democracy, at least the basis upon which a future progressive European democracy might be built, and did its extension, particularly to those countries in southern Europe emerging from fascist or fascistoid regimes, deserve the urgent support of the communists and other left forces – both from the point of view of helping the new democracies to consolidate their political systems and in the wider interests of creating a broader and deeper European union? Should the parties of the left place their perceived duty to the working-class of their own country before all other considerations, in the belief that true internationalism begins at home? Or should they be prepared to risk sacrificing the interests of their home constituency in order to contribute to building the Community? These questions reflect the counter-positions of the PCF and the PCI.

Altiero Spinelli, even when he was still a member of the European Commission, had criticised the Council of Ministers for its delaying tactics over Greece's application for membership of the Community. Spinelli's concerns were shared by the PCI and by its allies in the PCE and the Greek Eurocommunist party. The PCI argued that extension of the Community membership to southern Europe was not only necessary to prevent a return of rightwing dictatorship to the region, but was also a means by which the nature of the Community could be changed into a union founded on social solidarity between peoples and not simply a glorified market place. In other words, extension of Community membership was intrinsically linked to the economic, social and democratic development of the Community away from a simple market logic. The PCF rested its opposition to the Community primarily on its presentation of France's national interests, but could also point to the opposition of the Portuguese and Greek communist parties (PCP and KKE) as proof that its position was not merely nationalistic but 'internationalist'.

It is easy, of course, to depict the French as unreconstructed national chauvinists and the Italians as Europeanists. And there is certainly some truth in this. But this view is perhaps too unfair to the PCF in its simplicity. For behind the diametric opposition of views – which naturally saw the Group split yet again on a major issue confronting the Community – lay different perceptions of national interests. The fact is that the two parties had different perceptions of how their countries' interests related to the wider concerns of the Mediterranean basin, and consequently different views of how Mediterranean policy should develop within the Community. The PCI was acutely aware of the pressing problems of the Italian Mezzogiorno – indeed the Italian north–south divide was seen by PCI theorists and leaders as threatening the very existence of the Italian democratic republic and potentially undermining everything the party was seeking. The party saw a solution to the problem of the Mezzogiorno as certainly lying beyond the capacity or the political will of the Christian Democrat-dominated Italian State machine. A strong Mediterranean policy on the part of the European Community was essential to the future of Italy. Instead of closing the door on the rest of the Mediterranean countries and seeking to plead the case of the Mezzogiorno with the richer countries of northern Europe, the PCI calculated that its case would be strengthened by the admission to the Community of Spain, Portugal and Greece and by working to forge a new and better relationship between the Community and the non-European Mediterranean countries. Its strategic imperative, then, was the creation of a Mediterranean 'bloc' within, and on the fringes of, the Community (Spinelli Archives, cartella 33). The PCF, by contrast, did not see France's destiny as being tied so closely to that of the Mediterranean countries but rather as competing with Germany to resist German hegemony in Europe and assert France's role in the world. Resistance to German hegemony could, of course, be conceptualised as an act of solidarity with those peripheral countries which were next on the 'shopping list' of the German and American multinationals. The point is that the PCI's emphasis on solidarity with the new democratic political systems in Spain, Portugal and Greece and advocacy of a strong Community Mediterranean policy may be a lot more 'Europeanist' than the PCF's insistence that enlargement would threaten the French farmers of the Midi (amongst whom its support was not insubstantial); but both policy stances were in fact in line with the two parties' perceptions of their countries' interests.

Needless to say, the stresses and strains within the Group engendered by the debate over enlargement were magnified when Spain and Portugal entered the Community in 1986. The presence of PCE and PCP members in the Communists and Allies Group helped to sharpen the lines of confrontation. The PCF was no longer so isolated with the presence of the PCP (and earlier of the three KKE deputies whose presence, however, was somewhat offset by the one Greek Eurocommunist MEP who supported the PCI on the issue). The PCE not only lent new support to its Italian comrades but felt distinctly annoyed by the opposition of the French to Spain's application for Community membership; the latter had been lent a certain urgency in the minds of the Spanish left by the attempted military coup against the fragile Spanish democracy in 1981.

The failure to agree any common policy on enlargement certainly goes part of the way towards explaining the failure of the Communists and Allies Group as a transnational party actor. For the issue at stake was not simply whether Spain, Portugal or Greece should enter the Community; but whether the Community should continue to develop in both breadth and depth – in both its membership and in its range of activities. The events of 1989–90 were to see the familiar contours of the debate re-emerge: following the break-up of the Communists and Allies Group, the PCI- and PCE-led Group for a Unitary European Left would advocate strong Community support for the newly emergent democracies of Eastern Europe, seeing economic and political support as necessary to prevent those countries sliding back into demagogy and dictatorship, and clearly adopting a favourable predisposition towards East European membership of the Community, sooner rather than later. (A stance that, incidentally, was echoed by that old friend of the PCI and PCE, Alexander Dubcek. As speaker of the Czechoslovak National Assembly, Dubcek called for Czechoslovakia's admission to full EC membership at the earliest opportunity.) The French-led Left Unity Group was much less forthcoming, reflecting the fears of many of its constituent parties that Community membership represented the final nail in the coffin of 'actually existing socialism' and capitalist colonisation of the former 'socialist countries'.

Institutional development of the Community

Perhaps it was on the question of the institutional development of the European Community that the divisions within the Communists and Allies Group became most obvious. Of course, as commentators as diverse as Marchais and Spinelli, Amendola and Gérard Laprat, were keen to point out, such divisions ran through all European Parliament political groupings – and quite spectacularly through the Socialist Group, for example, in which the British Labour Party's opposition to the institutional development of the Community was as tenacious as that of the PCF. But the division was so striking within the Communists and Allies Group because of the exceptionally high profile that the Italian component of the Group adopted in advocating the cause of institutional development.

As early as 1976, the PCI had criticised the Report on European Union of Belgian Prime Minister Leo Tindemans as timid and inadequate, calling for a much stronger statement in favour of institutional reform. Spinelli accused Tindemans of having betrayed his mandate by producing a report designed to placate the immobilist and obstructionist stance of the Council of Ministers. Against Tindemans, the Italian communists and allies in the European Parliament argued that reliance upon inter-governmental consensus at summits between the heads of state would inevitably mean discontinuities in development. Movement forward towards the European ideal could only be sustained when competence was transferred in a definitive sense to a supranational authority. Moreover, the proposal for a two-tier Europe would, in the absence of a strong central authority capable of directing economic development to ensure that the peripheral countries did not fall behind, mean that the south of Europe would be discriminated against.

In striking contrast to the position of the PCI, the PCF members of the Communists and Allies Group based their opposition to the Tindemans report on the grounds that it advocated too much in the direction of European economic and political integration and was a threat to the sovereignty of France and to the interests of the European workers. When Tindemans was sent to France by the EC Council of Ministers to engage in consultations with the political forces, only the PCF refused to meet him or to enter into discussions (Timmermann, 1979, 37–8).

The PCI lent its support to Spinelli's campaign for an acceleration of European political union led by a revitalised and strengthened European Parliament. In an internal memo to PCI General Secretary Enrico Berlinguer, dated June 1978, Spinelli praised the PCI for having adopted 'correct positions' to date on the Community, and for having won the respect of many forces both within the Parliament and within the other Community institutions. But he implicitly criticised the fact that its contacts remained largely confined to its own Communists and Allies Group and to trade union allies on the Economic and Social Committee. What was needed, as a decisive moment in the struggle to accelerate the unification process arrived with the 1979 direct elections, was a new European programme which posited the PCI centre-stage as far as the European movement was concerned. The party should show itself ready to assume direct responsibility for the future of Europe – and claim co-responsibility with the Italian government from which the PCI was still excluded, for Italy's future in Europe. (Spinelli Archives, cartella 36.)

The choice facing the PCI, Spinelli insisted, was clear: either to react to events as they arose, trying to make the most of the European Community in the best interests of those who had elected it, or to go on the offensive, seeking to shape the new Europe in the making and, if not exactly establish an hegemonic position, then at least contribute to the emergence of new hegemonic 'Europeanism from the left'. The debate, Spinelli acknowledged, was already well underway within the Communists and Allies Group at Strasbourg. But, it was implied, the PCI was being held back from the fullest commitment to forging a new historic bloc of pro-EU forces by the logic of its Group alignment with the PCF. It was necessary to move beyond this and to pursue institutional reform and development ever more strongly.

Such an appeal was well calculated to fall on receptive ears. The notion of reaching out to other progressive forces, beyond the communist tradition, the idea of a historic compromise designed to facilitate the emergence of a new bloc of such forces, tied in well with existing PCI strategic thinking. Moreover, the idea that Europe might prove the big idea that would establish the PCI's governmental vocation and allow it to break the political deadlock within Italy was especially welcome to a PCI leadership embattled domestically with the growing disappointments of its historic compromise with the Christian Democratic Party (DC). The June 1979 direct elections to the European Parliament both inaugurated a new phase in the struggle for institutional reform, as Spinelli had desired, and marked the first electoral set-back for the PCI in 30 years; the abandonment of the party's historic compromise strategy domestically left a strategic and intellectual vacuum which Spinelli's European federalism increasingly filled.

In the new Parliament elected in 1979, the balance between PCI and PCF was much more even. The Group as a whole rose from 17 members to 44, with the PCF now holding 19 seats and the PCI 24 (the Danish SF held the remaining seat). Yet once again it was the PCI component that was the most consistently active at Strasbourg, especially on institutional matters. Almost immediately the PCI, acting upon Spinelli's advice, stepped up its efforts to play a more decisive part in the struggle for a stronger Community and a redress of the democratic deficit. In March 1980 (Spinelli Archives, cartella 36) Spinelli penned a memorandum to Guido Fanti, who had replaced the ailing Amendola as leader of the Communists and Allies Group after the elections, deploring the fact that despite much discussion the PCI had not moved quickly enough to 'rectify our position within the Political Commission [of the Parliament]'. Spinelli – who was the Group's representative on the body and was impatient that the PCI had not given him the clear authorisation he wanted – proposed that the party should move ahead of its French comrades decisively and support his proposals that the Commission of the Community be asked not to allow any of its powers to be transferred to the Council of Ministers, and that the Parliament should discuss the programme of the new Commission before the approval of its nomination and demand that, if the Commission did not seem to be committed in the direction required by the Parliament, the Parliament use its power of censure. The PCI subsequently supported this, and effectively endorsed his famous Crocodile Club initiative launched on 9 July 1980. This was an informal club of MEPs of all party groups dedicated to convincing the European Parliament that it should assume the task of drafting a treaty for the union of Europe. One of the first European Parliament deputies to join the Crocodile Club was PCI General Secretary Enrico Berlinguer, who subsequently travelled to Strasbourg for meetings of the club. Exactly one year later the Parliament, by a large majority, adopted the proposal and decided to constitute a commission, or committee, on institutional affairs from January 1982; the PCI backed the proposal unanimously, the PCF voted against.

The continuing involvement of the PCI under Spinelli's guidance in the affairs of the Parliament was to see the party's representatives play a significant role in the committees of the Parliament, particularly those concerned with further development of the Community. Spinelli himself became *relatore generale* of the Institutional Commission created on his initiative. The Draft Treaty for European Union produced by this body and approved by the Parliament in February 1984 was intended to set the movement towards European union firmly in train once more. It was an ambitious project, which pointed towards a politically united Europe, led by a strong and democratic parliament, and with the will to tackle at root common social and economic problems such as mass unemployment, regional disparities and social welfare and security.

The Draft Treaty placed particular emphasis, as had the PCI for some years, on the need above all for a relaunch of the European project through a comprehensive reform of Community institutions and a clear delineation of their competencies. It advocated that the European Council should assume the functions of a collective state president, nominating the president of the Commission and mandating him to form a new Commission. A Council of the Union, composed of representatives of the various governments, would share with the Parliament legislative power, the power to approve the budget and to supervise the Commission. The idea behind this was that the Parliament should cease decisively being a merely consultative body and instead become an integral part of the legislative authority. The Commission would become a veritable European government, subject to approval of its programme by the Parliament and a vote of confidence by the Parliament. The Parliament would have the power – by a strong qualified majority – to censure the Commission and force it to resign. The aim was to make a qualitative leap forward, which would break with the logic of national governments being able to obstruct further progress towards European unity in the name of national interests, by equipping the Community with institutions capable of effectively formulating and implementing common European policies; and to democratise the relationship between the Parliament and the other institutions of the Community.

Needless to say, the vote on the Draft Treaty – probably the single most important question placed before the 1979–84 European Parliament, saw the Communists and Allies Group divide yet again. Thirty-two of the by now forty-eight Group members were present for the vote (of the sixteen absentees, two were PCI, thirteen were PCF and one was KKE). The fact that two-thirds of the PCF members did not even bother to turn up for the vote was in itself eloquent testimony to the relative disinterest of the PCF in European affairs. Of these thirty-two, some twenty-two (all Italian) voted in favour of the Draft Treaty, nine (six PCF, two KKE and one SF) voted against, and the KKE-interior member abstained.

The actual Single European Act presented by the European Council in December 1985 was a grave disappointment to Spinelli and the PCI. The debate engendered by the Single Act again saw the Communists and Allies Group divide, with the PCI and PCE supporting ratification of the Act and the PCF, KKE and PCP naturally opposed. Although the Act upgraded the powers of the Parliament somewhat, it fell far short of the proposals contained in the Draft Treaty. The decisive shift from the Council to the Parliament had not taken place, and there seemed little likelihood of the Parliament being given full legislative, budgetary and supervisory powers. Moreover, the PCI regarded the emphasis placed upon the completion of the Single Market by 1992 as quite unmatched by an equal attention to social harmonisation and political unity. The support given to the Act by the PCI and PCE was far from uncritical, then, and Spinelli himself confessed to being bitterly disillusioned. In the new Parliament, elected in 1984, he called, however, for an increased struggle to match economic integration with work towards overcoming the democratic deficit and building a new United States of Europe. Spinelli urged that the Parliament set itself the goal of working to transform itself into a Constituent Assembly of a new Europe after the 1989 elections.

Spinelli did not live to see his struggle through to completion. But although his death in 1985 robbed the Communists and Allies Group of its foremost advocate of the European project, it did not lead to any slackening in the commitment of the PCI to pursue his dream. Indeed, the Italian communist Sergio Segre succeeded to the chairmanship of the Parliament's Institutional Affairs Committee.

The PCI group at Strasbourg sought the renewal of its mandate in 1989 on the basis of its work in favour of European union and its demand that the parliament become the constituent assembly of which Spinelli had spoken. It is scarcely surprising, then, that a party which had sought, in Spinelli's words, to play a 'guiding role' in bringing other political forces to drink from the European fountain, and which regarded the struggle for Europe as entering a critical phase in which an acceleration and an increase in the efficacy of its actions was necessary, should decide that the political price which keeping the fiction of the Communists and Allies Group alive imposed now outweighed any administrative benefits.

The role and function of the Communists and Allies Group

The parties which formed the Communists and Allies Group in October 1973 – the PCI and PCF, joined shortly by the Danish SF – agreed from the outset that relations within the Group should be governed by the old principle of non-interference in each party's internal affairs and respect for the right of each party to decide its own policy. In the face of glaring and increasing policy divergences between the Group components, both Italian and French leaders were to insist – almost until the eve of the Group's demise – that such disagreement was normal, mutually acceptable, and part of a healthy dialectic. Others, such as Spinelli, tended to point more pragmatically to the fact that divisions ran throughout all of the European Parliament groupings and that the really important line of division – that between those who supported further development of the Community and those who opposed it – would eventually crystallise into two political alignments. Until then, and since such a crystallisation was as yet premature, even for Spinelli it was as useful a Group as any, especially since it meant so little in practice.

In fact, the two principal components of the Group offered slightly different rationalisations of the situation. The PCF tended to emphasise the fact that autonomy of action and the lack of unanimity in voting was a sign of normal relations between fraternal communist parties in action. The party had not sent its representatives to Strasbourg to become part of any embryonic European party – a charge that it levelled scornfully at the other French political parties. But this in no way contradicted its decision to share a parliamentary grouping with sister-parties. The PCI, by contrast, tended rather to emphasise the fact that the decision not to impose either ideological unity nor Group discipline in voting was entirely in line with the precedent already adopted by the PCI in its relations inside the Italian parliament with the 'left independents' elected to the Chamber of Deputies on its electoral lists. In other words, it was the principle governing relations between member-parties of the international communist movement that rationalised, for the French, the mode of operation of the Group at Strasbourg. For the Italians, on the other hand, it was the important precedent established in its relations with non-party left independents elected on its lists, foreshadowing the abandonment of democratic centralism and the renunciation of any pretence at hegemony. The difference is one of emphasis, admittedly; but it is not unimportant.

The fragile nature of the Group, and the fact that even the facade of administrative unity depended upon observance of the unwritten rules of inter-party communist diplomacy, was of course frequently threatened (and in part eventually undermined) by the presence of, largely Italian, non-communist 'allies' such as

Spinelli. Spinelli's many initiatives in favour of European unity and his refusal to be muzzled in any way were a constant source of irritation and deep annoyance to the PCF. In February 1977, for example, the PCF responded angrily to a suggestion of Spinelli's that the party was 'anti-German'. An enraged editorial in the party daily, *l'Humanité*, on 19 February 1977, attacked the party's Group ally in unprecedented language. Rebutting the charge of anti-Germanism – the PCF cited as evidence to the contrary its solidarity with the German communists – the party newspaper continued: 'when one has been EEC industrial commissioner, like Altiero Spinelli, has one not contributed to the colonisation of the European economies by American monopolies? Is one not then particularly ill placed to present West European policy as a guarantor of independence against American hegemony?'

Spinelli returned to the attack with a rather damning critique of the PCF, which he penned in February 1979 (Spinelli Archives, cartella 36). The PCF had fallen back upon a position of leftwing nationalism. But this, in itself, he added, did not represent a novelty. It was typical of the position adopted by the West German Social Democrats at the end of the Second World War. The difference was that the German Social Democrats had since recognised their mistake and 'vomited' out their nationalism, whereas the PCF was still trapped in the logic of national chauvinism just at the moment when it was losing all relevance. The result was that the PCF presented itself to the French electorate on a platform towards Europe not dissimilar from that of the rightwing Gaullists. The insult was double-edged: in equating the PCF with the Gaullists, and even more to the point in suggesting that the PCF was a sort of primitive SPD. The same point was made in an article in *Le Monde* in the run-up to the European Parliament elections in June 1979. Asked for his opinion of the PCF, Spinelli declared that 'the contrast is clear, decisive, between Italian communists who fight for the development of the Community and French communists who don't want to hear talk of this. They mount a rearguard operation, occupying the position that the left had twenty years ago, beginning with the German social democrats' (*Le Monde*, 1 June 1979).

The point is of course not merely that members of the Communists and Allies Group were trading public polemics with each other on the issues which lay at the very heart of their divergences on European policy; but that the presence of 'allies' such as Spinelli permitted the 'fraternal' communist parties to accelerate the process by which they took their distance from each other on matters European without yet tearing apart the fragile unity of the Group altogether (until the end of the second directly elected Parliament). When they attacked Spinelli, elected on the PCI lists as an independent and so closely and intimately associated with the policy revision carried through by the PCI leadership, as a 'capitalist coloniser', the PCF were clearly attacking the perceived deviation and errors of their Italian comrades. When Spinelli, uninhibited by communist diplomacy, gave vent to his contempt for the PCF's backwardness, the PCI made no move to disassociate itself from his strictures or to hide its agreement with his basic analysis. Within the Group, there is evidence of strains between the Italian and French components over Spinelli's role. Spinelli's friend and fellow European federalist, Luciano Bolis, told the present writer that internal political struggles, sometimes bitter, preceded agreement to permit Spinelli to express his ideas in the name of the Group, whilst the PCF component proceeded to disassociate itself from many of his speeches and initiatives. Spinelli himself apparently made little or no effort to persuade the French comrades to change their minds, even avoiding personal or social contact with members of a party for which he had no political respect (Bolis interview, Florence, December 1989). Indeed, he publicly attributed the PCF's massive setback in the European elections of 1984 – when its share of the seats at Strasbourg fell from nineteen to ten, and the PCI's rose from twenty-four to twenty-eight, further unbalancing the Group in favour of the Italian position – to the fact that it had been punished by the French electorate for playing an 'antidemocratic and ultra nationalist role' (*Panorama*, 2 June 1984).

In such a way the administrative unity of the Group was gradually strained and twisted until, by 1989, it had lost all *raison d'être*. As late as 1985 Gérard Laprat, the PCF member who performed the role of General Secretary of the Communists and Allies Group, could claim that

la reconnaissance des réalités nationales au sein du Groupe communiste et apparentés n'a fait obstacle ni à une insertion au sein du travail parlementaire, ni à des rapports avec les autres groupes, ni surtout à un accroissement continu du travail de coopération entre les députés de diverses nationalités du groupe.

(The recognition of national realities within the Communists and Allies Group poses no obstacle either to its work within the Parliament or to its relations with other groups, nor, above all, to a continuing growth in collaborative work between the MEPs of different nationalities within the Group.) (Laprat, 1985a, 229)

The reality, however, was somewhat different. In fact, the French and Italian parties, each supported by its allies within the group, had effectively agreed to proceed practically as if they were two different groups. This was not merely a question of refusing to impose a Group discipline, complete with party whip, nor even of maintaining respect for the principle of party autonomy; what was involved, rather, was that the Communists and Allies Group had, by the end of the 1980s, ceased to exist or to function in anything other than a purely administrative sense: i.e., the fiction of the Group allowed the component parties to benefit from certain economies of scale as far as deployment of the Parliament's secretarial and financial support was concerned.

Indeed, as should be obvious by now, the Group was an anomaly from the moment in which it was formally created. As early as 1978, PCI member Nilde Jotti was quoted as declaring that the work of the Group had become so difficult due to conflicts between the French and the Italians that it was necessary to interrupt the Group's sessions to allow 'time for reflection' (quoted in Timmermann, 1979, 51). If such a secular equivalent of the 'pauses for prayer' which are common during difficult episcopal conferences was already necessary by 1978, how much more impossible was any real co-operation after another intense decade of strategic, policy and ideological divergence over key questions relating to the future of Europe?

The formal rupture came in the summer of 1989 – just months before the fall of the Berlin Wall and the events in Eastern Europe that would traumatise the communist parties and place the debate about the future of Europe back at the top of the political agenda.

The decision by the PCI, PCE, Greek Left and the Danish SF to constitute a new Group for a Unitary European Left, committed to pursuing the European agenda and the realignment of the Left in Europe which these parties had been working towards for some time, was really merely a question of clarifying an existing situation and making it correspond to reality. Nevertheless, the decision to put an end to the old Communists and Allies Group clearly provoked a degree of bitterness with the PCF. The French communists had felt much less inhibited and frustrated by the Communists and Allies Group and ran a much greater risk of being isolated inside the new Parliament – and perhaps, it seemed initially, not even being able to form a political group. René Piquet, the PCF representative who subsequently became president of the Left Unity Group, attributed full responsibility for the rupture to the Italians, highlighting the PCI's desire to join the Socialist International and eventually the Socialist Group as the reason for the split. He wrote that

> our Italian comrades have, with the others in the group, a fundamental difference on the institutional question. They want total supranationality, European political union. But for our part, this wasn't sufficient reason for not working together. We could have lived with that divergence. So what was the rest of the problem? Our Italian comrades have decided to enter into the Socialist International, and, in this Parliament, join the Socialist Group. So that is the reason why they couldn't stay with us and decided to leave. (Piquet, 1990, 16–17)

That may have been part of the reason; and certainly the Group subsequently formed by the PCI and PCE would be of a transitional nature. But the most important reason for the new departure was probably that the Communists and Allies Group was no longer an effective forum within which to pursue either an acceleration of the struggle for European union or a realignment of the European left.

The first indication of the change that was brewing came in April 1989 when PCI General Secretary Achille Occhetto chose a visit to Catalonia to discuss with both the Catalan communists and PCE General Secretary Julio Anguita the possibility of launching a new group within the European Parliament formed 'by CPs committed to the construction of Europe, by the Danish Popular Socialists, by the forces that today are a part of the Rainbow group, and by smaller groups' (quoted in *The Italian Communists*, April-June, 1989). Unfortunately, it was not to prove so easy to attract elements of the 'new social movements', which had not been represented in the old Communists and Allies Group, into the proposed new group; but the PCI worked hard throughout the Spring and Summer to win agreement between itself and the PCE, SF and Greek Left. The decision of the Danish SF to join with the Italians and Spaniards in a new European Parliamentary Group was in one crucial respect surprising: the SF was very far indeed from sharing the pro-EU views of the other parties. However, the 'new left' and anti-dogmatic nature of the SF mean that it was instinctively closer to the ethos of the formerly Eurocommunist parties than it would ever be to the hardline PCF or PCP.

After the European Parliament elections in June, the PCI executive declared the experience of the Communists and Allies Group over and mandated its European deputies to 'proceed with the constitution of a group coherent with its particular strategic choices' (*The Italian Communists*, July–September, 1989). Such a group would, however, seek from the outset to establish 'an organic relationship' with the Socialist Group – implying that the new group would act as a temporary 'stop-off point' for those communist parties seeking a convergence with the socialist mainstream but inhibited as yet by the power of veto which the existing socialist parties in their countries exercised over any moves they might make to join the Socialist International (in itself, a precondition for membership of the European Parliament's Socialist Group).

The PCI declared that its principal motivation for seeking to launch a new group was that its deputies in the new European Parliament were committed to working for 'an effective political integration, an authentic European unity, and to attribute new and more penetrating powers to Parliament in accordance with the Italian voters' very clear pronouncement through the referendum'. Therefore, it was necessary that the representation of the Italian communists at Strasbourg 'contributes from clear and coherent European stands in this battle ... avoiding the misunderstanding of permanency in the same group with those elected from parties whose strategic platform on the subject of European integration has proven irreconcilable with the PCI's' (*The Italian Communists*, July–September, 1989).

The new group which the PCI and its allies would form should 'carefully watch the possible evolution of other forces of the left in a consistently Europeanist sense. It will act to stimulate and consolidate it. It will work for the most vast [*sic*] convergence between the representatives of all the formations of the left, progressive and environmentalist forces, and of the federalist currents in the European Parliament'. The decision to seek a closer relationship with the Socialist Group from the outset was defined as an 'essential' move, falling 'within the framework of the strategy of renewal and of unitary strengthening of the Euroleft'. Giorgio Napolitano, in an interview conceded to *l'Unità* on 9 July (reported in *The Italian Communists*, July–September, 1989), highlighted differences with the PCF and PCP as particularly irreconcilable, and speculated that if negotiations aimed at the formation of the new group failed, then the PCI might still go ahead and constitute an informal grouping on its own.

The formal launch of the new Group for a Unitary European Left came on 20 July at a conference in Strasbourg. Occhetto was able to underline the 'coherently Europeanist orientation' of the group, the founding platform of which echoed all of the PCI's strategic priorities including the forging of a new 'organic' relationship with the socialists. The PCI representative Luigi Colajanni was elected Group president, with a Spaniard, Antonio Gutierrez Diaz, as vice-president. The PCI's farewell to the PCF was brief and to the point: 'This will not impede convergences, when possible. For our part, we hope that a change will take place in the PCF's position in regards to European integration' (Napolitano, quoted in *The Italian Communists*, July–September, 1989).

The formation of the Group for a Unitary European Left was followed, shortly afterwards, by the announcement that agreement had been reached between the PCF, the PCP and the KKE on the need to launch their own political grouping – although, surprisingly perhaps, they chose not to retain the 'Communists and Allies' title, but to name their new grouping 'Left Unity'. The Left Unity Group also subsequently attracted the one member of the Irish Workers' Party elected to the new parliament, thus giving the communists their first English-speaking representative.

The platform of Left Unity represented a considerable modification at least in terms of rhetoric, insofar as it avoided the anti-European integration language so frequently used by the constituent parties (with the exception of the Irish Workers' Party). Nevertheless, it was easy, reading between the lines, to detect the familiar contours of the PCF/PCP position: insistence that the Europe the Group supported consisted 'of all states of the continent and not merely those in the present European Community'; opposition to the Single Market's *laissez-faire* logic; and insistence upon a Europe that was neutral and non-aligned. In one important respect, a step forward seemed to be taken – perhaps partly in deference to the Irish Workers' Party, but also reflecting the ongoing debate even within the most hard-line communist parties – namely, the Group's platform pledged support for a strengthening of the Parliament's powers so as to narrow the democratic deficit. However, on closer inspection it is apparent that the Parliament's enhanced standing was to be at the expense of the Commission – not at the expense of the Council of Ministers. In other words, what was accepted was not any increase in supranationality, but a redistribution of powers, within the existing competencies of the Community, from an unelected to an elected body.

In the event, the dramatic collapse of the communist regimes in Eastern Europe and the subsequent transformation of the PCI into the PDS, and its adhesion to the Socialist International and the Socialist Group in the European Parliament, meant that both the new European Parliamentary groups founded in 1989 would be short-lived. For a variety of reasons the PCI's allies were unable to 'cross the Rubicon' and join the Socialist International. In part, this was because it made no political sense for small 'new left' or reform-communist formations, competing with larger social democratic parties in their respective countries, to do so: such a move would have called their existence into question. In part, it was because the larger social democratic parties in Spain, Greece and Denmark may well have vetoed any such move. The PCE-IU, Greek Left and Danish SF would thus remain isolated until, after the 1994 European Parliamentary elections, they would negotiate the formation of yet another new European Parliamentary group with the other communist parties – a move made easier by the subsequent entry of 'new left' parties from Finland and Sweden. This, however, is a matter I will return to later. For now, we may note that the 1980s ended, not with any emergence of a new Euro-left but with crippling divergences on European policy having driven the members of the former 'communist family' further apart from one another than ever.

3
CASE STUDIES:
EUROPEAN UNION POLICY AND THE
LEFT PARTIES

3.1 The Italian Communist Party (PCI) and its communist successor parties (PRC and PdCI)

Throughout the process that culminated in the signing of the Treaty of Rome in 1957, establishing the European Economic Community, the Italian Communist Party's attitude towards the Community was one of hostility. The PCI joined the Soviet Communist Party, and Western communist parties such as the French, in condemning the Community as a tool of imperialism that had the two-fold objective of subjugating Western Europe economically and politically to American capital, and strengthening imperialism's offensive against the socialist countries led by the Soviet Union.

In the atmosphere of the Cold War, the communist parties of Western Europe tended to regard all moves intended to promote integration between the states of Western Europe as part and parcel of the West's preparations for war against the USSR, and therefore contrary to the interests of 'peaceful and democratic nations' (Galante, 1988, 5).

What is significant in the case of the PCI, however, was the very early recognition that institutions of the Community, once established, could not simply be wished out of existence. As early as 1956–57, the party sought to intervene in debates in the Italian parliament and in public by proposing changes and amendments intended to 'redirect' the processes of integration while implicitly accepting 'political realities'. Thus, at the end of 1956, PCI leadership member Bruno Trentin attacked a mere maximalist stand of full-frontal opposition to the new European institutions and advocated greater realism:

> Di fronte a questa forza operante la classe operaia non può rimanere indifferente e nemmeno limitarsi ad assumere certe posizioni di principio, pur giuste e necessarie. Essa deve invece agire, con una sua politica, con un suo programma che affronti in generale e di volta in volta i problemi concreti posti in Italia dalla esistenza della Ceca, per influire con la lotta e con l'iniziativa politica sugli stessi orientamenti di questo organismo e sulle ripercussioni che esso esercita: per contrastare o limitare i riflessi più negativi della politica economica e sociale perseguita dall'Alta Autorità della Ceca; per imporre, se questo si dimostrerà possibile, la approvazione di determinati provvedimenti (in materia di investimenti, di

prezzi, di dogana, di salario e di orario di lavoro) suscettibili di favorire lo sviluppo e il rafforzamento dell'industria di base in Italia e di garantire migliori condizioni di vita per i lavoratori'.

(Faced with this reality, the working-class cannot remain indifferent and even less limit itself to assuming certain principled positions, however just and necessary. It must instead campaign, with its own policy, its own programme, that address both the general and specific problems caused in Italy by the existence of the ECSC, seeking to influence with its struggle and its political initiative the orientation and the impact of this body: to oppose or to limit the most negative outcomes of the political and economic policy followed by the High Authority of the ECSC; to impose, if this proves possible, the approval of measures (in terms of investments, prices policy, taxes, pay and hours of work) that favour the development and strengthening of the industrial sector in Italy and that guarantee better living conditions for the workers.) (quoted in Galante, 1988, 151)

In this passage we already have the makings of a reformist strategy towards the Community – accepting the process of integration as a given fact but seeking to involve the working-class movement in political action designed to extract greater improvements in conditions for the mass of the Italian people.

Although it was to be some time yet before the PCI leadership would explicitly adopt such a strategy, the resolution approved by the party Directorate in January 1957 sought to move away from a position of propagandistic attacks on the process of integration, which were only contributing to the party's isolation from other political forces. In a sense, the PCI leadership sought, even at this early stage, to 'de-ideologise' the party's opposition, arguing instead in terms of the practical political and economic consequences for Italy. In doing so, the PCI differed significantly in emphasis from the Soviet and French communist parties – a point that is sometimes overlooked by commentators who tend to emphasise the similarities in position between the parties at this juncture. The January 1957 resolution of the PCI Directorate called upon the party 'to make the problem of Europe its own concern, to incorporate the exigency of a development of European productive forces into its own programme, and not to close itself in a sterile position of preconceived opposition' (quoted in Galante, 1988, 152).

In the succeeding parliamentary debates on the treaties, the PCI intervened in a way designed to concretise this strategic orientation: proposing, for example, during the debate on the Euratom, controls designed to restrict the use of nuclear material to non-military purposes; and insisting, during the debate on the approval of the Treaty of Rome, on measures designed to alter the 'monopolistic and capitalistic' nature of the EEC such as protection for small enterprises, equal treatment for agriculture and industry, concentration of investment in deprived areas of the Italian Mezzogiorno and international control of the monopolies.

Needless to say, this did not represent, at this stage, a conversion to the camp of European integrationism or federalism. Rather it is the case that the PCI's opposition to the EEC, which undoubtedly remained strong during the late 1950s and early 1960s, was not expressed merely in dogmatic or ideological terms but already at this stage involved the party in a tortuous search for a programmatic alternative to the 'Europe of the monopolies'.

It is certainly true that a change in Soviet assessments of the nature and potential of the EEC came about in the period, 1959–62, when Moscow switched its emphasis from attacking the EEC as a tool of monopoly capital that was doomed to failure to acknowledging that the EEC was growing in significance as an economic and political actor on the international stage and demonstrating the capacity to regenerate the industrial structure of capitalism. This switch in emphasis suited the PCI. The Italian communists had concluded by the beginning of the 1960s that, in Luigi Longo's words, 'European integration was an essential element in the Italian economic leap forward' (quoted in Feld, 1968, 253). However, it would be wrong to conclude that the evolution of the PCI's position was merely a case of falling into line with Soviet foreign policy interests. In fact, the PCI's European policy was intimately related to its perceptions of its domestic position and the changing nature of the Italian social structure. That Moscow should at around this time shift its emphasis somewhat to demanding entrance for Soviet and East European goods on favourable terms to the new EEC market rather than the destruction of the EEC through a frontal assault was certainly welcome. But the PCI, at a conference of communist parties in Moscow in November 1962, went considerably beyond the Soviet position, effectively accepting that the process of economic integration was in itself a progressive and inevitable one that entailed not merely risks but great opportunities for the working-class movement.

In early 1963 (Feld, 1968, 254), the PCI finally abandoned its earlier oppositionist stance to the EEC, arguing not for the dissolution of the Community but for a 'democratic' revision of the Treaty of Rome to defend national and popular interests. Whilst this represented a considerable advance in the direction indicated by Trentin in 1956, it nevertheless remains that the PCI at this juncture envisaged a Community in which economic co-operation and co-ordination, combined with firm supranational control of the multinationals, laid the basis for progressive governments to pursue national roads to socialism, within a favourable European context. The party had not as yet come to embrace European political union, let alone European federalism, as a goal. However, the party did state – significantly – that the enlargement of the Community to embrace other states was a desirable end from the point of view of achieving the changes in the Community's structure and nature which it sought. The logic here seems to have two-fold: that through enlargement, the internal contradictions of the Community would also grow, opening up new possibilities for 'progressive and democratic' forces to exploit those contradictions; and that enlargement would also numerically strengthen the ranks of the working-class forces. Thus, the PCI supported the British application for membership, in contrast to the French communists, for example, who rejoiced in de Gaulle's veto.

From 1962 the PCI began to campaign for the right to have its members nominated by the national parliament to the European Parliament, from which the communist parties were excluded on prejudicial grounds. For the PCI, this step appears to be entirely in keeping with the logic of working to effect a transformation from within. The PCF, by contrast, continued for some time to regard participation in the European Parliament as the thin end of a revisionist wedge which would both weaken the communists' campaign to smash the Treaty of Rome and prove detrimental to the interests of France (i.e., to the ability of a French communist-led leftwing government to pursue its strategy of socialist transformation).

An important, albeit as yet somewhat tentative, divergence between the positions of the PCI and PCF can thus be detected even in the mid-1960s: tentative, because both parties were as yet united in decrying the 'Europe of the monopolies' as being anathema to the interests of progress. However, the PCI, accepting the process of economic integration in broad outline as 'objectively progressive', or at any rate in accordance with the historical tendencies of the epoch, can be seen as manoeuvring for position so as to influence future developments; the PCF, adopting a maximalist position of full-frontal opposition to the Community as being contrary to the interests of France and the working-class, can be regarded as seeking the best means of fighting further integration step by step.

However, in the 1960s this difference in analysis and in emphasis was somewhat clouded by the common position which the communist parties still shared in opposing political union. As yet, the PCI shared the French and Soviet opposition to any integrated political structure that might threaten national sovereignty. In 1966, the two parties spelt out their opposition to any transfer of decision-making power away from the national parliaments that would threaten the ability of socialist governments to carry out nationalisations and other reforms deemed desirable (Feld, 1968, 262-3). If it was the case, as Feld suggests, that the lack of enthusiasm of the PCI leadership at this stage for any increase in the powers of the European Parliament, for example, was due to their fear that the countries of northern Europe (where communists were politically weak) would show little sympathy for a progressive government in Italy, then it is surely also true that the subsequent conversion of the PCI to enthusiastic support for supranational political institutions and, above all, a strong European Parliament, is related to its despair at effecting a successful reformist strategy within the confines of the Italian nation-state. This would lead it to search for allies amongst the ranks of northern European social democracy. But this is somewhat to anticipate the argument.

By the end of the 1960s an important policy development can be noted. Following the entrance of PCI representatives into the European Parliament in March 1969, a debate got underway within the party as to the function and role of the Parliament. Two positions were argued. Giorgio Amendola, the leader of the PCI delegation to the Parliament, a close friend of Altiero Spinelli, and a key figure in the evolution of the party's European policy, argued for an increase in the powers of the European Parliament, a position echoed by PCI Senator Giovanni Bertoli who called for 'an immediate strengthening of the Parliament's powers in all matters in which the Commission has an autonomous power of decision, for example the administration of the EEC Social Fund' (quoted in Leich, 1971, 277). By contrast, others, including Nilde Jotti, argued that any increase in the powers of the Parliament in the absence of direct elections would be a step towards authoritarianism. The party's position, by the beginning of the 1970s, was one of support both for direct elections to the European Parliament and for a substantial increase in the European Parliament's powers vis-à-vis the Council of Ministers and the Commission. In other words, the PCI argued, in the name of greater democracy, for a transfer of power away from non-elected bodies within the Community's institutions to an elected body; although it was to be some time before the party would go a step further and argue for a transfer of powers from national parliaments to the European Parliament.

As already mentioned, the PCI at this juncture was far from advocating European political union – a project it was later to embrace. In fact, the party's European policy still had many points in common with that of the French communists: strong defence of the rights and interests of workers and small farmers within the country (the point being, of course, that the party was relating to its national constituency, rather than thinking explicitly in terms of transnational economic strategy), opposition to the erosion of the powers of EEC member states, and much rhetoric about the need for the Community to escape from dependence upon the American camp and to act as an autonomous force which could point the way towards a supersession of the blocs centred on the two superpowers.

However, participation in the institutions of the Community was to exercise a greater 'modifying' effect upon the PCI than the PCI was able to exercise upon the Community. Just as involvement in the democratic process within Italy was to result in a substantial mutation of PCI ideology and strategy as the party came closer to government, so the first communist party to participate in the European Parliament was to develop a stake in the protection and expansion of its foothold there. This process saw the PCI become an enthusiastic advocate of many of the ideas associated with the European federalist movement over the next ten years. The party, which had committed itself without the ambiguities of certain other communist parties to changing the direction of the integration process from within, just as it had committed itself to changing the direction of Italian parliamentary democracy from within, was to discover the potential of a powerful European Parliament for exercising influence upon an Italian governmental process from which it seemed permanently excluded. Certainly, the party's commitment to European union seemed, if anything, to take concrete shape ever more rapidly after the failure of its hopes of entering the government of Italy in the late 1970s. Of importance also was the party's growing sense of despair, accentuated by the collapse of the 'historic compromise', at the capacity of Italian democracy to survive. The fragile legitimacy of the Italian nation-state, the alleged degeneration of the political institutions and political parties, the recurrence of plots and counter-plots, conspiracies, subversion and terrorism, and the emergence of acute social and economic contradictions in the 1970s, all led the PCI – and other Italian political forces as well – to conclude that Italy's democratic stability was best protected by anchoring the country firmly within a politically united, as well as economically integrated, Europe. In a sense, the PCI's concern with the failure of its strategy to revitalise Italian democracy by securing acceptance of its own entrance into the governmental arena, led it to transfer its hopes increasingly to the European plane. In this respect, its view – which grew ever stronger over the years – that European union was the key to salvaging, renewing and relaunching Italian democracy mirrors the concern with democratic consolidation which underpinned the European policies of the PCE and the KKE-es, in Spain and Greece respectively, despite the fact that Italy had emerged from fascism some thirty years earlier.

An important influence upon the PCI during the 1970s was Altiero Spinelli, who may be regarded as having anticipated in many respects the party's evolutionary course. Spinelli, a founding father of European federalism and for many years one of Italy's EEC Commissioners, was approached by the PCI leadership after the Soviet invasion of Czechoslovakia in 1968 and asked to help them devise a PCI policy on Europe. As he recalled later: 'They had some vague idea that Europe was the road they ought to be taking, but they were not sure how to go about it' (Urban, 1978, 16).

Initially the PCI leadership – and in particular Giorgio Amendola – spoke in terms of a new peaceful, democratic Europe 'from the Atlantic to the Urals'. The vagueness of this concept – and the implication of fence sitting on the question of whether the party was in the 'Western camp' or the 'Soviet camp' – led the PCI leadership to a redefinition of its European policy, placing the emphasis on the unification of Western Europe. Incidentally, in describing the earlier rhetoric of a new Europe 'from the Atlantic to the Urals' as being Gaullist in nature, Spinelli might well have added that it was precisely the type of vague concept so beloved of the French Communist Party. (The seeming convergence between PCF and Gaullist positions on Europe was to exercise the minds of commentators right into the 1980s.)

The PCI's policy, then, was to undergo a number of qualitative refinements during the late 1960s and early-to-mid-1970s. Having specified Western Europe as the primary object of its political strategy for European unification, the party leadership first spoke in terms of a confederation of nation-states, before moving on to acceptance of the ideas of federalism.

Spinelli resigned his Commission in 1976 to accept nomination as an independent left candidate on the PCI's electoral lists in the Italian general election of that year. He was subsequently nominated as a delegate from the Italian national parliament to the European Parliament, being returned in the direct elections of 1979 and 1984.

As George Urban points out (1978, 7), Spinelli's decision to stand for election to parliament on the PCI's electoral lists was greeted with 'a mixture of horror and disbelief' by many of his colleagues. The conventional wisdom at the time was that he had lent himself, unwittingly or naively, as a Trojan horse by which the communist enemy could hope to penetrate and ultimately destroy the EEC citadel.

However, Spinelli justified his decision to accept nomination on the PCI's lists by arguing that the crisis of Italian democracy was so severe that only a historic compromise such as the PCI was proposing between the democratic forces could save the situation from catastrophe and halt what he saw as Italy's drift away from the Community. He accepted nomination, moreover, on the understanding that he would not take the Communist whip in parliament, being free to speak out on whatever issues he chose and to vote independently; this was the same principle which was later to apply when he entered the Communists and Allies Group at Strasbourg, leaving him free to pursue initiatives which, as we saw in the preceding chapter, certainly did not meet with the approval of all the members of the Group. Spinelli, though, could tell George Urban that 'I can influence the Party's policies in those areas which matter most to me – its policies on Europe. I do not think I am boasting when I say that the Party has, in fact, adopted the line which I had sought and supported for many years, especially the need to transcend economic unification and move towards a European political union' (Urban, 1978, 8).

Indeed, Spinelli brought his influence to bear on the PCI's strategic orientation in another, related, way, arguing that the leftwing forces in Europe could only assume the leadership of the struggle to build a new, politically united Europe if those communist parties, such as the PCI, which were focusing their horizons on such a Europe moved beyond the parameters of their own tradition to establish good working relationships on the programmatic and ideological levels with the European social democratic parties. With considerable acumen Spinelli boldly predicted what, at this juncture, critics and friends alike of the PCI were unwilling to believe:

> The Italian Communists are men and women whose principal concern is the welfare and general good of the Italian people, who want social reforms to that end, and who are perfectly prepared to ally themselves with others to that end. They are people of the stamp of the Austrian, Belgian and British socialists – in fact social democrats ... This is not a party of militants – it is a party of millions of ordinary, reform-hungry people, and the Apparat at grass-roots levels is also social democratic much more than Marxist or Leninist. (Urban, 1978, 10–11)

Certainly during the course of the 1970s the PCI moved substantially towards a much more positive European policy, locating Europe at the centre of its economic and political programme. The party had come, as we have seen, to relate the failures and shortcomings of the leftwing traditions – both communist and social democratic – to the limitations of the nation-state as an agency of radical change in the era of increasing internationalisation. As Pietro Ingrao, a much-respected leader of the PCI's radical left wing, put it:

> Sono fenomeni che hanno ridotto o mutato profondamente gli spazi di intervento su cui si è fondato per secoli lo Stato-nazione di tipo europeo e su cui si sono foggiate anche le politiche sperimentate e practicate, soprattutto nel secondo dopo-guerra, dalla sinistra europea e dal movimento operaio. In questo senso si può parlare di una connessione tra la crisi delle politiche del Welfare State e queste nuove dimensioni sovranazionali che riguardano ormai questioni fondamentali come l'organizzazione della pace e della sicurezza, la risposta all

sfida dell'innovazione tecnologica, il gravissimo livello che sta assumendo la disoccupazione di massa in Europa e nel mondo, l'organizzazione di sistemi mondiali di informazione, una politica per l'ambiente all'altezza dei problemi e non limitata all difesa di qualche 'pezzo' di natura da conservare indenne.

(There are phenomena that have reduced or changed profoundly the room for interventions on which was founded for centuries the nation-state of the European type, and on which basis also the European left and the workers' movement fashioned its policies, above all in the post-war period. In this sense, one can talk of a connection between the crisis of the policies of the Welfare State and these supranational dimensions regarding what are by now fundamental questions such as the organisation of peace and security, the response to the challenge of technological innovation, the very serious levels that mass unemployment is assuming in Europe and in the world, the organisation of world systems of information, and an environmental policy that is up to the problems and not limited to conserving some 'piece' of nature undamaged.) (Garzia, 1985, 8)

The urgency with which the party had come to view the necessity for a comprehensive 'European road to socialism', based on a programmatic convergence between the major leftwing forces in Western Europe, was underlined in the run-up to the 1979 elections to the European Parliament. In 1978, the PCI was the organiser of a major convention on problems of European integration at which members of the German SPD and the French PS participated. This was to herald a series of initiatives by the PCI over the next decade with the intention of facilitating mutual exchange of ideas and ultimately programmatic convergence on European themes between the major leftwing parties.

In June 1979, the PCI programme for the European elections reflected the clear European choice that had been endorsed by the party's Fifteenth Congress in March of that year. (The summary that follows is based on the analysis of the programmes of the Italian and French communist parties in a special issue of the journal *l'Italia e l'Europa*, in March 1980.) The programme called for a European plan to confront the crisis of the capitalist system through controls upon the multinational corporations, although acceptance of the role of the market was made explicit. The PCI sought to counterpose the 'negative' integration achieved to date – the grave imbalances within the European Community, the recurrence of mass migration from the weaker areas to the core – which it attributed to the neo-liberal nature of the integration process, to the desired 'positive' integration. By this, it meant, following Spinelli, the urgent necessity to pass to social harmonisation and political union so as to tackle regional imbalances and facilitate supranational control of market forces in the interests of social and economic democracy. In other words, the PCI was at this stage clearly and unambiguously pronouncing itself in favour of European unification to a much greater extent than the French PS or the British Labour party (not to mention the PCF).

The democratisation of the Community's institutions was restated as a fundamental objective of the party. This was not only because of the desire to see a stronger European Parliament advance the cause of pan-European economic planning or social engineering, but also because the PCI argued that the then structure of the Community – with a strong Council of Ministers exercising effective power – prevented true integration. The Council of Ministers' decisions necessarily reflected the interests of the dominant nation-states rather than a vision of Europe's destiny as a whole. The influence of Spinelli here can be readily discerned. Nevertheless, some contradiction remained between the declaration of support for a strong European Parliament and the declared wish that this should not be at the expense of the powers of the national parliaments.

Strong support for the development of effective social and regional policies – deemed of urgency in the case of the Italian Mezzogiorno – went hand in hand with an advocacy of a profound realignment of political forces within the European ambit. The PCI declared itself favourable to the broadest possible co-operation, not just with the socialists, but also with Christian democratic and secular parties of every inspiration, which were prepared to fight for a relaunch and renewal of the European dream. In essence, the party was moving towards an extension of its domestic national strategy of the historic compromise to the level of the Community. Although a realignment of the European left began to figure very prominently from this stage on as a strategic goal of the party, the PCI did not confine its drive to enlist support for an extension of the European integration process to the social and political to the forces of the left: Spinelli had long argued that the real political dividing line where the future of the Community was concerned was not between right and left at all but between those who were prepared to fight for European unity and those who either resisted and opposed the European project or wanted to confine it to the completion of a free market in labour and capital only. The PCI had come by the end of the 1970s to embrace this view.

The party declared itself in favour of European monetary and economic union, regarding currency barriers as having a detrimental effect on industrial and agricultural policy. But it criticised what it saw as the failure of European policy to address problems of regional and sectoral imbalances that lay at the heart of the economic crisis. In this respect the PCI called for an effective co-ordination of the economies of the member states with a programming of economic growth in order to facilitate a more balanced development of the Community; the re-examination after an initial period of the workings of the European Monetary System (EMS) with particular attention to the problems experienced by the weaker countries and with a view to regulating relations with the dollar and encouraging the participation of sterling; the creation of a European currency unit as a step towards a common currency; and the elaboration by the Community of a common project for the reform of the international monetary system. The party also committed itself to a considerable strengthening of regional policy, calling for the amount of money made available through the regional fund to be increased by almost 300 per cent.

The Community was seen as having a considerable potential in tackling the problem of mass unemployment, both through the transformation of the Social Fund into a source of support for the temporarily unemployed and for retraining schemes, and through the promotion by the Community of agricultural and industrial co-operatives. Indeed, what emerges in the programme of the PCI is a vision of a European Community which breaks decisively with the logic of monopoly capital in the direction of a strong supranational reformism – co-ordinating scientific and technological research and directing its results towards the sectors deemed most in need of help; harmonising employment legislation and guaranteeing the rights of trade unions; promoting small – and medium-size enterprises and co-operatives by facilitating their access to technological innovations; controlling large-scale investments and involving the trade unions in the programming of investments throughout the Community; and creating a European Central Bank.

The Community that the PCI envisaged would be one that asserted its autonomy and acted as a force for détente and disarmament, engaging in economic co-operation with Eastern Europe and assuming a position that was neither 'anti-American nor anti-Soviet'. The party programme was therefore at pains to emphasise opposition to any notion that Europe should become a new military bloc, and to call for a ban on European arms exports to the Third World. Amongst the concrete measures proposed to ensure that the new Europe should embody the PCI's new internationalism were: support by the Community for peoples struggling against racist or oppressive regimes; renewal of the Lomé agreement, ensuring full access to EC markets for the agricultural and industrial products of the developing countries; realisation of economic agreements with the countries of Latin America and Asia; preferential trade terms for the poorest countries of the Third World; and promotion by the Community of a major programme of investment on terms favourable to the Third World, which would enable them to break free of dependence upon the multinationals alone.

One can see also a progressive evolution in the nature of the PCI's thinking on European defence and security. By the mid-1970s, the PCI had clearly accepted Italy's membership of the North Atlantic Treaty Organisation (NATO), arguing that to call the country's strategic placement into question would upset the balance of power in Europe and do nothing to secure peace and mutual disarmament. Moreover, as Enrico Berlinguer pointed out, a PCI-led Italian government would probably feel safer behind the NATO shield than with a position of neutrality, given the USSR's record in Czechoslovakia in 1968.

Acceptance of NATO, and concomitant rejection of the demands of communist left-wingers for neutrality or non-alignment, led logically to advocacy of a common European defence and security policy – anathema to the French Communists. In the PCI's view, by the end of the 1970s, a common European defence policy would strengthen the European pillar of NATO, making it more difficult for Washington to go over the heads of Europe in dealing with Moscow, and consolidating Europe as a force between the superpowers. To critics of the party leadership, both internal and external, the acceptance of a common European defence policy ran counter to the party's professed support for a 'Europe of peace' which leaned neither to East nor to West. Indeed, the party's opposition to the deployment of US missiles in Western Europe (itself balanced by PCI opposition to the deployment of Soviet SS-20 missiles in Eastern Europe) did not entirely overcome the tension evident in the party's policy.

The PCI, throughout the late 1970s and the 1980s, was to find itself faced with this dilemma: how to signal the party's firm and unequivocal anchorage in the Western camp whilst at the same time opposing Western militarism and arguing for a policy of peace, which, in the eyes of conservative critics, undermined Western interests. The party had not succeeded in overcoming this dilemma, even by the time of the majority faction's mutation into the PDS in 1991. The election of Achille Occhetto as General Secretary of the new PDS in February 1991 was marred by the opposition of the party's right wing in protest at the party's opposition to Western involvement in the Gulf War. Once again, the Italian (ex-) communists found themselves caught between commitment to a Europe that was subservient to neither the USA nor the USSR, and huge media pressure to 'prove' their democratic credentials by falling into line with the foreign policy of Washington. (By the end of the 1990s, the PDS leadership had enthusiastically endorsed the Blair–Clinton axis in both foreign and economic policy, sealing its conversion to a very moderate form of 'third way' social democracy by effectively abandoning the earlier attempts by the PCI to carve out a principled and nuanced left-of-centre position.)

Many of the proposals and policies outlined in the PCI's manifesto for the first direct elections were to remain central to the party's agenda for Europe during the next decade. However, one can also see a progressive maturation of the party's 'European choice' after 1984. That was of course the year in which the European Parliament approved the project of European political union, of which Altiero Spinelli had been the prime mover. The vote on the Draft Treaty had seen the PCI and the majority of the Socialists vote in favour, with the PCF voting against. The PCI, with Spinelli once again on its electoral lists, returned to Strasbourg after the 1984 European elections with its position reinforced; helped by the wave of sympathy which followed the tragic death of Enrico Berlinguer during the election campaign, the party polled a third of the national vote and won twenty-six seats. Thereafter the urgency with which the party insisted that the actual processes of integration were failing to keep pace with the challenges of the time, and were in fact leading towards immobilism and a dangerous increase in the Community's 'democratic deficit' increased markedly.

The PCI was dismayed by what it saw as conservative feet dragging on two essential questions: political union, and a democratic redress of the balance between the Council of Ministers, the Commission and the European Parliament. The party had concluded that resistance to European unity by certain governments, particularly the British, and the attempt by political forces of the right to restrict the expression of the European ideal to the completion of a free market in goods, services, capital and labour, were not merely threatening to de-rail the European project, with the exclusion from the unification process of 'broad democratic masses', but were creating a 'small Europe', which would prove incapable of responding to the new challenges of the day, from the processes of change underway in the USSR and Eastern Europe to the crisis of third-world debt and the third-world population explosion. The failure of the governments of the Community to incorporate a firm commitment to European democracy within the Single Act was bemoaned as being grossly inadequate, although the PCI supported the Single Act as a stepping stone towards what it was hoped would be more concrete moves in the future.

The PCI had come, during the course of the 1980s, not only to embrace European federalism, but also to share Spinelli's belief that what was at stake was nothing less than the future of European democracy itself. The party redefined its socialist internationalism – its commitment to universal democracy, peace between all peoples and a new relationship between Europe and the countries of the Third World – precisely in terms of European supranationality, believing that anything short of supranational European democracy would leave Europe a prisoner of the logic of the political right. Gianni Cervetti, president of the Communists and Allies Group in the European Parliament, argued that the PCI had come to 'see in the political unity of the European Community the concrete realisation, in this part of the world, of the idea of supranationality', and he quoted Gramsci in support of the view that the historical process leads to European union as it was only within such a union that productive forces and democratic potential could be fully developed; and that the development of European union would, within a matter of years, render the concept of nationalism as being of 'archaeological value' (Cervetti, 1986, 52).

The party, in other words, had reached the conclusion that any hesitation with respect to the necessity of pushing ahead in favour of the construction of a supranational European democracy could only mean that the leadership of Europe was forfeited to rightwing forces whose ideological, moral and cultural hegemony constituted a barrier to true integration between the European peoples. The heirs of Churchill, Adenauer and de Gasperi were Thatcher and Kohl – not champions of Europeanism but of pursuit of profit at the expense of the weaker European regions. In 1987, Cervetti, writing in the PCI daily newspaper *l'Unità* (25 March 1987), argued explicitly for an acceleration in the left's (and the PCI's) 'Europeanisation' as the only possible effective response to stagnation in remedying the democratic deficit. Another prominent party leader, Giorgio Napolitano, declared in the party's theoretical journal in 1988 that it would be disastrous not to 'advance courageously on the path of integration, to lose direction, to leave to conservative forces the banner of European unity'. The left must respond with a vision of a politically united, socially integrated and democratic Europe that translated itself into concrete proposals. The role of the European Parliament was increasingly seen as the nucleus of a constituent assembly for just such a united European state. Significantly, it was the PCI (in the person of Gianni Cervetti) that moved a bill proposing that the European Parliament be given a constituent mandate; the measure was approved by the Italian electorate in a referendum held on the same day as the European elections. This effectively authorised the European Parliament to formulate a Constitution for the political union of Europe.

The party's programme for the 1989 European elections reflected this firm embrace of European federalism. No longer was the PCI simply arguing that

European integration was inevitable, and that the best way to ensure the defence of working-class and Italian interests was to work from within the Community's institutions for change; rather the party was arguing that European integration and unity were essential and constituted the key cornerstone of all the party's political initiatives.

The 1989 programme (reproduced in *The Italian Communists*, April–June 1989) declared that 'battle has been joined' between 'progressive, far-sighted forces, able to inject fresh energy into Europe's unique civil and democratic heritage, using it as an instrument for the progress of all the world' and 'other forces representing oligarchic groups and neo-conservative policies'. Central to the struggle was overcoming the limitations of the Single European Act. This could only be accomplished by laying the basis of an institutional and political framework 'profoundly different from the present one. A reduction and control of the powers of lobbies, trusts, and great financial and industrial agglomerates is necessary'. This actually sounded more radical than it was, as subsequent passages in the programme would make clear.

The party laid great emphasis upon the social dimension of the single market, which, it argued, should be strengthened and progressively expanded: 'the function of a Single European Market must not mean that business Europe, the Europe of the huge economic agglomerates and the rich, prevails. This is why liberalisation policies are not enough. [N.B., liberalisation policies were not, however, rejected.] Social policies must constitute the essential and pre-eminent aspect of the new phase of integration.' Yet this could only come to pass with a strong and democratic European state, capable of intervening decisively in all spheres of life. Here, the PCI restated the case for social democracy – but at the European level where success alone might be achieved:

> It is a question of intervening in various fields: reform of the social state, efficiency of services, which involves a clear distinction in public administration between safeguarding employees and representing the customers' more general interests; anti-trust legislation and the democratisation of the firm; budget policies that permit a different distribution of income and the more rational allocation of resources; the creation of new forms of entrepreneurship. But above all economic democracy should be qualified as a growth in the workers' opportunities for access to knowledge of the firm's transformations, and as an informed participation, not only in governing these transformations and their human and social implications, but also the processes of accumulation through democratically governed collective funds and financial instruments.

This was a platform that by now had come to involve a very limited concept of economic democracy. The party was not so much rejecting the neo-liberal nature of the sort of European integration on offer, as trying to ameliorate it with some reformist measures. The programme did not go beyond the logic of capitalism but rather sought to repropose certain familiar social democratic themes at a supranational European level. Already, in 1989, it is arguable that the PCI platform on Europe reveals a party that no longer merits the label 'Left party', in the sense of a party that contests capitalism. (It is also worth noting that the PCI fielded as a candidate in the 1989 European elections, the French political scientist and constitutionalist Maurice Duverger, who stressed the similarities between the party and the French PS.) Certainly, within a few years of the majority faction's transmutation into the Left Democrats (PDS), this transformation would be more or less complete. PDS leader Massimo d'Alema would lead his party into elections in the late 1990s and in 2001 arguing that there was no feasible alternative to liberal globalisation and that welfare spending cuts were necessary in order to 'build Europe' (Gilbert, 1998).

The PCI in 1989 also outlined a vision of the new Europe's international role. A 'more equitable structure in international economic relations' was urged through an up-grading of the Lomé convention, a cancellation of foreign debt for the poorest countries and for others a rescheduling of debt, reduction of interest rates and transformation into investment funds, and 'a transfer of resources, technology and economic, financial and professional means to the countries of the Third World'. Strong support for a common defence policy and calls for a strengthening of the European pillar of NATO were coupled with opposition to any modernisation of NATO's armaments, and a call for an acceleration of nuclear disarmament. In fact, the PCI clearly saw a strengthening of European defence co-operation as offering the best escape from subordination to the American defence industry whose interest in comprehensive disarmament in Europe was still doubted. The party agreed with a proposal from the Community's socialist parties to create an independent European security institution.

Whereas the PCF, and other such communist parties, viewed EC approaches to Eastern Europe with grave suspicion – detecting a capitalist plot to destabilise the 'socialist' countries – the PCI stressed the importance of the EC as a source for democratic stability and encouragement of economic growth. The party welcomed the extension of the community through both membership and associate membership to the countries of Eastern Europe and to the EFTA countries.

The acceleration of moves towards monetary union was also seen as necessary to control speculation and as laying the foundation for an assertion of economic autonomy from the United States: 'the dollar now seems inappropriate to continue in its role as the world monetary system's only foundation. The currency of a single country, the US dollar, administered in a completely autonomous way and according to the United States' exclusive interests, can no longer be the sole international currency par excellence.' The party expressed undiluted enthusiasm for European Monetary Union and a European Central Bank – defined as a 'decisive political step towards Europe's political unity'.

The PCI manifesto proposed four concrete measures which should be undertaken to strengthen the political unity of the Community and point towards a united European state:

1 Confer on the European Parliament the legislative powers necessary for elaborating and controlling, together with the Council of Ministers, Community policies, i.e., its regulations and directives;

2 Give the new Parliament the task of drawing up a new project for European union (or of indicating the constitutional bases for the Community to become a true European political union), with the contribution of other Community institutions and ratification set within the competence of the national parliaments;
3 Give different powers and new authority to the Commission, so that it becomes a true 'Community Government'. The Commission's membership must be decided with the European Parliament's decisive concourse, and it must ask the Parliament for a vote of confidence on the basis of its programme and respond to it for what it does;
4 Inaugurate as of now regular co-operation relations, forms of mutual consultation, and eventual moments of co-ordination for important supranational Community problems between the European Parliament and its national confreres. (*The Italian Communists*, April–June 1989)

The party did insist, however, that progress towards European union could not be based on supranational institutions alone but required a new relationship between the Community and its regions. To this end, the PCI proposed a considerable strengthening of the social and regional funds and a decentralisation of their management; and a new industrial policy for the Community that would necessitate a more than doubling of the funds of the European Investment Bank.

Finally, much emphasis was placed upon the need for a common transport policy, co-ordination of scientific and research efforts, a revision of the and a common European policy on culture, training and education.

The PCI's programme for the 1989 European elections was the last major policy statement on EU matters before the dissolution of the PCI and its replacement by its successor parties, the PDS and the Party of Communist Refoundation (PRC). It is significant as a measure of how far the party had travelled in the preceding three decades in that it constituted the most clear and unambiguous statement of the party's European federalist vocation to date and underlined what was by now beyond doubt: that of all the parties of the left in Western Europe – communist, post-communist or social democratic – it had travelled furthest in relocating its ideological, strategic and programmatic thinking on the supranational European plane. But the programme is significant in another respect. It is not only an unambiguously pro-integrationist and pro-federalist document. It is also a classic statement by a social democratic party that seeks to manage capitalism in a more equitable, just and sensible manner than the political right, but which has abandoned a vision of transcending capitalism or of contesting the fundamental nature of the European integration process that is currently underway. Driven in part by its sense of isolation within the Italian political system, and in part by the limitations of the Eurocommunist experience, and motivated also by its strongly ingrained preference for pragmatic reformist perceived solutions over ideology, the party had undergone a transformation that was even more profound than the rebranding of 'New Labour' under Tony Blair. There is no doubt that the strategic reorientation towards the centre of politics gained momentum after the death in 1984 of Enrico Berlinguer – perhaps the last great, charismatic Italian communist leader who continued to be imbued with the culture, morals and intellectual ethos of Gramscian Marxism. Berlinguer, as we have seen, did much to lead his party towards a pro-European federalist position; however, he remained an idealist at heart whose vision of a socialist Europe had helped to lift his party members' eyes beyond the narrow horizon of 'a growth in the workers' opportunities for access to knowledge of the firm's transformations'. His ideological legacy would prove to be a difficult one, if not downright embarrassing (Valentini, 1997).

The transformation of the majority faction of the PCI into the eminently moderate, social democratic PDS in 1991 would of course be followed by the birth of a smaller Party of Communist Refoundation (PRC), dedicated as its name suggests to refounding the Italian communist movement. In truth, the subsequent evolution of the European policy of the PDS (renamed the DS in 1998, after it merged with various social democratic and left-Christian democratic factions) lies outside the scope of the present book. It is clearly a social democratic, rather than a Left, party; in government (from 1996 to 2001) it has chosen to swim with the tide of neo-liberal globalisation rather than to challenge its claim to hegemony in any fundamental way. The DS entered the twenty-first century having 'ditched red for blue, state ownership for privatisation and class warfare for pop music', and having enlisted the endorsement of Tony Blair at its first congress of the new century (Carroll, 2000). The failures of Eurocommunism had in a sense forced the PCI leadership to look to socialist and social democratic parties in Western Europe as potential partners in a revitalised European left. In the 1980s, it still hoped that it might act as the leftwing of social democracy, recalling social democratic parties in France, Germany and elsewhere to the possibilities of a relaunch of a strong social democratic reformism at the European federalist level. It was the party's tragedy, perhaps, that just as political isolation had undermined its political strategy at home and abroad in the 1970s and 1980s, so in the 1990s those social democratic parties with whom it sought convergence were following neo-liberal policies more or less uncritically (and often in the name of European integration). What many within the European centre-left would seek in the 1990s was not so much a strong social democratic reformism, using the EU as a weapon with which to fight against monopolies and inequality, but rather a slightly modified version of Clintonism or Blairism. Small wonder, perhaps, that the PDS in government would quickly assimilate to such 'minimalism', especially as it had a strong minority within its ranks who had lost all faith in the traditions of the European left and urged the party to refound itself yet again as an Italian version of the US Democratic Party.

However, we cannot conclude this analysis of the evolution of the European policies of the Italian communists without looking at the Party of Communist Refoundation, whose ranks include Enrico Berlinguer's son, Marco. That party would see two splits in its ranks (in 1995 and again in 1998), both due to tactical and strategic disagreements over how to position itself politically in relation to competition between the Berlusconi-led rightwing forces and the PDS-led centre-left. These splits, the last of which produced the small Party of Italian Communists (PdCI), would weaken what remains of the communist tradition in Italy. Nevertheless, the PRC and the PdCI together command between 5 and 8 per cent of the vote in Italy and in seeking to define their political identity they have developed broad approaches to European integration that relate to the historical legacy of the PCI in interesting ways.

The PRC was born in February 1991 at a rally in Rome, which saw thousands of party founders chanting the name of Enrico Berlinguer, and laying claim to the legacy of the PCI (Menichini, 1991). Those founding the PRC were a fairly heterogeneous group – they included 'new left' radicals, left-leaning *Berlingueriani* (or left-Eurocommunists), members of the minority pro-Soviet wing of the old PCI led by Armando Cossutta, and members of small far-left groups such as *Democrazia Proletaria*. They were united by a belief that a radical anti-capitalist politics remained both valid and necessary. However, the PRC was from the outset a different sort of party than the old PCI had been. Not only was the PRC a much smaller party in terms of membership and electoral support (perhaps between 100,000 and 200,000 members and between 4 and 8 per cent of the vote, compared to around 1.4 million members and 27 per cent of the vote for the PCI at the time of its demise). It was clearly a much more leftwing party, with narrower social bases of support and a tendency towards dogmatism that had been wholly subdued in the PCI. Many of the working-class members and supporters of the old PCI from the industrial north and farm workers from the south moved over to the PRC, giving its politics a more aggressive class 'edge' than had been the case with the PCI. At the same time, it sought to appeal to that radical and anti-capitalist idealism, especially amongst the young, that the PCI had essentially turned its back on.

In European policy, the PRC departed from the strongly pro-integrationist stance of the PCI, adopting a much more critical attitude towards the neo-liberal nature of the integration process. An early opportunity to distinguish itself from the PDS came during the vote on the Maastricht Treaty in the Italian parliament in October 1992. Whilst the PDS supported the Treaty, notwithstanding its criticism of Maastricht's failure to adopt measures to promote stronger political union and social integration, the PRC deputies voted against. In the early 1990s, the party concentrated its fire on the neo-liberalism and monetarism that it saw as characteristic of Maastricht. According to Luigi Vinci, head of the PRC delegation to the European Parliament and a key figure in developing the party's EU policies throughout the 1990s, 'the pace of events [during the early and mid-1990s] rarely allowed us to enrich our political struggle with all the necessary reflection. We fought the 1994 European election campaign with a policy of maximum criticism of the Maastricht Treaty and the single currency, but this wasn't accompanied by a better defined programme' (letter to author, dated 3 July 1997). The thrust of the PRC's criticism of Maastricht was that the Treaty enshrined a narrow monetarist concept of economics that was leading to mass unemployment, social disaster, and erosion of popular support for the very notion of the European Union, and it concentrated political power in the hands of technocrats who were beyond political accountability. The left could 'not ignore that the forms and contents of European institutional construction today are intrinsically and organically capitalist' (Vinci, 1995, 20). In a clear break with the tradition of the PCI, Vinci argued also that democracy in the EU required a return of powers to the level of the nation-state because 'democracy ... cannot be effectively built at the European and regional levels alone'. The PRC, he argued, should reject pressure for the EU to develop into a federal union but at the same time accept that the left could not hope to govern the economy effectively except at a pan-European level. Therefore, the party should argue for a 'polycentric' approach to the question of sovereignty – strengthening both national parliaments and the European Parliament, and relations between them, at the expense of the technocrats.

In a direct criticism of the approach taken by social democratic parties – including the PDS, which the PRC characterised as a 'neo-liberal centre-left party' – the PRC argued that these parties made a fundamental error when they gave support to 'the political forms of capitalist globalisation, among which is the European Union designed by the Maastricht Treaty.' Instead, they should struggle to make reconnections between politics and economic policy, creating new forums for interventions designed to politicise economic debates and confront technocracy with democracy (Vinci, 1996a, 4). Yet, after 1996 of course, the PRC found itself supporting a minority centre-left government led by the PDS. (The party had already suffered a minor schism in 1995 when a number of its deputies resigned in protest at the PRC leadership's refusal to support the 'government of technocrats' that President Scalfaro had appointed following the collapse of the first Berlusconi government.) The centre-left government, from 1996 to 1998, attempted to prepare Italy for participation in the single currency by implementing budget cuts. The PRC secured, as the price of its support, an agreement to halt cuts to pensions and health spending. It failed, however, in its attempt to have Italy's participation in the single currency postponed for a few years to ease pressure on social policy. The PDS was able to portray it as effectively having swallowed the Maastricht Treaty by supporting the government. Clearly this rankled with the PRC leaders. The party was attempting a difficult, if not impossible (for a small party) political balancing act. On the one hand, it rejected Maastricht as 'a European attempt at neo-liberal management of the process of capitalist globalisation' and argued that both the old PCI and the PDS had fallen into a trap by accepting this in its fundamentals. On the other hand, it wanted to avoid becoming 'enclosed within national borders, ignoring the necessity of constructing another course of democratic and socially progressive political intervention, in the process of capitalist globalisation' (Vinci, 1996b, 6). It sought to challenge the basis upon which the single currency was being introduced, without rejecting the idea of monetary union per se. As Vinci argued, 'The Europe of Maastricht is just one of the ways – that of the capitalist right – of building a Europe that is equipped with common institutions' (Vinci, 1996c). Unfortunately, an alternative way of building such a Europe has remained vague and elusive for the party.

Tensions within the PRC came to the fore at the Third Party Congress in December 1996. Some members argued for the abandonment of the support given to the centre-left government, on the basis that this support had involved the PRC in a U-turn on European policy and on the party's anti-capitalist stand in general. In 1998 tensions resulted in an open split, when Armando Cossutta led a group of party leaders and members in a walkout to protest at the decision to withdraw support from the government. The Party of Italian Communists (PdCI) that he founded then participated in the centre-left government and fought elections as part of the PDS-led 'Olive tree' coalition. Interestingly, the PdCI defines itself as 'the left of the centre-left', criticising the DS for abandoning traditional social democracy in favour of Blairism and the PRC for retreating into a leftist oppositionism that 'cuts its roots with the history of the PCI' (Diliberto, 2001).

The PdCI is clearly a very small party, of no more perhaps than a few thousand members and between one and two per cent of the vote. It is, moreover, questionable whether the party would survive the departure or retirement of its two best-known leaders – Armando Cossutta and Oliviero Diliberto. Nevertheless a very brief consideration of its intervention in the arena of EU policy is worthwhile. While criticising the neo-liberalism of the DS, the PdCI has consciously sought to wrap itself in the pro-integrationist and pro-federalist clothes of the old PCI. In a joint statement with the European Federalist Movement in 1999, the party argued that 'whoever works against a federal Europe, against a European Constitution based on universal civil and social rights, against a common government of the economy and foreign policy, against enlargement of the EU, knowingly or otherwise, reinforces that process of unipolar globalisation that places the planet under the control of a handful of powerful actors' (Party of Italian Communists (PdCI), 1999). This was a clear dig at the PRC, accused of actually reinforcing American domination by retreating from a positive European federalism of the left. The PdCI called for the transformation of the European Commission into a true federal government, answerable to the European Parliament, for a strong common security and foreign policy, for common taxation and economic policies as a prerequisite of more effective control over capitalism, and for the political unity of Europe to be recognised by the left as a necessary condition for the creation of a more just and sustainable international order. PdCI leader Cossutta, now presenting himself as the authentic heir of Togliatti and Berlinguer, notwithstanding his pro-Soviet past, explicitly called for reform and strengthening of supranational institutions within the EU. The party's European policy was presented, in other words, as fully in keeping with PCI traditions, but further to the left.

The PRC, by contrast, continues to find difficulty in clearly defining its vision of how the EU should develop. The PRC fought the 1999 European Parliament elections on a platform that harshly criticised both the conduct of NATO's war against Yugoslavia – the Clinton–Blair axis was described as a 'more dangerous' and 'more aggressive and violent' version of the Reagan–Thatcher axis of the 1980s – and the role of European governments in accepting US imperialist dominance of the globe. Strongly anti-capitalist in its rhetoric, the manifesto attacked the neo-liberal basis upon which the single currency was introduced. Nevertheless, the PRC seemed to move forward from a position of 'oppositionism' by recognising that the single currency could become an instrument of European autonomy, vis-à-vis the dollar, and indeed that it could form the basis for a progressive and 'expansive' economic policy (Party of Communist Refoundation (PRC), 1999). Indeed, the actual reforms proposed in the manifesto were, as the PRC admitted, tantamount to a form of neo-Keynesianism. Demands for reforms to make the EU more receptive to refugees and to establish a common right of asylum, and to increase internal EU democracy by strengthening both the European Parliament (giving it the right to decide the contours of economic policy to be followed by the European Central Bank) and national parliaments, added to the picture of a party moving towards a more positive elaboration of policy.

At the start of the new century, the party was again embroiled in internal debate over its European and international policies. It sought to combine a strong critique of capitalism and globalisation (reminiscent of the French and Portuguese communist parties) with reassurances that it was not anti-EU but rather wanted a more durable and just form of political integration and common foreign policy that established European autonomy from the USA and brought Europe into a better relationship with developing countries. It also signalled a clear disagreement with communist parties such as the Portuguese by calling for the creation of 'a force, here in Europe, capable of competing with the Party of European Socialists for hegemony ... and to be a supranational reference point for the working classes and social movements from all over Europe' (Party of Communist Refoundation (PRC), 2000). The PRC recognised that this would mean overcoming ideological resistance on the part of some communist parties to the creation of some sort of Europe-wide party federation or confederation.

In conclusion, it is as yet difficult to clearly locate the PRC on the pro-integration/anti-integration spectrum. The party seems caught between contradictory impulses and conflicting ideological and political legacies on the European question. Moreover, like the PCF, the party faces the dilemma of defining its strategy in relation to a social democratic centre-left that is not only ardently pro-integrationist, but increasingly neo-liberal as well.

3.2 The French Communist Party (PCF)

The PCF's policy towards the European Community shares a common point of departure with that of the PCI: the post-war communist hostility to any move in the direction of greater economic, political or military co-ordination between the capitalist powers. This was perceived, in the context of the Cold War, as a threat to Soviet security and to the interests of the European working-class movement. However, certain divergences between the PCI and PCF can be traced back to the 1960s.

Whilst the PCI moved in the early 1960s to accept 'existing realities' and work with the grain of European integration, the PCF stuck rigidly throughout the 1960s to the fundamentals of the earlier communist position. It sought a mobilisation of 'patriotic' and 'democratic' forces against any reduction in national sovereignty – waging a battle against every step in the direction of greater economic and political integration. It demanded replacement of the EEC by a council which would facilitate all-European economic co-operation, thus helping to diversify West European trade, reducing involvement with the American and world capitalist economy and increasing contacts with the USSR and Eastern Europe. And it advocated total opposition to any element of supranational organisation, including even those supranational agencies to control monopolies that the PCI saw as an important part of its strategy to democratise the Community at this stage. For the PCF, such a suggestion threatened the reduction of the powers of the nation-state and consequently impaired the ability of progressive governments to pursue paths to socialism. PCF General Secretary Waldeck Rochet is quoted by Feld (1968, 261) as stating in September 1967 that 'we are hostile to the installation of a supranational government for the "Little Europe" of the six because it would have the result of depriving us of our national independence and place West Europe under German hegemony and American tutelage'.

At the November 1960 conference of communist parties in Moscow, the PCF disagreed with the emerging Italian reassessment of the nature and likely progress of European economic integration and instead 'sought to defend the notion that the Common Market was merely an instrument for strengthening the American monopolies in Europe which would increase the dependence of the European countries on the United States and the dependence of France on a revanchist and reactionary Germany' (Feld, 1968, 253). To back up this position the PCF, in common with many other communist parties at this stage, insisted that the EEC was leading to a progressive deterioration in the living standards of the working class – an analysis that was hotly rejected by the Italians.

During the late 1960s and early 1970s, the PCF was effectively excluded from participation in the European Parliament due to the reluctance of the French Government to concede its right to participate in the French National Assembly delegation to that body. The PCF itself was caught between a desire to remove doubts about its democratic legitimacy and to have its fair share of the French seats at Strasbourg, and its fear that participation in the parliament might mark the beginning of a reformist process. The party was also anxious to consolidate its new alliance with the French socialists – the Union of the Left, signed in 1972 – which, it was hoped, would allow both the growth of the left as a whole and, equally (or more) importantly, the growth of the weight of the PCF inside it. Hence such considerations of political strategy prompted the declaration in 1972 that the PCF would 'participate in building the European Economic Community, its institutions and its common policies, with the will to act to free it from the domination of large capitalist enterprises, to democratise its institutions, to support the demands of workers and to orientate the achievements of the Community in their interests' (quoted in Irving, 1977, 418).

CASE STUDIES 93

In 1973, the French government acceded to PCF representation and the party entered the European Parliament. Between 1972 and 1977 a series of tactical compromises suggested to commentators that a fundamental change in PCF attitudes toward the Community was taking place. Most importantly, in April 1977 the PCF announced its acceptance of the principle of direct elections to the European Parliament, which was greeted at the time as proof that the PCF was moving towards the position of the PCI. Commentators also pointed out that PCF declarations in favour of French national sovereignty and advocacy of autarkic solutions to French economic problems expressed a fundamental contradiction at the heart of party strategy and, to some writers, even constituted double standards (Irving, 1977; Sacco, 1979).

In actual fact, the contradiction was more in the minds of those who misread the PCF's motivation. The party was driven toward a tactical compromise on the question of participation in the European Parliament and support for direct elections by the demands of domestic political strategy and by the desire, once present inside the European Parliament, to maintain the forms of communist internationalism by at least meeting the PCI half-way on the terrain of tactics. However, on the fundamentals of PCF thinking on Europe – rejection of supranational economic programming and belief in socialism in one country behind autarkic and protectionist policies; and rejection of any increase in the powers of the European Parliament or other Community bodies in the name of French sovereignty – there was no movement whatsoever towards the Italian and Spanish position. Indeed, simultaneous with support for direct elections, the PCF voted in the French National Assembly to veto any increase in the powers of the European Parliament to the detriment of the French parliament. As Webb put it, in the run-up to the first direct elections, 'it is difficult to find traces of the deep-seated conversion of the party to the kind of economic analysis which underpins the PCI's position on European integration' (Webb, 1979, 148).

When direct elections came, in June 1979, the two parties could agree only on vague and general statements about the need to fight against the growth in unemployment, to fight for social reforms which would benefit the working-class, to champion détente and campaign for a new relationship between Europe and the Third World and to defend the rights of migrant workers. On more concrete questions relating to the future of the Community, the French communists fought on the basis of positions that not merely diverged from those of the PCI, but were diametrically opposed in certain key respects. The issue of the expansion of the Community – to embrace the new democracies of southern Europe: Spain, Portugal and Greece – figured prominently in discussions at this stage. The PCF strongly opposed expansion as a threat to the interests of French farmers, especially those small farmers in the Midi whose votes the party sought.

The PCF manifesto for the 1979 elections was based upon the declaration of the party central committee issued in December 1978. This document, entitled *Pour une France indepéndante et une Europe démocratique*, was distinguished by the total refusal to countenance any supranational development of the Community.

The PCF in many respects approached the position then held by the British Labour Party – or at least by significant sections of it – in equating national sovereignty with liberty and democracy and in deducing that any improvement in the economic and social standing of the working-class was linked to the capacity of a leftwing government to utilise the nation-state as an instrument of struggle against the multinationals.

The party entered the 1979 elections convinced that the process of European integration was part of the strategy of the international bourgeoisie, aided by the forces of social democracy (above all, German social democracy), to stabilise once and for all the subordination of Western Europe to American and German capital; this characterisation of social democracy as a key component of a bourgeois strategy which aimed at effecting a decisive shift in the balance of forces away from the working-class and progressive elements was to grow more shrill after the final rupture of the 'Union of the Left'. Already, at this stage, it contained an implicit criticism of the PCI, which was then engaged in a dialogue with the SPD. It was to be another ten years, however, before the PCF would openly call into question the class nature of the PCI.

The PCF insisted that the Community's agenda included an aggressive and expansionist orientation towards the Soviet Union and the so-called socialist countries of Eastern Europe which stood in sharp contrast to the PCF's call for a 'Europe of the peoples, from the Atlantic to the Urals'. The party declared itself in full support of a united struggle by the workers of the continent in defence of their common interests, but insisted that this struggle could only be conducted and carried to victory if France and other countries insisted on the maintenance and defence of their national sovereignty. The party was to indignantly dismiss suggestions that it was guilty of chauvinism, nationalism or racism, pointing to its support for the elimination of discrimination throughout the Community – citing the example of the West German employment ban on communists working in the public service.

In the economic sphere, the party committed itself to oppose any move towards monetary union, which was interpreted merely as an act of subordination of the French franc to the Deutschmark. Strong support was given to the idea that France should insist upon a renegotiation with West Germany of all commercial, industrial, agricultural and financial exchanges in order to defend French national interests. The suggested enlargement of the Community to embrace Greece, Spain and Portugal was also seen as a fundamental threat to French prosperity and autonomy, which demanded application of the French veto.

The PCF declared itself opposed to any European common defence policy, and to the long-term formation of a European army, voicing the concern that this would give West Germany access to nuclear weapons and would be intended as an instrument of aggression against the East.

Finally, declarations of support for the democratisation of the European Community were carefully circumscribed by insistence that this involved increased participation by the trade unions and other popular organisations in the economic and social committees of the Community and in the administration of the

CASE STUDIES 95

Community's Regional and Social Funds – not in any increase in powers of the Parliament.

The period following the first direct elections saw the PCF move significantly away from even a superficial convergence with the Italian position towards wholehearted concentration upon the themes indicated in its manifesto. The dynamics of this turn are much debated; but it does appear that the PCF, reacting to the collapse of the Union of the Left in France, sought to overcome its isolation (or at least to rejoice in the new found purity of its position, and to rally its members and supporters by strengthening the communist sub-culture) by portraying itself as the defender of French national interests and by making the EC the scapegoat for all of France's social and economic ills. Throughout the 1980s the party position was to remain one of total opposition to any increase in the powers of the European Parliament, any transfer of authority from the French state to the Community and any further move in the direction of economic, social or political integration.

Already, in June 1979, the PCF politburo presented an analysis of the results of the European Parliament elections that acclaimed the high level of abstentionism in France as 'a flagrant defeat for all the political forces which set up the Common Market and which are working for its extension and for more vigorous integration along supranational lines', adding that 'the supranational projects ran up against the people's profound adherence to national realities' (quoted in Szajkowski, 1980, 307–9). What was certainly not in question was the PCF's profound adherence to 'national realities'. The decade that opened with the PCF realigning itself with the USSR, stiffening its stance against 'revisionism' and American imperialism, and reasserting the validity of its 'socialism in the colours of France', witnessed an upsurge in nationalist rhetoric. Typical, was the contribution of Politburo member Maxime Gremetz in a series of articles in the party's theoretical journal *Cahiers du Communisme*. For example, in March 1981, Gremetz highlighted the PCF's attack upon the alleged subordination of the other French parties to American hegemony as a major theme in the party's presidential campaign in language rich in nationalist pride:

> Non. La France n'est pas un pays de second rang. Elle a une grande influence dans le monde, elle peut et doit y jouer un grand rôle ... Elle doit parler de sa propre voix, sans se réfugier au sein des Neuf pour masquer son silence ou sa passivité, nu attendre le feu vert des Etats-Unis, de la RFA ou de tout autre pays, pour promouvoir des initiatives. Elle doit donc refuser tout alignement sur Bonn et toute allégeance à Washington ... Nous voulons une France forte, indépendante, active, respectant les autres et se faisant respecter.
>
> (No. France is not a second-rate country. It has a big influence in the world; it can and must play a great role ... It must speak in its own voice, without taking refuge behind the Nine to mark its silence or its passivity, or awaiting the green light of the United States, of the FRG or of any other country, to promote its initiatives. It must refuse all alignment with Bonn and all allegiance to Washington ... we want a strong France, independent, active, respecting others and making itself respected.) (Gremetz, 1981)

And yet the PCF did not call for the withdrawal of France from the Community. Rather, as the party's Twenty-fourth Congress in February 1982 recognised, France was a member of both the EEC and of NATO and the party would respect existing international agreements and alliances. 'A member of the EEC, our country, whilst preserving in all circumstances its freedom of action and its legitimate national interests, can and must play an active role in favour of a Europe of the workers that is democratic, truly independent and open to the world: a Europe that remains, all too evidently, to be constructed' (Marchais, 1982).

The fundamental contradiction that this position involved meant that the party was unable to break out of a defensive mode and lead an all-out nationalist or 'national democratic' offensive to take France out of the Community, which is what the PCF analysis of the Community would seem to imply as being in the interests of the country. Instead, the PCF was committed to remaining inside an organisation that it alleged was developing in a way that was disastrous for France and for the interests of the working class throughout Europe. The party was on record as disagreeing with the PCI and PCE about the capacity of the Community to be democratically transformed, step-by-step. And yet its alternative consisted of little more than vague generalities about a 'Europe of the Peoples' and calls for a new international economic order, the institutional forms of which were never clear. The PCF, therefore, seemed condemned to wage a purely defensive struggle to prevent any further supranational development of the Community: a struggle to simply halt the European train at the station it had reached – and perhaps go into reverse for a few stations – but without either indicating clearly another direction the train might take, or changing carriage.

Naturally, the party opposed the ratification by the European Parliament of the Single European Act, dismissing the various initiatives of Altiero Spinelli as being detrimental to the interests of France, the working-class, the cause of peace and détente. The electoral setback that the party received at the European elections of June 1984 – when its share of the vote fell to just over 11 per cent and its number of MEPs declined from 19 to just 10 – did nothing to force a change of direction. Rationalising its disappointing performance, which it attributed to the 'anticommunist' campaign allegedly waged against it by the other parties, the PCF took comfort in a further reinforcement of the increasingly rigid lines of demarcation between itself and the Socialist Party. The June 1984 European elections coincided, of course, with a final showdown in PCF–PS relations; a month later the PCF withdrew its ministers from the government, formally initiating the period of frontal struggle against the Mitterrand administrations.

The PCF, which had attacked the activities of the social democratic parties, and especially the SPD, as part-and-parcel of European capital's designs to subjugate the forces of labour, and which had come to regard the Europeanisation of these parties' programmes as proof of their betrayal of both national and working-class interests to the needs of the multinationals, was increasingly isolated also within the Communists and Allies Group at Strasbourg. In 1986, reflecting upon the recent congress of the PCI at which that party had declared itself an 'integral part of the

European left', the PCF was forced to the obvious conclusion that its group partner inside the Strasbourg assembly had undergone a profoundly dangerous change in its basic nature. The PCI, through its 'privileged relations' with certain socialist and social democratic parties, had come (it was implied) to side with the American camp. 'The PCI no longer presents itself as a revolutionary party dedicated to transformatory goals, but as a modern reformist party' (Laroche, 1986b).

The latter part of the 1980s saw the PCF draw the various strands of its opposition to European integration together into a concerted drive to frustrate the Single Market project. Four themes in particular featured prominently in the party's campaign. First, the party argued that the logic behind the Single European Act was simply 'to adapt the Europe of the Twelve to the needs of the multinationals' as Gérard Laprat, the secretary of the Communists and Allies Group at Strasbourg, put it (Laprat, 1987, 80). By removing all barriers on the movement of capital, goods and people, the needs of the multinationals to maximise profits by relocating investments would be served. Conversely, any chance that a progressive government might have of defending the living standards of its people through controlling capital flows would be removed. Regional and sectoral imbalances would inevitably grow as a result. The effect of this removal of such restraints as bourgeois democracy had hitherto imposed upon the activities of monopoly capital would be to undermine the possibility of true co-operation between the peoples of Europe:

> A qui fera-t-on croire que l'aggravation des déséquilibres régionaux, l'accélération brutale de la restructuration industrielle, l'ouverture des marchés européens à tous les vents, et surtout ceux d'outre-Atlantique signifient une amélioration de la coopération européenne! Bien au contraire, le grand marché cassera les quelques mécanismes européens qui, s'ils avaient été utilisés avec une tout autre volonté politique, auraient pu être utilisés dans le sens de coopération mutuellement avantageuses.
>
> (Who can believe that the aggravation of regional imbalances, the brutal acceleration of industrial restructuring, the opening of European markets to all comers, and above all those that come from the other side of the Atlantic, signifies an improvement in European co-operation! On the contrary, the Single Market crushes those European mechanisms that, if they had been used with a proper political will, might have contributed to advantageous mutual co-operation.) (Laprat, 1987, 83)

Second, the PCF maintained that the completion of the Single Market by 1992 represented a grave danger and a threat to the French people because it also involved a concerted attempt to force lower living standards and lower standards of social welfare and employment protection upon the country. Attacks upon the public sector through privatisations, attempts to redress the balance between profits and salaries in favour of the former and utilisation of increased employment insecurity in order to force down wages were all portrayed as essential preparations for the completion of the Single Market on the part of a French bourgeoisie that aimed to resolve its internal contradictions by renouncing national sovereignty and welding its fortunes to those of American and German capital. In this respect also, talk of a 'social space', upon which the PCI and the socialist parties placed so much hope, was dismissed as a deception. PCF central committee member, Bernard Marx, wrote that 'Jacques Delors ... says that the creation of a "European social space" by 1992 implies the establishment of a "minimum base" for working people's social rights in the various EEC countries. This clearly shows that their objective is to deny all rights, because the base will be set as low as possible' (Marx, 1989a, 80).

Third, the PCF saw the 1992 project as aiming to seal the domination of German capital over the rest of Europe, and in particular to subordinate France to Germany through monetary union. The loss of national control over the currency would lead inevitably to the German control over France's economic destiny. And behind Germany, of course, stood the USA and Japan – already seeking ways of combining with German-based multinational companies. The resurgence of a reactionary and revanchist Germany would thus pave the way for the reestablishment of American hegemony over the European continent, threatening the socialist countries of the East as well as the working-class of the West. In this sense the Community was the 'Trojan horse of American imperialism' (Derycke, 1988, 76).

Fourth, the party argued that an essential component of the European integration project was the formulation of a common defence policy. The advocates of 1992 were seen as believing that 'military integration constitutes, after money and finance, the second pillar in the process of European integration' (Marx, 1989a, 81). The PCF's objection to such integration was based on the belief that, far from constituting any base from which to fight for a European defence alliance autonomous from the United States, this was just an attempt to maximise profits through an acceleration of the arms race in which Europe would out-bid others in arms sales to the Third World in particular. A common defence policy was also seen as contributing to instability in the continent as a whole and as constituting a threat to the security of the USSR (Gremetz, 1987). The party, moreover, saw increased Franco-German military co-operation both as threatening France's position outside NATO's integrated military structure and as undermining the country's self-sufficiency in arms production. Once again, the argument against European defence integration rested not merely upon the claim that it was 'reactionary' (i.e., detrimental to working-class interests or to the cause of peace) but upon a strong measure of French nationalism. PCF central committee member and foreign policy specialist Yves Choliere said in 1989:

> Our party is opposed to the creation of NATO's European nucleus and to the integration of the French armed forces into its structure (including the establishment of a Franco-West German brigade, of a Joint Defence Council, or of any joint command). We are against France's covert or open re-entry into NATO's integrated military organisation and against any kind of European effort to manufacture the arms the nation needs for purposes of defence.

The PCF's electoral lists in the 1989 elections to the European Parliament were led by Philippe Herzog, a key member of the party Politburo, whose 300-page book, published in time for the contest (Herzog, 1989), both summarised all the arguments that the party had been developing over the preceding twenty years and constituted in effect the most elaborate statement of the party's position to date. Herzog argued that the European project that all the other political forces in France had endorsed involved the appropriation by the dominant multinational corporations of the national resources of the European states, the destruction of the democratic and social gains of working people and the creation of a European society saturated with unemployment, underemployment, casual and unprotected labour and a divided working-class movement. Such a project was central to the restructuring and relaunch of the world capitalist system as a whole. It would adversely affect the interests of the peoples of the Third World, for instead of a 'Europe of the Peoples' promoting balanced development they would be faced with a Europe of the multinationals intent upon extraction of profit. It threatened the USSR and the processes of 'socialist renewal' in the East and it promised an acceleration of arms manufacture. Against this, the PCF promised a struggle in the national interests of the country. As Bernard Marx put it, 'only by re-establishing its sovereignty will France be strong enough to act in the international arena for accord between the peoples and for new forms of co-operation which each country needs for economic growth and full employment' (Marx, 1989a, 81).

But here, precisely, was the party's greatest weakness: as before, the failure to articulate what precise forms such 'accord' and 'co-operation' might take, and what future it saw for a European Community that was halted in its tracks. In the event, the response to the PCF's appeal for a vote 'for friendship, solidarity and co-operation between the peoples of the entire world' was disappointing. The party slumped to just 7.7 per cent and seven MEPs – its worse performance ever in a non-presidential election.

The 1990s were to be a disastrous decade for the PCF. The collapse of the USSR and the 'socialist' countries in the East drew forth a confused response from the PCF leadership that only hastened the loss of political credibility and the growth of internal dissent, as waves of would-be reformers, 'renovators' and 'reconstructors' were forced out of the party (Hopkins, 1990). The belated and half-hearted attempts at renewal by Robert Hue (who succeeded Marchais as General Secretary in December1994) only underlined the loss of ideological coherence and of political direction. Falling electoral support and (on the basis of such evidence as the PCF releases) membership formed a constant backdrop to the growing sense of crisis within the party. Participation in a centre-left government from 1997 to 2002 would only accelerate the decline. By 2002, party support had dropped to an absolutely abysmal 3.4 per cent in the presidential elections and a scarcely less catastrophic 4.8 per cent in the subsequent general elections. This background of relentless decline is essential to keep in mind when seeking to understand the evolution of EU policy during the 1990s for, despite the often dogmatic certainty that characterises PCF rhetoric on EU integration, the loss of coherence and meaning was also to extend to this aspect of party policy.

One of the first battles the PCF faced in the early 1990s was the referendum campaign on the Maastricht Treaty in autumn 1992. Naturally, the party fought hard to sustain a 'No' vote, with central committee member Pierre Zarka telling the annual Fête de l'Humanité that Maastricht was designed to strengthen international capital at the expense of ordinary workers and to secure German political and economic dominance over other European countries (Webster, 1992). For PCF theorist Gilles Masson, 'either a country is sovereign, or it is under foreign domination. There is no middle way' (Masson, 1992, 33). Maastricht involved a fundamental violation of national sovereignty. The PCF Central Committee in its appeal to French voters went further: Maastricht represented the repudiation of the heritage of the French revolution – liberty, equality and fraternity (French Communist Party (PCF), 1992). Central Committee member Jacques Le Digabel would clarify this by arguing that Maastricht heralded 'an antidemocratic Europe full of danger for the rights and liberties of man'. The German model of denying immigrants their full legal and citizenship rights would become the norm (Le Digabel, 1992, 21). The PCF referendum campaign emphasised the threat to workers' jobs and working conditions, the erosion of social justice, and the betrayal of French democracy and sovereignty that the Maastricht Treaty was said to involve.

But the PCF fought its campaign in unfavourable conditions. First, the party message was almost drowned out by the much greater media attention paid to the far right and rightwing Gaullist lobbying against Maastricht. The rise in nationalist rhetoric, which almost saw the French electorate reject the Treaty, would in turn tempt the PCF, which spent part of the mid-1990s fighting off allegations that it was contributing to an informal 'red-brown' alliance of communists and rightists against European integration. Second, the party faced stiff competition for the anti-Maastricht vote from a new protectionist republican left-of-centre movement, the Citizens' Movement, established by former Socialist Party Minister Jean-Pierre Chevènement. This movement would attract the support of several prominent ex-PCF leaders, disillusioned by the lack of reform within that party. Third, the early 1990s saw increasing party fragmentation. Not only did former leaders defect to both the Socialist Party and the Citizens' Movement; others who remained within the PCF became increasingly vocal in their criticism of the Marchais leadership. The critics included Philippe Herzog and (former Politburo member) Charles Fiterman.

Another disappointing performance in the 1994 European Parliamentary elections, when the PCF vote fell to under 7 per cent, was followed by the election of Robert Hue as party leader. The Twenty-ninth Party Congress in December 1996 cleared the way for the signing of a joint declaration with the Socialists in April 1997. This, in turn, helped prepare the ground for the formation of a left coalition government from June 1997 onwards. Although it was badly split on the terms of the coalition deal, with opponents including the leading writer on EU matters Maxime Gremetz (Bell, 1998, 131), the PCF benefited electorally from the end to its isolation, polling 9.9 per cent in the 1997 National Assembly elections and increasing its number of deputies from 23 to 36. However, participation in government involved significant policy compromises which would arguably prove ultimately very damaging to the PCF's political credibility and sense of identity. Although the PCF continued to attack the single currency as increasing unemployment and eroding national sovereignty by handing economic power to the European Central Bank, it did not press for the joint platform for government to include its demand for a referendum on the issue. In fact, both the PCF and PS accepted that their policy positions were near-well incompatible on this issue and chose instead to focus on the need to work for a stronger 'social Europe'. In reality, of course, this would mean that the position of the bigger and stronger party would prevail. Socialist Party leader Lionel Jospin had emphasised during the election campaign that his party would not endorse the single currency at any social price, even though it was highly desirable in itself, and that his government would seek to reverse rightwing spending cuts. In a sense, this rhetoric allowed the PCF leadership to claim some influence over PS policy. In reality, the opposite was true. The two parties agreed to demand four conditions to France's acceptance of monetary union: the establishment of a political counter-weight to the European Central Bank; the inclusion of Spain and Italy in the first wave; a decision to prevent the euro being overvalued against the dollar and the yen; and the Stability Pact agreed at the Dublin EU summit to be set aside in favour of a 'pact of solidarity and growth' (cited in *The Irish Times*, 22 May 1997). In effect, this was the basis upon which the new government took office, and it was of course a position that implicitly endorsed French involvement in monetary union. It was the PCF that had shifted ground. Indeed, in advance of the second round of voting in 1997, Robert Hue announced that 'the Communist Party is not europhobic' and denied that the PCF's alliance with the PS threatened European integration (*The Irish Times*, 27 May 1997).

At the same time as it was sending reassuring signals to the Socialists that the PCF's policy on European integration would not be allowed to get in the way of its commitment to coalition government, the party continued to expound a very different vision of how the EU should develop, at least at the rhetorical level. In the run-up to the Twenty-ninth Party Congress, the leading PCF MEP Francis Wurtz spelt out a decidedly anti-integrationist message. European construction should be about helping nation-states to formulate effective answers to the 'defects of internationalisation'. A 'new ECU' should not seek to replace national currencies, but on the contrary aim to facilitate monetary co-operation designed to strengthen existing national currencies against market speculators. Movements of capital should be taxed and the revenue raised should be used to fight unemployment. Alongside the EU, a new forum should be created involving Russia, Ukraine and Belarus which would seek to 'regroup' all the nation states of the continent (Wurtz, 1996). The single currency, designed by Maastricht, was intended to ensure that a larger slice of the cake was given to those big financial concerns based in the Deutschmark zone – at the expense of French and other European workers

(Manaille, 1996, 25). The call for the replacement of plans for the single currency with a new 'European fund for co-development' based on the defence of national currencies also featured in the PCF's 1997 election campaign (Cirera, 1997, 13). And yet, once in government these calls were all but abandoned in practice.

Between 1997 and 2002 the centre-left government effectively prepared France for participation in the single currency, as well as presiding over a programme of quite ambitious privatisations. In EU policy, the government programme ran completely counter to what the PCF had been arguing for decades. Yet PCF ministers participated in the enactment of that programme. Within a week of taking office as prime minister, Jospin signed the Stability Pact to prepare for the single currency, abandoning the pre-election pledge to renegotiate it 'without a squeak from the PCF' (Budgen, 2002, 34). The new government's privatisation programme involved more sell-offs than the previous six governments combined, and the Socialists 'made deficit reduction and lower taxes their priorities, holding public-spending increase down to an annual 2 per cent between 1997 and 2001' (Budgen, 2002, 35). In September 2000, a programme of tax cuts, including cuts to the top rate of tax, was announced. The Socialists, by far the largest party in the left coalition, could count on support from the generally pro-European integrationist Greens and Radicals.

By the end of the 1990s, not only was support for the mainstream left beginning to weaken, but within the mainstream left pro-integrationist parties and politicians were seemingly gaining the upper hand over anti-integrationists. Thus, in the 1999 European Parliament elections, the Greens, their electoral list headed by an enthusiastically pro-integrationist Daniel Cohn-Bendit, overtook the PCF, polling nearly 10 per cent to the latter's 6.8 per cent. Indeed, the PCF had desperately (and unsuccessfully) tried to broaden its appeal by opening its lists to non-communists, and softening its own line on European integration to such an extent that the Socialist Minister for European Affairs, Pierre Moscovici, could declare shortly after the results were in that 'the Communist Party has changed and is now totally constructive about Europe'. Ominously for the PCF, not only did its new-found moderation fail to win it voters back from the PS; to many on the radical left it inevitably appeared like naked opportunism, designed to keep the party afloat as a 'party of government' at all costs. Ideological and policy disorientation was further underlined by the party's stance on the Balkan war. Although the leadership officially opposed the NATO bombing of Yugoslavia, it remained within a government that supported it and several figures on the 1999 electoral list for the European Parliamentary elections, including Philippe Herzog, endorsed the NATO bombing. In the 1999 European Parliamentary elections, the far-left Trotskyist parties polled almost as many votes as the PCF, entering the European Parliament with five MEPs (to the PCF's six); in the Presidential elections of 2002 they decisively overtook the PCF, polling over 10 per cent to the Communists' 3.4 per cent. The party polled just 3 per cent amongst white-collar workers and a derisive 1 per cent amongst 18 to 24-year-old voters (Budgen, 2002, 49). In the run-up to these elections, on 14 March 2002, Robert Hue was jostled and jeered by communist trade union militants of the

CASE STUDIES

CGT at a rally against job losses – an unprecedented event that underlined once again the turmoil and sense of existential crisis within the party.

By 2002, the Socialists hoped that a 35-hour working week, a significant drop in unemployment and a rise in growth levels would 'compensate' for measures that were distasteful to left voters. This was clearly proven wrong in the first round of voting in the 2002 Presidential elections, when widespread abstention by left voters and the dramatic surge in support for the Trotskyist parties cost Jospin his place in the second round and led to the psychologically devastating spectacle of Chirac facing far right leader Jean-Marie Le Pen in that deciding contest. The PCF was undoubtedly the biggest loser in 2002. It had virtually nothing to show for its participation in government and had, in the eyes of many voters, lost all credibility.

At the time of writing, the future of the PCF is very unclear. It is true that political commentators have pronounced the party 'dead' on many previous occasions. This time, however, its disorientation is perhaps more profound, its morale more badly shaken and its unity under greater threat than at any time since 1945. The party's turmoil on the question of Europe – so central to its vision of how France should develop in economic, political and cultural terms, and so implicated in its implicit endorsement in government of the tax cuts, privatisations and welfare spending limits that its rhetoric decries – is at the heart of its loss of direction. It is not so much that the PCF has evolved a new policy position on the central issues of European integration that is unpalatable to its traditional voters. It is rather that it has continued to pay lip-service to one set of policies while participating in a government that has implemented the very opposite of those policies in key respects. The result has been to leave many left voters, and indeed party faithful, wondering what exactly the PCF stands for nowadays. There is undoubtedly electoral mileage in France for a party of the left that takes a clear-headed, convincing and strategic stance on European integration that is either anti-integrationist or alternatively is critically supportive of integration. What is less clear is whether left voters will return in significant numbers to a party that seems to say one thing and then to do another. Of all the left parties considered in the present study, the PCF is perhaps the one that currently seems least well equipped to measure up to the challenges of the future.

3.3 The Communist Party of Greece (KKE) and the Coalition of Left and Progress (Synaspismos)

The KKE, as we have seen, split into two factions in February 1968. Since then the European policy of the two organisations – the pro-Soviet KKE and the Eurocommunist KKE-es (which was renamed the Greek Left – EA – in 1986, and finally claimed a post-communist identity for itself in the 1990s when it was reborn as the Coalition of Left and Progress, or Synaspismos) – has diverged completely.

The KKE has maintained a position of total opposition to Greek membership of the European Union, playing a leading role in the campaign against Greece's entry in 1981. The KKE here converged with the positions of the French Communist Party. During a visit to Greece in February 1979, PCF General Secretary George Marchais met with a warm welcome when he declared that the PCF was opposed to any enlargement of the Community to include Greece or the Iberian countries. KKE General Secretary Harilaos Florakis replied that his party shared this position entirely, being convinced that membership would be detrimental to the interests of Greek farmers and to the independence of Greece. Both parties signed a joint communiqué to this effect (Kapetanyannis, 1979, 454).

The theme of protecting Greek independence was to feature prominently in the propaganda of the KKE – and was to have a not inconsiderable resonance in a country where the left especially displays a marked hostility towards American and Western interference in internal politics. One has to bear in mind here the historical legacy of the Greek civil war which saw Western forces, led by the British and later the Americans, intervene in order to crush the Communist-led partisan movement. The important role of the American presence in bringing pressure to bear upon internal Greek political settlements has been noted by a number of writers (e.g., Featherstone and Katsoudas, 1987), and suspicion has persisted of a CIA role in the Colonels' coup of 1967 that led to the Papadopoulos dictatorship. One also has to bear in mind the culturally ambiguous relationship of Greece to the rest of Europe (Kourvetaris and Dobratz, 1987). It is relatively easy to understand why such a vehemently anti-EC and anti-Western stand was attractive when the KKE emerged from repression in 1974.

Moreover, the Pan-Hellenic Socialist Movement (PASOK) initially displayed hostility towards the European Community and all things Western, seeing Greece's international vocation as lying in closer economic ties with the East and diplomatic support for and identification with third-world liberation movements, during the period 1974–81. Although, upon attaining governmental office PASOK was to modify its position considerably, the point is that the anti-EU rhetoric of the KKE was by no means out of place within the Greek left as a whole, during the run-up to Greek membership of the EC.

The KKE, during the 1970s and early 1980s, sought to denounce the EEC as an organisation that was completely dependent upon American capital, and could therefore be expected to follow the American line in supporting Turkish interests at the expense of Greece; that had no potential to develop away from its existing format – an instrument of monopoly capital – in the sort of direction suggested as feasible by the Italians; that would contribute to growing regional and sectoral imbalances within the Greek economy; and that, far from consolidating Greek democracy, would not hesitate to act in the interests of the foreign monopolies by helping to impose another dictatorship if the interests of the monopolies so required (Featherstone and Katsoudas, 1987, 260). This view reflected, of course, the KKE's dismissive attitude towards 'bourgeois democracy' in general – seen as little more than a fig leaf behind which lurked monopoly capitalist exploitation.

Following Greek membership of the EC in 1981, the KKE General Secretary Harilaos Florakis called on his party to step up its condemnation of PASOK's 'betrayal' on the issue. At the Eleventh Party Congress in 1983 the anti-EC and anti-Western tone was unmistakable: 'we should remind them [the working-class] what PASOK used to say before the elections, and what it is actually doing now. What happened with PASOK's promises to withdraw from NATO and the EEC and to close down American bases? If PASOK has forgotten such promises the people have not. It is consequently our duty to keep such memories alive ...' (quoted in Loulis, 1986). The congress approved a resolution from the Politburo calling for an economic strategy based upon nationalisation of the monopolies, development of the home market through protectionist policies and exploitation of natural resources by the state.

The KKE hoped to benefit from disillusionment with PASOK's change of heart on the EC issue in the European elections of 1984, which it fought on a staunchly anti-EC platform. In the event, though PASOK's vote dropped by nearly 7 percentage points, the KKE's share also fell from the previous European elections (from 12.8 per cent to 11.6 per cent).

The KKE reacted to the proposal for a Single European Market with predictable hostility, emphasising that Greece had entered the international division of labour on unfavourable terms and 'as a result of West European integration, it is becoming a country of cheap services (primarily tourist services) with a poorly developed industry and virtually no modern technological base'. The Twelfth Congress of the KKE in May 1987 reaffirmed the party's commitment to withdrawal from both NATO and the EC. Whilst willing to co-operate with forces not committed to an immediate withdrawal from the EC, the party leadership stressed its confidence in winning such allies around to the view that membership of the Community constituted 'a denial of progress and change' (Verney, 1987).

In March 1988 the KKE published its *Red Book* as a response to the predictions of the European Commission concerning the likely impact of 1992. Hailed at the time as proof that movement was underway within the party, and that the KKE was finally 'entering Europe', the document was a belated recognition that simply saying 'No' was not a sufficient response to the acceleration of Greek preparations for 1992. The dogmatic nature of the party's stance on Europe had always been a bone of contention in its relations with the KKE-es-turned-Greek Left, and the party's strategic shift from envisaging an alliance with PASOK to seeking to lead a Left Coalition with Greek Left was another motivation for a reconsideration of tactics. According to Susannah Verney, an additional factor forcing some reconsideration of line was the changing Soviet attitude towards the Community, with the USSR seeking new EC–CMEA trading agreements (Verney, 1988).

The new tone contained in the *Red Book*, however, did not go very far. Although stating that differences on European policy should no longer constitute a source of division on the left, the KKE proposed a co-ordination of struggle against the consequences of 1992. The concessions in the direction of new thinking that were made – for example, suggesting that struggle within the Community to exploit its internal contradictions might well result in a change in the Community's nature, acknowledging that some EC directives (for example, on pollution) had a positive impact upon Greece, and shifting the emphasis somewhat from protectionism towards a recognition of the internationalisation of economic life – turned out to be short-lived. Politburo member Grigoris Pharakos pointed out that although for tactical reasons immediate withdrawal from the Community might not be on the agenda, a future leftwing government would certainly move in that direction. By late June 1988 Harilaos Florakis was once again emphasising opposition to the EC rather than accommodation, not least because the slightest move in the direction of change had already provoked a backlash from party hardliners led by Aleka Papariga (who would shortly succeed him as General Secretary).

Struggle between 'renewers' within the party, who favoured at least a tactical change of line on Europe to facilitate a Left Coalition, and traditionalists, insisting upon Greek withdrawal from the EC, continued throughout late 1988 and 1989. A Joint Statement of the KKE and the Greek Left, intended to form the base for a joint European election manifesto in 1989, stressed the need for more structural funding, common sectoral policies and enhanced powers for the European Parliament, in language borrowed from longstanding Greek Left policy positions. In the European elections of 1989 the KKE and the Greek Left, fighting together under the banner of the Left Coalition, Synaspismos (the term would soon become associated exclusively with the smaller, reformist party, when the KKE pulled out of the tactical alliance and retreated into its hardline positions), succeeded in polling 14.5 per cent which allowed the two parties to return three and one MEPs respectively. (The brief alliance between the two formations was facilitated by two other developments. First, the KKE-es's transformation into the Greek Left eased KKE sensitivities about co-operation with a rival claimant to the title of 'communist'. Second, both parties briefly participated in an unprecedented and short-lived coalition government with the conservative New Democracy party in 1989, the sole purpose of which was to root out corruption associated with PASOK.)

Subsequent events, however, belied the KKE's change of heart. The Thirteenth Congress of the KKE in February 1991 saw a resurgence of the European theme. It also witnessed the political victory of traditionalist elements over the so-called renewers. The congress had been preceded by fierce debate within the KKE over the impending collapse of the Soviet Union and the downfall of allied regimes in Eastern Europe. Demands for change from leaders such as Grigoris Pharakos were denounced by Stalinists led by Florakis and Papariga as 'a piece of academic opportunism.' Amongst the demands that were defeated at the congress was the call for the party to change its policy of withdrawal from the EC. The election of Aleka Papariga – the very leadership member who had led the backlash against any modification of the party's European line in 1988 – as the new KKE General Secretary indicated that the KKE had turned its back once more upon any abandonment of its age-old hostility to the Western European political and economic model. In July 1991 the KKE announced its withdrawal from the Coalition of Left and Progress (Synaspismos). KKE reformers, led by Maria Damanaki, in turn resigned from the KKE and pledged their loyalty to Synaspismos – which in effect now became an enlarged version of the post-communist Greek Left party. Needless to say, the split in the KKE, and the defection of its most open-minded members to Synaspismos would further strengthen the traditionalist orientation of the party. In August 1991, the KKE under Papariga supported the Moscow coup against President Gorbachev and the Fourteenth Party Congress in December saw Gorbachev denounced as a traitor, with the KKE firmly retrenching behind Stalinist lines. A purge of 'bourgeois counter-revolutionaries' was ordered within the party, a term of abuse that was also applied to those arguing for any change of policy of European integration.

Throughout the 1990s the KKE has stuck rigidly to its traditionalist positions and it is impossible to speak of any 'evolution' of its policies on European integration. It campaigned in the 1993 general election vigorously denouncing the Maastricht Treaty as the underlying cause of mass unemployment and harsh austerity policies. Since the mid-1990s it has attacked both ratification of the Amsterdam Treaty and the decision by PASOK and New Democracy to press ahead with Greek membership of the single currency. According to the party central committee, the process of European integration 'accentuates again the reactionary character of the EU'. The proposal to advance towards political union was backed by 'dominant capitalist concerns' which were anxious to evade 'every democratic control'. The EU itself is 'an anti-democratic and bureaucratic mechanism at the service of the interests of the monopolies'. The convergence criteria that governed which countries could qualify for participation in the single currency were designed to 'reinforce the position of European monopoly capital, led by German monopoly capital, in its struggle with American and Japanese capital, so that it can exploit the workers and countries of the entire world, including the ex-socialist countries'. The 'total domination of the European Central Bank under German control' would guarantee the destruction of national independence. For Greece, the single currency would be a disaster as industries would close, 'one after the other', becoming replaced with slimmed-down local operations dominated by multinationals that had no regard for the 'progress of the country'. The public sector would be plundered through the policies of massive sell-offs and small farmers would be cleared off the land at an ever-increasing rate. Against this vision of economic, political and cultural catastrophe, the KKE argued for a total rejection of the EU 'in its entirety'. No progressive outcome could result from any revision of the Maastricht Treaty; instead, a 'total rupture' with the choices involved in the construction of the EU had to be made (all quotations taken from Communist Party of Greece (KKE), 1995).

The problem for the KKE is that membership of the EU has helped bring about a profound transformation of the Greek economy and society. While it is true that traditional industries and poor farmers have been hit by restructuring, and this has affected the support base of the party, it is an illusion to argue that the country as a whole has simply become poorer. The party had argued at the start of the 1990s that its staunch and uncompromising opposition to European integration would enable it to mobilise growing numbers of Greeks who were alienated by the integration process. It would not only survive, but would expand. In actual fact, the party has continued its decline throughout the past decade. In the 1999 European Parliamentary elections it polled less than 9 per cent of the vote and in the general elections of 2000 it fell to 5.5 per cent. Undoubtedly, its decline would be more rapid were it not for the fact that Greek political culture was historically highly polarised between left and right by the experience of the Greek civil war, and the party retains a lingering emotional appeal to the older generation of left voters in particular.

The most recent KKE party congress – the Sixteenth Congress in December 2000 – saw a further hardening of position. The euro was accused of deepening divisions within the EU between 'the leading imperialist forces'. The EU was plotting with the USA to encircle Russia 'and any other countries that want to demand a leading position in the imperialist system. They want to stabilise capitalism in Russia but without that country becoming a leading power in the imperialist system.' (Here the KKE's analysis seems to veer between traditional solidarity for 'besieged Russia' and recognition that the 'traitors' in Moscow were queuing up to join the imperialist core, but were being prevented from doing so.) Astonishingly the party claimed that the processes of economic change associated with European integration and globalisation meant that 'the *only winners* are the country's financial oligarchy, the international monopolies and the small group that shares in the squandering of community funds. The working class and other strata of the people live under conditions of increasing relative and absolute poverty' (emphasis added). The party reaffirmed its call for withdrawal from the EU and for wholesale nationalisation of the economy, adding however that it didn't envisage 'total, universal' public ownership – it was prepared to allow for 'a productive co-operative system for people with small and medium-sized farm holdings and businesses'. The final twist in this surreal retreat into a purist Marxist-Leninist solipsism came in the congress's call for the party's future strategy to revolve around the formation of an 'Anti-imperialist, Anti-monopoly Democratic Front of struggle (AADF)'. Given that the only other obvious participant in such an AADF is the party's youth movement, the congress's concern that the AADF should not be allowed to submerge the party's own identity is perhaps a mite exaggerated. The December 2000 Party Congress also heard a call from Harilaos Florakis (now the honorary president of the KKE) to defend the memory of the USSR – 'a regime which was the hope and the expectation of all people and the homeland of all the fighters worldwide'. Florakis also declared that the implementation of the Maastricht, Amsterdam and Nice Treaties proved the national treachery of bourgeois forces and quoted with approval Stalin's exhortation to the Communist Parties delegations from capitalist countries attending the Nineteenth Congress of the Soviet Communist Party to 'hold that banner [of national independence and sovereignty] high and defend it, if you want to be patriots, if you wish to become your nation's leading force' (all quotations taken from Communist Party of Greece, 2000). And so the KKE marches into the twenty-first century, armed with Stalin's analysis of Europe at the outset of the Cold War.

The Eurocommunist KKE-es displayed from a very early stage in its existence a markedly different approach towards Europe from that of the KKE, incurring the charge during the 1970s of being 'to the right' of PASOK. The influence upon this small political formation (many of whose intellectuals and leaders were Western-educated) of the theoreticians of the PCI and PCE was obvious from the start. During the 1970s the KKE-es adopted a resolutely nationalistic line on questions such as Cyprus and the 'Turkish threat' – positions which Synaspismos would totally reverse in the 1990s – but followed the lead of the PCI in opposing any unilateral Greek withdrawal from NATO on the grounds that it would represent an upset to the strategic balance in the area and would lead to destabilisation in the Balkans (Kapetanyannis, 1979, 458).

The party also supported Greek entrance into the EC – the only party of the Greek left to do so – whilst criticising the terms of membership negotiated by the rightwing New Democracy government. KKE-es basically followed the PCI line, as it evolved throughout the 1970s and 1980s, arguing that 'the cause of socialism must be seen and fought in its European context' (Kapetanyannis, 1979, 458). In essence the KKE-es not merely saw membership of the Community as a way of anchoring Greek democracy to sound foundations: it also shared the PCI view of the Community as a potential site of struggle, capable of being 'captured' from within and transformed from a 'Europe of the monopolies' into a 'Europe of working people'. In March 1981 the party denounced the policies of the KKE and PASOK against membership as encouraging Greek people to adopt a passive attitude and thus fail to exploit to the full the new opportunities that membership of the EC afforded. The party called for Greek workers to obtain the same rights as workers in other EC countries, and to participate alongside their 'comrades' in other EC countries in pressing for more progressive policies. The Greek economy should embrace the opportunity for a participation in the international division of labour that did not tie it to the old dependency patterns of the past (Communist Party of Greece-Interior (KKE-es), 1981).

However, the party's moderate and conciliatory line on the European question, accepting Greek membership in an effort to consolidate Greek democracy and appealing to a trans-class rather than a working-class constituency, was to cost it dear electorally. 'Not communist enough to attract traditionalists and fundamentalists and not liberal enough to lure the non-communist vote' (Kapetanyannis, 1987, 154), it never succeeded in establishing any clear identity for itself, with a vote that has ranged at between 2 and 5 per cent. This in turn was to inhibit the development of any truly autonomous European policy, with the result that the KKE-es was to run the risk of appearing to take its intellectual cue in European matters from the PCI. This would really only change during the 1990s when, following the disappearance of the PCI and the transformation of the Greek Eurocommunists into the post-communist Synaspismos, the heirs of the KKE-es would attract greater attention.

We have already noted the developments that led to the transformation of the KKE-es into first the Greek Left party, and ultimately, following merger with reform-minded KKE dissidents and others, into Synaspismos. At first, this was a fairly loose coalition of parties and groups. However, following the withdrawal of the hardline KKE from any association with Synaspismos in 1991, a decision was taken to transform Synaspismos into a party. The formal launch of this new structure (retaining the old name) came in June 1992. Maria Damanaki became the first leader, following her defection from the KKE; Nicos Constantopoulos succeeded her as leader in December 1993. The party was self-consciously post-communist, identifying with 'the ideas and values of democratic socialism, ecology, feminism and anti-militarism. It believes in pluralism and considers the defence of human rights non-negotiable' (Coalition of Left and Progress (Synaspismos), 2002). In some respect, the new party is not only much more open-minded on policy and strategy than the KKE; it is also much more democratic. For example, secret ballots of the entire membership determine major issues such as the composition of lists for national and European elections.

It has to be said that the record of Synaspismos since 1991 combines both policy innovation and electoral disappointment. The party has never really risen above the level of electoral support obtained by the old KKE-es. For example, in the 1999 European Parliamentary elections it polled 5.2 per cent and in the 2000 general elections it got 3.2 per cent. Its best performance to date has been 6.2 per cent (European Parliamentary elections of 1994) and its most disappointing was the 2.94 per cent it obtained in the general elections of 1993. There is no doubt that Synaspismos is a party of intellectuals and white-collar workers, a classic example of the so-called 'post-materialist' New Left, and that it has little base amongst the working-class and other lower social strata.

The most obvious and comprehensive statement of the fundamental divergence between the European perspectives of the KKE and Synaspismos came in the 'Proposals for a radical re-orientation of Greek foreign policy', adopted by the Central Political Committee of Synaspismos in May 1996. Attacking the tendency towards US domination of the post-Cold War world, economically and militarily, under the pretence of a 'new world order' and stating its total opposition to NATO expansion (a stance influenced by its commitment to anti-militarism), Synaspismos nevertheless declared that 'in our party's opinion the European option constitutes the basic orientation of our national strategy and of a multidimensional foreign policy. Europe, which should promote the presently embryonic common foreign policy and defence policy of the EU in the process of its political unification, is the most favourable ground for Greece. This firm European option is followed by our equally firm opposition to the conservative choices prevailing today in the course of this unification.' The party identified Greek nationalism, aggravated by anti-Turkish feeling and hysteria over the position of the Former Yugoslav Republic of Macedonia (FYROM), the legitimacy of which Greek extremists sought to undermine in the name of a Greek monopoly of 'Macedonianism', as dangerous. The promotion by nationalists among the Greek population of 'the sense of a brotherless, encircled nation' that could rise to the status of a regional Balkan power with US help was a lethal illusion. Relations with the EU should not be downgraded by pursuit of either regional hegemony or a new dependent relationship on the USA. A compromise on the Cyprus problem was urged, and Cypriot membership of the EU was seen as fundamental in securing this: 'The resolution of the Council of Ministers of the EU of March 6, 1995 [concerning eventual Cypriot membership of the EU] may prove important in the course of restoring Cyprus' true independence.'

Indeed, throughout this important document the EU is seen as having a potentially very progressive role to play in securing a better and less antagonistic role for Greece internationally. By contrast, those who wished to detach Greece from the EU (the KKE, implicitly, amongst them) were accused of feeding a 'dangerous nationalist wave, which strengthened jingoism, xenophobia, the concept of a brotherless, select and thus proudly isolated nation'. A much stronger EU role in the Balkans was seen as the best way of securing a more progressive resolution of problems. As for the KKE – its 'deep antiEuropeanism limited its role to that of an embarrassed observer [during the crisis over the FYROM], unable to formulate a coherent proposal for a way out of the impasse'. Synaspismos, by contrast, 'decisively supports full EU membership for all the Balkan countries.' Greek opposition to Turkish membership of the EU was criticised and, by contrast, Synaspismos emphasised that 'it is in the interests of Greece if Turkey follows a European orientation and ceases to be a backward Eastern country prone to Islamic fundamentalism and to the acceptance of a role in the Middle East where it will be under absolute American control'. In short, EU membership was not only a good thing in itself – it was seen as potentially the antidote to ugly nationalism, bloody regional conflict in the Balkans, American domination over both Greece and Turkey through exploitation of their rivalries, and continuing division in Cyprus. (All quotations are from Coalition of Left and Progress, 1996.) A starker contrast with the KKE view of the international role of the EU would be harder to find.

In subsequent policy elaborations, Synaspismos – which had in the early 1990s criticised Maastricht for falling short of what was needed to advance towards a socially just and politically united federal Europe – attacked the failure of EU governments to go much further than they actually did at Amsterdam. The Amsterdam Treaty did not constitute the 'necessary social and democratic turn in the course of European unification'. Much more was needed to break with the neoliberal logic of Maastricht and to democratise the Union. The party argued that 'it is imperative to continue and to strengthen the struggle for the intensification and adoption of the social and political element in the unification process'. It would have preferred a strong commitment to common foreign and defence policies. All-European efforts for employment and social cohesion should be strengthened in the context of monetary union. Greece should introduce the euro (Coalition of Left and Progress (Synaspismos), 1997).

The party subsequently decided to signal its disappointment at the limited results achieved in Amsterdam by abstaining on ratification of the Treaty. Once again, it is important to note that its analysis was diametrically opposed to that of the KKE. Synaspismos advocated both much stronger progress in the direction of a federal United States of Europe, and specific measures to balance the power of the European Central Bank with an 'economic government of the European

Union'; that is to say, the European Parliament should be given legislative power and control over economic policy. The party thus justified its decision to abstain on the parliamentary vote in order to 'insist firmly on its [Synaspismos's] European orientation and struggles so that the future of the necessary European integration carries the seal of a "Left Europeanism"'. The KKE was implicitly attacked for advocating 'strategies of reverting to national isolation by the cultivation of dead end anti-European stances' (Coalition of Left and Progress (Synaspismos), 1998).

In the European Parliamentary elections of 1999 Synaspismos highlighted its opposition to the war in Yugoslavia and to the subordination of European common foreign and defence policy initiatives to (a US-dominated) NATO. At the same time, it emphasised its commitment to European integration. 'The necessary introduction of a common currency (Euro)' should be accompanied 'by a wider change in the financial and social policies currently being implemented, with a radical, social and democratic change in the way it is being built'. The EU should be 'a place of real convergence, development and social cohesion, where the social model is strengthened, working hours are reduced without a reduction in wages ... a Europe of environmental protection, of equality between the sexes'. 'More rapid progress in the direction of the political unification of Europe' was needed. The KKE policy of withdrawal from the EU was explicitly attacked as a 'flight to nowhere' stance (Coalition of Left and Progress (Synaspismos), 1999).

Finally, at the end of 2000, in its consideration of the Nice summit on reform of the institutions of the EU, Synaspismos called for the introduction of a 'democratic European Constitution', the elevation of the European Parliament into a proper legislative power, the introduction of a much stronger Charter of Human Rights than that proposed, and a 'radical revision' of the basic Treaties of the EU, 'aiming at a democratic political unification and social cohesion of the European Union' (Coalition of Left and Progress (Synaspismos), 2000b).

From this brief summary we may conclude that left European federalist idealism is alive and well within a party such as Synaspismos. Deeply hostile to neo-liberalism, to American economic, political and military domination, and to NATO militarism, it remains convinced that the only realistic way to combat all of these realities is to work for a stronger European Union, not a weaker one: to fight for a politically more united, socially more integrated and harmonised, and economically more egalitarian European Union in which the elected European Parliament acquires new and decisive powers. Such an analysis is of course diametrically opposed to the outlook of some of the parties with which it shares membership of the Confederal Group of the European Unitary Left/Nordic Green Left (GUE/NGL), including the KKE from which it is more divided than ever on these fundamental strategic issues. Thus, Synaspismos's calls for the establishment of a 'party of the European Radical and Democratic Left' on the left flank of the Party of European Socialists, whilst echoing views expressed by the Italian PRC and some others, remains a highly controversial position – a strategic problem to which I will return in the final chapter.

3.4 The Portuguese Communist Party (PCP)

The PCP, from the moment of its legalisation after the anti-fascist revolution of 25 April 1974, strongly opposed the idea of Portuguese membership of the European Community. The party shared in full the PCF's analysis of the EC as an invention of monopoly capital, designed to secure the political domination of the multinationals and to perpetuate American/German hegemony over the weaker European states. Membership of the Community, it was argued, would lead to increasing unemployment and hardship for the Portuguese working-class with growing emigration to the capitalist core and a weakening of the democratic gains of the Portuguese revolution; to Portuguese small farmers being drawn into conditions of dependency and impoverishment; and to the destruction of many small businesses and marginalisation of those petty bourgeois strata seen by the PCP as potential allies in an 'anti-monopoly capital alliance'. Indeed, the argument that EC membership threatened the gains of the Portuguese revolution would remain a central theme of a party that increasingly based its appeal, and its legitimacy, on nostalgia for the 'heroic' period of the mid-1970s.

Thus, whilst the Portuguese Socialist Party under Mario Soares saw the EC as a guarantor of the new democratic order, the PCP saw in Portugal's application for membership only a plot to subvert the gains of the April revolution – such as collectivisation of land in the Alentejo, nationalisation of banks and the seizure of industrial monopolies – and to consolidate the leading role of foreign capital within the Portuguese economy. As Melo Antunes (1985, 172) has put it, 'for the PSP (or for its leadership) political democracy could only become a durable reality in Portugal when the country was fully integrated with those countries whose political model is that of Western Europe and whose economic model is that which is subordinate to the laws of the market economy'. For the PCP, as for the PCF, the socialists' abandonment of any attempt to construct a non-capitalist society – their ultimate 'betrayal' of the working-class – was precisely linked to their Europeanism. Portugal's membership of the EC in 1986 thus marked a further 'counter-revolutionary turn' in the country's history.

While the Socialist Party joined with the rightwing Portuguese parties in declaring full support for a European Parliament elected on the basis of direct universal suffrage, not surprisingly the PCP, detecting further proof of plots to subvert the 'gains of April', placed itself at the head of those forces totally and radically opposed to direct elections. The great fear of the PCP – as in the case of the PCF and KKE – was of course that a European Parliament elected in such a way would acquire de facto greater legitimacy and ultimately would inevitably supplant the powers and prerogatives of the national parliament.

The essential dilemma for the PCP was that of coming to terms with the model of society prevalent in Western Europe. Even more so than the PCF, or the KKE, the PCP has clung to the dream of national-communism – of a 'socialist' Portugal led by the communist party. Two factors are important in understanding the psychology of the Portuguese party, which has earned itself the reputation of being amongst the more Stalinist of all Western European communist parties: first, the fact that Portugal was, throughout the long years of the Salazar-Caetano dictatorship, relatively more isolated from the European capitalist core than any other country (including Spain and Greece); and second, that Portugal alone amongst Western European countries almost witnessed a successful seizure of state power (in 1974–75) by a communist party that tended to conceptualise the economic and political situation of the country as if it was akin to a third-world country rather than an emergent European capitalist democracy.

The PCP, then, convinced itself of the possibility of making a real break with the capitalist world economy, radically rejecting the political as well as economic model of Western Europe. It would continue for many years to cling to its Leninist concepts both of society and of the role of the party, not in the defensive and contradictory manner of the French, but with real conviction – rejecting all compromise with an economic and political order, the consolidation of which it refused to accept as inevitable. When the party began to lose that sense of conviction, after the collapse of the USSR, it would flounder for a coherent message to put in its place.

The PCP had greatly appreciated the assistance of the PCF in campaigning against Portugal's application to join the Community. That both parties had cited the defence of their national constituencies scarcely detracted from this display of 'proletarian internationalism', which was founded on an objective convergence between the two parties.

The PCP in fact had been reluctant to accept the reality of Portugal's move towards Community membership, clinging to the hope that the EC's internal problems would prevent it from extending membership to Portugal and Spain. When the treaty of accession was signed, the party demanded that the government be dismissed for 'betraying the Portuguese people' and called for dissolution of parliament and early elections (Gaspar, 1990, 53). Following a setback in the elections that took place after ratification of the accession treaty, the party somewhat switched its tactics to calling for a renegotiation of the terms of Portuguese entry, perhaps recognising that this seemed a more realistic policy from the electorate's point of view than simple calls for withdrawal. However, it would seem that this represented more an attempt to gain politically from the support of those disrupted by the impact of membership – as the PCP was the only major party to attack the Community – than an actual change of heart about the nature of the Community.

The PCP participated of course in the Portuguese 1987 elections to the European Parliament and secured three seats with 11.5 per cent of the vote. A clear indication of the party's intended course of action inside the European Party was given when the party sent to Strasbourg at the head of its delegation Angelo Veloso, a tough PCP militant and long-time critic of the Italian and Spanish 'revisionists'. Party General Secretary Alvaro Cunhal returned to the theme of Community membership in his address to the Twenty-sixth Congress of the PCF in December

1987. The rightwing government in power in Portugal, he claimed, was intent upon the erosion of the gains of the April Revolution and had now found in the EEC a new instrument with which to effect this: '[membership of the EC] is disastrous for our industry, for our agriculture, for our fisheries, and for our national independence'.

The PCP, alone of the parties represented in the Portuguese National Assembly, voted against ratification of the Single European Act. The Twelfth Congress of the PCP, which took place in December 1988, heard a very negative assessment of the balance sheet since Portugal joined the Community. Dismissing claims that the Single Market would open up a market of 320 million consumers to Portuguese manufacturers, Alvaro Cunhal claimed that the truth was that 'it is a market of 10 million Portuguese which is opened to an invasion of products from the EEC' (quoted in *Cahiers du Communisme*, February 1989). The country's deficit with the rest of the Community had passed from 2 billion escudos in 1985 to 283 billion in 1987, and this could be expected to increase dramatically after 1992. Foreign investments had rocketed, resulting in the plundering of national wealth. The congress committed the party to fight 'without reserve' against all further processes of integration, against the supranational character of decision-making processes, and against any upgrading of the West European Union in the direction of a common defence policy. Attempts by a group of would-be reformers within the party's ranks, led by politburo member Zita Seabra, to reopen the question of the party's wholly negative approach to Community membership were crushed. Seabra, who had argued that the party's one-track strategy vis-à-vis the EC and other issues had contributed to the party's political decline, was finally expelled from the PCP in January 1990.

Nevertheless, a tactical change could be detected in the congress's emphasis on action needed to frustrate any further developments in the direction of European integration, rather than calling for a campaign for outright withdrawal from the Community. A certain deliberate vagueness permitted the party to appear more flexible than it actually was in practice. Carlos Brito, member of the politburo of the PCP, talked, for example, of the need to develop 'relations with the EEC countries on the basis of mutual benefit and the defence of national interests and of national sovereignty' (Brito, 1989, 50). The 1988 Party Congress's call for a struggle against the negative effects of EC membership and acknowledgement that such a struggle could result in a policy of 'using for the benefit of the nation all the opportunities connected with incorporation into the Common Market' (Brito, 1989, 50) might thus be interpreted as a softening of the party's line, but was probably more concerned with retaining maximum tactical flexibility in order to reap full electoral benefit from harnessing the grievances of those various groups adversely economically and socially affected by the restructuring necessitated by preparations for 1992. It might also have been deemed a useful tactical response to the growing internal pressure for party change. As various writers have pointed out, the end of the 1980s saw successive waves of dissent within the PCP, which the party leadership sought to contain and/or crush (Raby, 1989, and Patricio, 1990).

The party entered the European elections of 1989 with a platform that reflected in almost every respect the concerns and views of the French communists. The PCP hoped to benefit from the discontent of many workers in traditional industries and small business people and small farmers who felt threatened from the considerable upheaval which Portuguese adjustment to the requirements of the completion of the Single Market entailed. The party, and its electoral allies in the United Democratic Coalition (CDU), actually polled 14.4 per cent of the vote and won three seats in the Strasbourg assembly – a result which was sufficiently pleasing to ensure the subsequent defeat of reformers arguing for a change in the party's European line. This, in turn, ensured that the PCP entered the 1990s with a European policy that in effect sought to attract the support of those in the sectors of the economy most vulnerable to modernisation and change. This was especially true of the two main groups that formed the 'bedrock' of party support – rural workers in the south and urban manual workers in the urban area of Setubal. Unfortunately for the PCP, industrial restructuring would hit both groups badly and gradually erode the party's electoral support throughout the 1990s.

Already by the time of the 1989 European Parliamentary elections there were portents of trouble to come. Patricio (1990, 205–7) points out that in the European Parliamentary elections the local PCP administration in Almada supported an independent leftist candidate instead of the official PCP candidate, and that a much more pragmatic attitude towards the European Community was evident amongst party militants and MEPs than amongst the politburo. Indeed, the MEP Barros Moura would subsequently leave the PCP for the Socialist Party. The Twelfth Party Congress in May 1990 was held against the background of falling membership and the enormous political fall-out from the collapse of the Stalinist regimes in Eastern Europe, as well as the impending collapse of the USSR. The Cunhal leadership had never made any secret of its hostility towards the Soviet reform process, and Gorbachev in particular. Party dissenters called for an overhaul of such attitudes, the abandonment of 'democratic centralism' and even for the resignation of Cunhal. Dissenters included the leading Portuguese writer and intellectual, José Saramago, who resigned in early 1990, and the trade union leader José Luis Judas, who urged a critique of Soviet-style Marxism-Leninism and a positive evaluation of the European Community as enhancing modernisation and development in Portugal – an attitude that Patricio claims was shared by many communist trade unionists. (Judas was deselected as a congress delegate because of his stand.)

In the early and mid-1990s, the PCP shifted the emphasis of its campaigning work to fighting against any deepening of European integration. Its policy statement attacking the Maastricht Treaty and calling for a referendum on the issue stressed its support for a form of European construction 'founded on free nations and on sovereign and independent states' as opposed to a federal Europe, which could only destroy national independence and democracy, place the smaller member states at the mercy of the larger, impoverish workers and small farmers, and increase the power of the capitalist technocracy (Portuguese Communist Party (PCP), 1992). The PCP manifesto for the 1994 European Parliamentary elections continued the fight against

Maastricht. The blueprint for European integration that Maastricht contained was 'detrimental to national interests and determined by the interests of the most powerful countries and by big capital'. The implementation of the Treaty had contributed to rising unemployment and serious economic recession. The Treaty 'plays down social policies, strengthens the trend towards the consolidation of existing inequalities in development and challenges the rules of political democracy, namely in what concerns the powers of national parliaments. It implies sacrifices for the people, particularly as a result of the untenable insistence on achieving the goals of nominal convergence to pave the way for Economic and Monetary Union.' Although the Treaty was in force, the struggle to change its 'underlying logic' should be stepped up. The best way to do this was to elect PCP MEPs who were committed 'to the firm defence of national interests and sovereignty' (Portuguese Communist Party (PCP), 1994a). At the same time, the manifesto, whilst prioritising the party's opposition to the allegedly negative aspects of federalist integration, also listed a number of potential positive developments that the party would welcome. These included 'effective social policies, based on the principle of progressive harmonisation of living and working conditions', 'a regional policy which may actually contribute to correct inequalities and asymmetries', and a stronger environmental and consumers' policy. Certainly, these proposals can be seen as involving an implicit acknowledgement that the EU had progressive potential, provided it could be turned away from the neo-liberal and federalist path mapped out in Maastricht. Indeed, the PCP 1994 manifesto called for 'a necessary change of course in the policy of European integration' and for a 'struggle to fully use the new powers of the European Parliament' against the Commission and the EU bureaucracy. However, these policy innovations – for undoubtedly they were such – tended to get lost amid the heavy rhetoric about defending national independence and defeating European federalism. (In the event, the 1994 European Parliamentary elections saw support for the communist-led CDU fall to 11.2 per cent; not only did the CDU lose one of its four European Parliamentary seats, but one of the remaining three seats went to the Greens, the minor partner in the CDU).

A year later, the party and its allies slumped to just 8.6 per cent in the Portuguese general elections. The result suggested that the defeated party reformers' warnings of inexorable decline might be becoming reality. As Goldey puts it, '[the PCP was] prevented from destalinizing by the grand old man of the party, Alvaro Cunhal, but losing traditional support to mortality everywhere, demoralization and migration in Alentejo, and privatization and restructuring of loss-making former nationalized industries in the Lisbon area' (Goldey, 1997, 247). The problem for the PCP was, of course, that Portugal's growing immersion in the international division of labour encouraged by deeper European integration, and the industrial restructuring that went with that, were eroding its support base and confronting it with an ever-starker choice. Should it cling to the defence of a shrinking and increasingly marginalised section of the working-class, or should it embrace modernisation, both in the sense of greater internal party democracy and new political thinking and in the sense of pitching its appeal at more 'dynamic' sections of the workforce, which, its trade union leaders such as Judas had recognised, had much to gain from a positive European agenda? Such an agenda might have involved the party in campaigning for Portugal to draw upon EU funds for environmental projects; or in attacking the misuse of EU funds for retraining by the ruling parties for patronage purposes; or in campaigning for greater EU spending on education and infrastructural development and for a strong Charter of workers' rights. In the event, the party attempted a belated and partial destalinisation, coupled with a continuing attack upon the nature and direction of European integration, in which the rhetoric about the evils of the single currency would drown out the potentially more innovative policy elements that its 1994 European Parliamentary election manifesto had hinted at.

In 1995, the PCP published its agenda for the forthcoming Intergovernmental Conference that would finalise the arrangements for the launch of the single currency. The party called for a decisive rejection of the single currency, blaming the Maastricht criteria for 'the destruction of our productive capacity, the decline in economic growth, the large increase in unemployment, and worsening social problems and a growing dependence on external factors' (Portuguese Communist Party, 1995). In opposition to Portuguese adoption of the euro, the PCP called for 'reaffirmation of the national dimension of economies'. As Cunha (2000, 97–8) argues, the PCP saw Portugal's participation in the single currency as returning the country to the sort of economic dependence that existed before the revolution in 1974. Moreover, 'agricultural independence would be threatened by EU and US imports'. The party called for a referendum on its proposed revision to the Maastricht Treaty as well as on participation in the single currency. Dismissing the government view that there was no alternative to implementation of the Maastricht criteria, the PCP called for employment and social justice to be prioritised and argued that monetary union would divide the EU between rich and poor nations and increase poverty within member states (Cunha, 2000, 100). It maintained that the Portuguese economy was not ready to sustain the harsh penalties imposed by the Maastricht convergence criteria and that it would lose more in the long term that it had gained, in the short term, through subsidies. In the words of party General Secretary Carlos Carvalhas, 'They gave us the sausage in order to take the pig!' (quoted in Cunha, 2000, 101).

Carvalhas had succeeded the veteran Stalinist Alvaro Cunhal as General Secretary in 1992. A loyal member of the party leadership, he had cautiously taken his distance from Stalinism shortly after his election and, throughout the 1990s, he sought to edge the party forwards from the preoccupations of the Cunhal generation of veterans without any rupture with its revolutionary past. To an extent, this involved making moves in the direction suggested by groups of party reformers – after those reformers had been silenced or forced out of leading party positions. In the face of electoral and membership decline 'rumours of renewed aspirations for renovation resurfaced' in 1996 and 1997 (Cunha, 2000, 104). The 1999 European elections saw the party vote decline to 10.3 per cent (the CDU lost one of its three seats), and in the general elections in October 1999, the party polled 9.02 per cent.

Actually, this was considered something of a success, as worse results had been feared. Amid increasing calls for change as the Sixteenth Party Congress approached in December 2000, a public row broke out between Carvalhas and his predecessor. Cunhal had attacked any notion of abandoning Marxism–Leninism, warning that this would be the death of a true communist party, and called for a ban to be adopted to stop the party entering coalition governments with the socialists. Both these notions ran counter to the Carvalhas line. Carvalhas had made clear his willingness to discuss voting alliances with the socialists after the 1999 elections and, in response to Cunhal, he argued that it 'would be an error' if the PCP were to refuse to contemplate change. In February 2000, the party central committee decided to abandon the historic attachment to Marxism–Leninism, to elect the leadership in future through a secret ballot of party members, and to open a dialogue with the socialists. The December 2000 congress confirmed these important reforms, with Carvalhas dismissing the accusation that he was presiding over a social democratisation of the party and arguing that 'the dogmatisation of Marxism–Leninism was one of … the causes of the defeat of socialism in the East … because it led to serious deformations and mistakes in the policies and practice of Party and State' (Carvalhas, 2000, 14).

However, it may well be that the changes embarked upon are 'too little, too late', as the party's decline has not apparently been halted. The Portuguese general elections on March 2002 saw the PCP and its allies poll their worst result ever – a mere 6.97 per cent. The problem the party faces may not be so much rhetorical adherence to Marxism–Leninism but rather overcoming the image that it is a weakened, defensive, rearguard and backward-looking party with an ageing membership and a shrinking class base. Ironically, the renewal of its policies on European integration may be central to any prospects of a revival. As Cunha argues (2000, 104), 'The PCP's attitude towards the EU has been a main issue of contention between the renovators and the orthodox leaders. The renovators generally viewed the latter's inability to understand and adapt to the transformations which the EU facilitated in Portugal as one of the justifications to change [sic] the party's positions.' And he concludes that the issue of EU membership and participation in further integration has become a measurement of the party's potential for change. On this reasoning, the process of renovation is far from successful.

The party's 'programmatic declaration' for the 1999 European Parliamentary elections unambiguously associated federalism with neo-liberalism, identifying any further move towards deeper integration as an attack on democracy, on national independence and on the well-being of the Portuguese people (Portuguese Communist Party (PCP), 1999). The manifesto for the 1999 general elections went further. It spelt out the 'principles, fundamentals and basic measures' which must govern European construction. These included: respect for national sovereignty; limiting EU interventions strictly to areas in which it could clearly justify its intervention; giving national parliaments a greater say in EU policy-making; maintaining the national veto over areas of major policy concern; achieving greater control of the European Commission; bringing the European Central Bank under greater political control;

fully maintening the voting rights, representation and language rights of the smaller member states; and achieving a greater transparency in EU decision-making. It also called for a renegotiation of the Stability Pact to prioritise employment creation; a reform of the EU budget to make it an instrument of economic and social cohesion; reform of the CAP and the Common Fisheries Policy; and an end to the policy of privatisations. Clearly, this list includes many proposals that all Left parties would endorse, some proposals that are not incompatible with a strengthening of the EU's role, and a great many proposals that are concerned with strengthening the nation-state and 'rolling back' the integration process.

The 2000 Party Congress reaffirmed the PCP's hostility towards a policy of 'always submitting to the decisions of the European Union' and attacked the socialists in government for 'conformism towards the European Union, where the PS [Socialist Party] is at the forefront of the federalist projects' (Carvalhas, 2000, 6-7). The congress adopted a statement on the international situation that went much further, in its rhetoric, than General Secretary Carvalhas. Deriding the 'European Union's process of militarisation', it accused the EU of leading 'counter-revolutionary processes' that included the 'dismantling of the socialist regimes which existed in [Eastern Europe] and engaging in a take-over of the former socialist countries in the interests of German and American capital'. The 'three main imperialist poles' in the world were identified as the USA, Japan and 'the EU/Germany'. Social democratic parties, governments and trade unions were accused of 'confirming their historic role' by surrendering to neo-liberalism. All in all, the analysis contained in this document confirms that any fundamental rethink of the nature and potential of the European integration process is not in sight at present and might be expected to meet with fierce internal opposition were it ever to be a likely prospect.

Cunha (2000, 105) has argued that:

> The PCP is poised to take advantage of governmental mistakes in handling forthcoming crises. If the party does not intend to change its revolutionary rhetoric in the short to medium term, joining the Euro may provide it with political benefits. The party's recent backlash as a result of its losses in the local elections could be halted by citizen frustration with Euro side effects. As the only party to oppose the [Euro], the PCP stands to benefit depending on the political inclination of the voters, If joining the Euro does lead to further neo-liberal capitalist integration and increased unemployment, PCP support may rise. However, if communist negative projections do not occur, the party will again have missed an opportunity to reform, leading to further decline in support.

This is a perceptive summary of the position that the PCP now finds itself in. Faced with electoral losses in March 2002, the leadership seems to have decided that the road to electoral recovery lies in a hardening of its opposition to the euro and further European integration in general, in anticipation that it will benefit from a popular backlash against the effects of the single currency and further neo-liberal reforms. Thus, Carlos Carvalhas sought to rally the party faithful at the annual Festival of the party newspaper *Avante!* in September 2002 by predicting that among the dire consequences of the introduction of the euro would be a rise in the prices of essential goods and services, job losses, cuts in public services, drastic cuts in public investment as a result of the Stability Pact and the transformation of Portugal into 'a peripheral region of the European Union, a simple spot known for its sunshine, cheap manpower and clandestine immigration. This model is doomed to failure and regression' (Carvalhas, 2002b, 1-4). The best case scenario for the PCP would, of course, see it benefit from a rise in the protest vote as disillusionment with European integration grows in Portugal. That might also, of course, reinforce the unwillingness of party hardliners to contemplate the need for any further reform or rethinking of old dogmatic positions. The danger, however, is that if the party proves unwilling or unable to adjust its analysis to take into account the positive effects of European integration on the more dynamic sectors of the Portuguese economy, it risks being seen as a party that likes to say 'no' but lacks an alternative, coherent vision for Portugal and Europe. That might lead it to becoming locked into a spiral of atrophy and decline.

3.5 The Communist Party of Spain/United Left (PCE/IU)

The PCE, following its emergence from forty years of repression and clandestinity imposed by the Franco dictatorship, supported Spanish membership of the European Community. The party appears initially to have been influenced by a desire to erase the black propaganda of the Franco years, which painted the PCE as the enemy of all things Spanish, and also by a strategic conviction that Spanish democracy could best be protected by being anchored within the European Community. This view went hand in hand with the belief that the task of democratic consolidation should be the first priority of the Communist Party; both beliefs tied in well with the PCE's version of Eurocommunism during the 1970s. Undoubtedly, PCE leaders were also influenced by PCI thinking upon the nature and potential of the Community.

Commitment to Spanish membership of the Community also served the purpose of substantiating the party's assertion of autonomy from the USSR, offering clear evidence of its democratic credibility and locating it in the mainstream of post-Franco political thinking on the future course of the country's destiny. Indeed, Mujal-León has suggested that the treatment which the PCE leadership in exile had received at the hands of the Soviets intensified the desire to 'Europeanise' communism – to relocate the party's strategy on the terrain of a Europe, autonomous and independent of both major superpowers (Mujal-León, 1983, 117). Thus, 'a stubborn streak of Spanish nationalism was transfigured into a commitment for Europe'.

This European commitment, first developed during the 1960s and elaborated ever since, marked a fundamental departure from the earlier positions of the party, which had of course reflected the hostility of the international communist movement to the European Economic Community. The PCE, like the PCP and the KKE, did not have to take a specific stand on issues that demanded a response from the Italian and French parties during the 1970s – such as direct elections to the European Parliament – because of course Spain, Portugal and Greece did not enter the Community until the 1980s. (Greece became a member of the EC in 1981, returning one Communist MEP, nominated by the national parliament, and holding direct elections in 1982 when four Communist MEPs were elected. Spain and Portugal joined in 1986, with Spain returning three Communist MEPs, nominated by national parliament, until direct elections in October 1987, which saw five representatives of the newly formed United Left (IU) coalition returned.) Nevertheless, from the outset, the PCE sought to emphasise that support for EC membership did not imply uncritical acceptance of the monopolistic nature of the existent European Community but demanded strenuous efforts to democratise and change the nature of the Community through precisely such developments as a democratisation of the Community's institutions and a strengthening of the powers of the Parliament. PCE foreign policy chief Manuel Azcárate declared in 1979 that 'we support the adhesion of Spain ... not in order to maintain the EEC as it is today, but with the perspectives of transforming it ... in a progressive sense' (quoted in Diaz Lopez, 1979, 356–7). In an article in the PCE's theoretical journal *Nuestra Bandera* in May 1979 (quoted in Szajkowski, 1980, 309–19), Azcárate elaborated on this point:

> The amplification of the Common Market with the incorporation of Spain, Greece and Portugal will undoubtedly be a factor for change pointing towards a new equilibrium in the European structure, a lessening of the present domination by the Europe of the North, an increase in the importance of the Europe of the South, with strong labour and popular movements, with areas almost underdeveloped, and with growing demands for a new transforming social and regional policy.

The PCE further argued that direct elections to the European Parliament would lead to an increase in the importance of the Parliament – an event to be welcomed. The growing importance of the Parliament would increase rather than diminish the role and function of national parliaments: 'it will permit and potentiate [*sic*] a truly European debate (which in fact already exists), it will be of assistance in every country to the masses in assuming responsibility for the great European problems, and in putting into a European framework, often decisive for studying and getting down to real solutions, the problems experienced by each nation' (also taken from *Nuestra Bandera*, quoted in Szajkowski, 1980).

The increase in the standing of the European Parliament after 1979 would also contribute to two other processes: democratisation and debureaucratisation of the Community: 'and these two objectives will be decisive for reducing the role of the monopolies, for advancing towards a people's Europe, because all this is taking place at a time when a crisis is shaking Western Europe, with dreadful unemployment figures, with industries such as steel and textiles in decline, at a time when capitalism is demonstrating in a more and more visible way its inability to resolve contemporary problems' (same source as before). Of course, the actual experience was to prove more disappointing. The European Parliament, even today, is not the strong legislative body that the PCE had argued for, and the power of corporate lobbyists to 'persuade' MEPs continues to dismay and disillusion parties of the left that had hoped the European Parliament might be in the forefront of attempts to challenge corporate power and bring it under some sort of democratic control. Nevertheless, the struggle to strengthen the European Parliament remains a priority of the PCE and its allies in the IU.

The convergence with the positions of the PCI during the 1970s and 1980s was obvious. In stressing the need for a new internationalism 'capable of uniting not only the workers but all the progressive and anti-imperialist forces', and of the urgency of dialogue with the social democratic forces to order to achieve this, the PCE was also signalling its rejection of the PCF's characterisation of the nature of social democracy as well as its attitude towards further European integration.

Following the entrance of PCE parliamentarians into the European Parliament in 1986, the PCE aligned itself firmly with the Italian line inside the Communists and Allies Group. The party argued, for example, that the completion of the Single Market would almost certainly involve economies of scale, benefits to consumers and an increase in productive efficiency but at the expense of workers and of the weaker regions of the Community unless decisive measures were taken at a supranational level to control the processes of integration. It argued that two steps were essential. First, a redistribution of responsibilities between the institutions of the Community, broadening the powers of the European Parliament and the executive mandate of the Commission. This was judged necessary because of the inadequacy of the European currency system. The PCE shared the PCI's fears that if currency policy remained the domain of national governments then this would lead to a jiggling of exchange rates, causing instability and unhinging the entire single market of goods and services. The peripheral regions of the Community would suffer most of all. Second, EC bodies should play a much more significant role in the regional policies of the Community. The PCE called for a substantial increase in the funding of regional and social policies, to be used to combat unemployment. Again, given the strength of regional feeling within Spain, and the fact that the PCE itself is a highly regionalised party – for example, it has historically been present in Catalonia, not as the PCE at all but as the semi-autonomous sister party, the United Socialist Party of Catalonia (PSUC) – it is not surprising that the struggle for a stronger EU regional policy has remained a priority. The party nurtures the hope that a 'Europe of the regions' might offer a solution to the crisis of the Spanish nation-state, to which the question of democratic consolidation is intrinsically linked. In the 1980s, the PCE shared the view of the PCI that it was necessary for the left as a whole to fight for a revision of regional policy. Moreover, the PCE in 1989 sought to introduce a measure similar to that promoted by the Italian communists, which would have given the European Parliament constituent powers and committed the Spanish government to accept this; the measure was rejected by the Spanish courts and not put to a referendum.

By the time of the November 1990 Congress of the IU coalition, PCE foreign policy secretary Francisco Palero was able to inform the weekly paper of the British Communist Party (*Changes*, 10–23 November, 1990) that not only were the PCE and the IU 'deeply committed' to the development of the European Community, but 'our opinion has become stronger and we have worked upon the development of various initiatives which could speed up the construction of a political union in the European Community'. This stands in sharp contrast to David Bell's claim that the Spanish Communists became more 'anti-European' during the 1990s, an alleged development that Bell attributes to the collapse of the 'Italian model', the growing mood of Euro-scepticism in Spain, and the fact that opposition to Maastricht on patriotic grounds offered good cover for the loss of communist identity (Bell, 1996b, 250). In fact, this is quite unfair to the PCE/IU. The party and its allies were indeed highly critical of the monetarist nature of the Maastricht Treaty, and its potential negative impact on employment and social security spending. But, to be critical of neo-liberalism does not necessarily mean to be opposed to European integration. And, even in the face of grave misgivings about Maastricht, the party did not follow the example of PCF, PCP, KKE or PRC parliamentarians and vote against the Treaty. On the contrary, the leadership recommended that its deputies abstain; eight of them even defied this call to vote in favour of ratification; the only deputies in the Spanish Cortes to vote 'no' were the three representatives of *Herri Batasuna*, political wing of the Basque ETA.

Before we can trace the elaboration of party policy on European integration during the 1990s it is necessary to clarify the relationship between the PCE and the IU. This is because the PCE presents itself at elections under the banner of the IU, sits in both the Spanish and European Parliaments as part of the IU, and presents joint policy initiatives with its partners in the IU. Nevertheless, there have always been, and continue to be, tensions within the alliance – not least between the PCE's determination to maintain its separate identity as a communist party instead of 'dissolving' itself into a wider post-communist formation (such as the Finnish Left Alliance or the Greek Synaspismos) and the ambition of many within the IU, and in particular within its Catalan wing, the IC (Initiative for Catalonia), to develop a post-communist identity. However, these tensions are not so much between PCE members and members of other parties within the IU; rather, they are tensions between different factions of the PCE. Although the party formally prohibits organised factions, it is in actuality highly fragmented. For example, at the Sixth Congress of the IU in 2000 all three candidates for the post of IU co-ordinator were leaders of different tendencies within the PCE. The existence of the IU has in fact offered a way in which many of these divergences can be aired without destroying the PCE's unity completely.

Indeed the formation of the IU coalition has its roots in the horrendous factionalism, disunity and fratricidal strive which almost destroyed the Spanish communist movement during the late 1970s and early 1980s. Santiago Carrillo, who had led the party since the early 1960s, may have earnt a reputation as a Eurocommunist and critic of the USSR, but in his style of leadership he was conspicuously authoritarian, purging from the party those who disagreed with him. Carrillo's growing authoritarianism and hyper-centralised control were singularly unhelpful in a party committed to democratic consolidation and regional autonomy and helped to create a reservoir of internal alienation. His virtual 'excommunication' by the Soviets following publication of his book *'Eurocommunism' and the State* in the mid-1970s meant that Soviet interference – in the form of aid and encouragement to those Spanish communists willing to split from the PCE in opposition to Carrillo – further complicated matters. By the early 1980s, the party was badly fragmented and in 1982 its vote fell to around 4 per cent (from nearly 10 per cent). Forced out of the leadership, Carrillo would set up another breakaway party before moving into the orbit of the social democratic PSOE. Meanwhile his successor, Gerardo Iglesias, sought to heal the wounds and save the PCE from extinction by launching the coalition just weeks before the 1986 general election. Those joining the IU included the breakaway Communist Party of the Peoples of Spain (PCPE) led by Ignacio Gallego (who eventually rejoined the PCE, under the banner of the IU), the Party of Socialist Action (PASOC) led by Alonso Puerta, which was composed mainly of PSOE dissidents, and the tiny Republican Left (Gillespie, 1990, 119). The launch was facilitated by co-operation between these groups in opposition to NATO membership and in opposition to signs of growing corruption within the PSOE governments of Felipe Gonzalez.

The IU's electoral success was patchy at first. Nevertheless, by the end of the 1980s its vote was back up to 9 per cent and modest growth continued into the 1990s as the coalition benefited from growing disillusionment with the PSOE in power. In the European elections of 1994, it polled over 13 per cent, winning nine MEPs, and in the 1996 general election (when PSOE was finally ousted from power), it polled 10.6 per cent. It thus achieved the purpose of imposing greater unity within PCE ranks, stabilising the party and reversing its decline, and enabling it to reach out to new electors. The coalition, however, suffered from a number of critical weaknesses and internal contradictions and, for reasons that we will examine shortly, it entered the twenty-first century in very considerable disarray. At this point, it is important to bear in mind that the PCE was always by far the dominant force within the IU, supplying the overwhelming majority of militants, election workers, leaders and resources. Indeed, from inception until 1998, the PCE General Secretary was also IU co-ordinator. It is therefore somewhat pointless to examine PCE and IU policy evolution on the European question as if they are distinct.

As we have already seen, the IU reacted critically to the neo-liberal nature of Maastricht but, motivated by its overall pro-European convictions, refused to oppose the Treaty outright. The leadership advocated abstention in parliament; eight deputies chose nevertheless to vote in favour of Maastricht. The IU's position was pretty close to that of the Greek Synaspismos – namely, that Maastricht did not go far enough in the direction of the politically united, socially just, and democratised European Union that the movement favoured. In its evaluation of the Treaty, the Catalan component of the IU argued that 'the steps forward in the consolidation of the EC represent, for all their weaknesses, the introduction of organisational measures that potentially work against neoliberalism and act as a check on the hegemony of the USA' (Initiative for Catalonia, 1992). The creation of a 'European Union' was a 'positive step coherent with our European vocation', even if Maastricht left a serious democratic deficit to be filled. Economic and social cohesion, necessary for the success of the single currency (which the coalition supported as 'indispensable'), required stronger structural and cohesion funds. The Social Chapter received a basically positive evaluation, as did the introduction of a concept of EU citizenship. However, the coalition called for much stronger regional and environmental policies. In principle, the concept of a common foreign and security policy was praised but the IU/IC insisted that any common foreign or defence policy should not be subordinate to the USA (via NATO). Maastricht, however, was criticised for what it excluded, namely: fiscal harmonisation, reform of the CAP, the rights of workers from outside the EU, the rights of minority languages, and the failure to specify how expansion of the EU would be financed and new member states fully integrated.

Four years later, the IU was sounding much more critical about the progress that had been made with Maastricht. The experience in Bosnia and Chechnya proved that common foreign and security policies 'had not developed in a coherent way' (IC, 1996). The persistence of high levels of structural unemployment (Spanish unemployment rates were amongst the highest in the EU) and the blinkered neo-liberal approach to implementation of the convergence criteria for the single currency was feeding disillusionment on the left. Nevertheless, the IU/IC declared itself 'a fully pro-European' political movement, convinced that the EU remained 'an essential tool to face the great economic and ecological challenges' that lay ahead. The process of European construction needed adjustment, above all in two respects. First, the concepts of citizenship and workers' rights needed strengthening. Second, the EU required urgent action to democratise its decision-making processes and devolve powers to the regions. Under no circumstances should the left back away from its commitment to a federal political union; to do so would be to cede ground to the rightist and conservative forces.

In the debate leading up to revision of the Maastricht Treaty (which eventually produced the Amsterdam Treaty in 1998), the IU stressed its twin-track approach: total support for European federalism combined with criticism of neo-liberalism and high unemployment. IU co-ordinator and PCE General Secretary Julio Anguita wrote in 1996 that the tenth anniversary of Spain joining the EU should be used to demonstrate two things: 'the optimism of the Spanish people, their willingness to participate actively in the EU' – notwithstanding the fact that the negative aspects of Maastricht caused great hardship in some Spanish productive sectors – and the fact that 'change is needed in Europe' (Anguita, 1996a). He argued that 'a United Europe needs a constitution. An alternative Europe – economically and socially cohesive – cannot be based solely on the common market. Political union will be slowed down.' Therefore, the left should push for revision of the Treaty in the direction of measures designed to tame the market and curb neo-liberalism.

Euro-scepticism, however, was firmly rejected as irrelevant – 'Spain cannot find solutions for fundamental problems outside the EU.' In a further article, in the IU magazine *Europa* (produced by the MEPs), Anguita argued that 'for IU, a single market without a United Europe means to disarm society and governments before the multinationals' (Anguita, 1996b, 14–19). To reject the neo-liberal model of European construction was not to be 'anti-European'. Rather, the IU fought for 'a true economic and social cohesion that consolidates a European construction that advances not only on the economic front, but also on the political and social fronts'. In the absence of a considerably strengthened cohesion fund, the danger was that the single currency would maintain already existing inequalities between states while reducing the possibility for governments to intervene to correct dangerous disequilibria.

In 1997, these points were repeated and significantly amplified in a major policy document produced by the IU delegation in the European Parliament and approved by the IU federal leadership. (It is worth noting that at this point the IU, with its nine MEPs, was the largest single component in the GUE/NGL group and therefore carried considerable weight.) This document gave few concessions to the anti-integrationist views of several other Left parties allied to the IU within the European Parliament. It argued for deeper and more rapid progress towards a federal political union based on social and economic cohesion; for a European constitution that included a strong concept of EU citizenship; for full legislative powers to the European Parliament; for monetary union based on real convergence brought about through redistribution of wealth and resources within the EU; and for strong common foreign and defence policies that were not co-ordinated by NATO (the IU, at this point, still maintained its opposition to Spain's membership of NATO) (United Left (IU), 1997).

By the late 1990s, then, the PCE and its allies within the IU had clearly elaborated a position on European integration that was unambiguously pro-integration (indeed pro-federalist) but highly critical of the lack of strategic vision and obsession with narrow neo-liberal economics, to the detriment of social justice and the health of democracy, that it associated with the current direction of European construction. It was also highly critical of the social democratic and conservative governments that were adapting wholesale to the logic of the market rather than trying to harness the market to a broader vision of Europe. Like the PCI in the 1970s and Synaspismos today, it saw itself as keeping alive the flame of 'left Europeanist' idealism. And yet it was at precisely this point that tensions and contradictions came to the surface that threatened the future of both the PCE and the IU.

One such tension was between the nature of the PCE and that of the IU. The establishment of the IU had allowed the PCE to restore a considerable measure of party unity. But many divergences of opinion continued to exist within the party. Gorbachev and the reform process in the USSR during the late 1980s had paradoxically helped with the reintegration of hardline pro-Soviet communists into the PCE (for one thing, the external lifeline which Moscow had supplied was withdrawn).

This, in turn, led by the start of the 1990s to a renewed emphasis on the Marxist (or even Marxist-Leninist) nature of the party. Having rejected merger with Gonzalez's PSOE or integration into the social democratic mainstream (as the PCI had chosen), the party sought to emphasis its own distinct identity. Yet there are obvious problems for a democratic and reformist communist party in trying to manage the different aspirations and interpretations of Marxism of those who come from opposing Eurocommunist and pro-Soviet backgrounds. The IU formula could mask these contradictions but it did not remove them. In a sense, the PCE was trying to have it both ways: to remain a communist party, with its hammer and sickle emblem, and yet to present itself to the Spanish people as part of a post-communist 'new left' movement. Inevitably there were many who began to question the continuing relevance of the PCE and to contemplate full absorption into the IU (along the lines of Synaspismos in Greece) and many who began to resent the existence of the IU and to question whether the PCE ought to preserve its identity by 'going it alone'. Another tension was between the PCE's strong anti-NATO and anti-US stance and its support for a common EU defence and foreign policy. Logically, this is not necessarily a contradictory position to hold; the problem arises when the EU chooses to act through NATO, and to envisage any common European security and defence system operating as the European arm of NATO.

In 1998 and 1999, the PCE/IU leadership made a number of serious strategic blunders. The coalition was torn by internal dissent over its role in negotiating the so-called Pact of Lizarra in the Basque country in 1998. This Pact involved Basque separatists (included ETA's political wing Herri Batasuna – soon to be outlawed by the Spanish government) joining forces with other Basque parties and trade unions to press the central government for greater independence. It was to prove controversial precisely because of the involvement of ETA's supporters. The PCE had always taken a strong stand against terrorism and in favour of the defence of democracy against ETA's assassination of politicians, etc. – and it still does take such a stand. However, the leading role it played in negotiating the Pact allowed opponents to brand it as soft on ETA and provoked strong internal dissent. Many non-Basque leftist voters were alienated from the IU. A much more serious blunder came over the war in Kosovo. The IU alone amongst Spanish parties condemned the action taken by NATO against the Milosevic regime, and urged Spanish pilots serving with NATO to become war objectors. That was consistent with its anti-NATO and anti-US tradition, though critics might argue that such a tradition rather blinded it to the possibility that sometimes NATO might actually have right on its side. However, outrage followed when Anguita branded NATO Secretary-General, the Spanish socialist Javier Solana, as a 'war criminal' and even went so far as to suggest that Milosevic was a 'man of the left'. Whatever the intention, the impression was created that the old unreconstructed communist strain in the PCE/IU still hankered with nostalgia after the last of the East European neo-Stalinist leaders – although, in this case, a neo-Stalinist turned genocidal nationalist. The incident was enormously damaging. The media sought to question the movement's adherence to Western values, and its maturity as a political force. IU federations in Madrid, Asturias and Valencia criticised the leadership and demanded that the coalition denounce the crimes of Milosevic. In the European and regional elections in June 1999, the IU vote collapsed dramatically. In the European elections, it fell from 13.44 per cent (in 1994) and nine MEPs to 5.77 per cent and four MEPs. And in the regional elections it polled just over 6 per cent and suffered devastating losses. Over a decade of political progress had been wiped out. The IU was basically back at the electoral low point reached by the PCE in the early and mid-1980s. Undoubtedly, the fact that its growth years had coincided with disillusionment with the corruption of the PSOE in government was also important. Since 1996, the PSOE were back in opposition, the rightwing Popular Party formed the government, and the PSOE could play the anti-corruption card against the incumbents. This of course emphasises the extent to which PCE/IU success depends on it being able to position itself as a more radical but still acceptable force to the left of the PSOE, attractive to disillusioned PSOE voters.

In the aftermath of the 1999 debacle, the IU was thrown into chaos. Anguita offered to resign as IU co-ordinator (he had already been succeeded as PCE General Secretary by Francisco Frutos in 1998), and then withdrew his resignation. He finally resigned in 2000, being replaced at the head of the IU by Gaspar Llamazares. Further confusion and disorientation followed. With general elections approaching in 2000, the PCE/IU seems to have been thrown back in panic.

In February 2000, apparently in an effort to consolidate its position and to repair the damage caused by the portrayal of it as irresponsible and extremist, and by its very real divisions, the IU signed an electoral pact with the PSOE for the forthcoming general elections. Those IU regional federations who had been most outraged by the alleged pro-Milosevic stance were among the bodies pressing hardest for the electoral pact with the PSOE, anxious to avoid a repeat of the electoral collapse. The two parties heralded the agreement as being modelled on the French example and predicted that it would deliver a left government. As with the PCF, however, though without the 'benefit' of actually enjoying governmental office, the IU would pay a heavy price for the subsequent loss of policy coherence. It agreed to ditch its demand for Spain's withdrawal from NATO and to soft-peddle on policies such as calling for renationalisation of privatised companies, increases in the minimum wage, and increased EU spending. Moreover, PSOE leader Joaquín Almunia reassured employers during the campaign that the electoral pact with the IU did not deviate in any way from the requirements of the European Stability Pact. The implication was clear: that, in return for a role in government, the IU was willing to abandon the more radical and anti-neo-liberal elements of its own carefully nurtured EU policy.

The subsequent general election was a disaster for the left. Not only did the rightwing Popular Party gain an overall majority for the first time, the IU lost thirteen of its twenty-one seats in parliament and polled just 5.46 per cent of the popular vote. The subsequent loss of income from the Spanish state – which subsidises parties on the basis of votes won in elections – led to a financial crisis on top of the political crisis. The IU was forced to make two-thirds of its full-time staff redundant. It was thus a mood of real crisis that dominated both the Sixth Congress of the IU in October 2000 and the Sixteenth Congress of the PCE in May 2002.

In broad terms, the Sixteenth Congress of the PCE reaffirmed the long-standing policy of the party on European integration, albeit in more radical language than had often been used in the past. Apart from attacking the weakening of the EU's structural and cohesion funds, bemoaning the negative impact of the Stability Pact on social inequalities, and calling for the price of enlargement to the East (which the PCE supports) not to be paid by the poorer member states in the South, the congress defended three 'central ideas' on which the party's policy should rest. The first was that capital was opposed to a democratic development of the European Union. 'Different fractions of the bourgeoisie' were united in their desire to see power concentrated in the hands of bureaucracies that lacked democratic legitimacy (e.g. the board of the European Central Bank), both because of their desire to weaken workers' rights and because of their subservience to US capital and the US administration. The second 'central idea' was that the 'European transformatory left' needed to favour the development of a sovereign and democratic EU, politically and economically independent from the USA and NATO, as part of the drive to combat neo-liberalism and ultimately to build a socialist society. Greater co-ordination of Left parties at the European level and the development of an alternative programme of EU development was part of this task. Finally, the PCE argued that the construction of a democratic EU based on a strong constitution, full powers to the European Parliament, and a strong concept of European citizenship could contribute to a more just relationship between Europe and the Southern hemisphere. Such an EU could 'develop the conditions for a more multipolar world, limiting the power of the USA' and helping the countries of the Southern hemisphere to find their voice (Communist Party of Spain (PCE), 2002).

Beyond this, the congress saw unprecedented dissension. Some delegates expressed dismay at the presence of observers from the Chinese and North Korean communist parties. Former PCE trade union leader Julio Setien saw this as evidence that 'enormous confusion continued at the international level, with the PCE remaining imprisoned in the political loyalties of the old "international communist movement"' (Setien, 2002). Obviously, such signs of 'confusion' concern those who would like to move beyond the communist model of the past. More importantly, perhaps, the congress saw, for the first time, rival platforms being voted upon. General secretary Frutos secured the backing of 59 per cent of delegates, IU co-ordinator Llamazares secured 20 per cent and the leader of a leftist Partido Vivo ('living party') slate, Ángeles Maestro, secured 21 per cent. Whilst Frutos and Llamazares form an effective alliance for the time being, the relatively high support for Maestro is interesting from the point of view of future developments. His platform involved a radical rejection of capitalism, of social democracy as 'a structural element of the new imperialism', and of any electoral pact with the PSOE, and a call to the PCE to abandon the path of consensus it had pursued since the death of Franco and return to working-class militancy. Its goal, the PCE left wing believes, should be to link up with the anti-globalisation movement in such a way as to bring about 'intensification of the class struggle' (Maestro, 2002). Such a strategy might well involve a repudiation of the essentially reformist approach to European integration that the PCE has evolved over the years. (Maestro was unsparing in his rejection of 'left reformist positions that scarcely conceal the adoption of neo-liberal policies and complicity with war', citing both the PCF and the Olive Tree coalition in Italy as examples of this). Whilst this is unlikely to happen in the near future, the presence of a strong current of radical militancy within the party indicates that the crisis within the PCE and the IU is far from resolved.

3.6 The Danish Socialist People's Party (SF)

The SF was founded in 1958–9 as a result of a split within the Danish Communist Party (DKP). The charismatic leader of the DKP, Aksel Larsen, who had led the party since the 1930s and had gained a reputation as considerably less dogmatic and more independent-minded than many of his European counter-parts, was ousted from the party leadership over his refusal to accept the party's attempts to mute the deStalinisation process unleashed by Khrushchev at the Twentieth Soviet Party Congress. The Socialist People's Party, which he founded, was characterised from the outset by a more creative and less doctrinaire application of Marxist theory from that of the Communist Party and also by a pride in its Danish identity and its freedom from external control and influence.

The party – which polled 6.1 per cent of the national vote and won eleven parliamentary seats in 1960 – grew somewhat in influence in the 1960s, partly because its informal alliance with the Social Democrats both made possible a minority Social Democrat government and effectively made it a more respectable leftwing alternative to the latter. The SF, and not the communists or the many far left groups which the Danish left has spawned, tended to benefit most from the growing moderation of the Social Democrats, not least because of the SF's readiness to respond to the significant strength of anti-American feeling in the country which grew with the Vietnam war. Christensen (1996, 527) has pointed out that policy disagreements about foreign policy and NATO membership were central to the birth of both the SF in Denmark and the Norwegian Left Socialists; and that the 'new left' agenda around which these parties organised included anti-militarism, opposition to undemocratic hierarchical patterns of social organisation, solidarity with the 'Third World' and hostility to both the Soviet and US 'models'. These tenets of new left ideological thinking were to underpin SF hostility to European integration, which the party attacked as elitist, undemocratic and driven by the needs of big business.

Part of the SF's ideological heritage, then, was certainly a non-dogmatic and non-Leninist interpretation of Marxism, which was to draw it closer to the Eurocommunist Italian and Spanish parties – indeed, its critical support for the

Social Democrats during the early 1960s led to defections from its ranks from those who suspected that the party had become the leftwing of social democracy. Another part of that heritage was a strong sense of national identity, which coloured the party's attitude towards moves in the direction of European integration. Denouncing the EEC as an undemocratic body, which threatened to subordinate Denmark to American and German hegemony, the SF played a leading role in the campaign against Danish membership of the Community; indeed, it was the only party represented in the Danish Parliament to take such a stance during the 1972 referendum on membership. Although it lost this battle, it benefited from the contest in terms of ideological cohesion – badly needed after the death of Aksel Larsen in 1971. The contest enabled it to project an image as a patriotic and popular new-left party.

Unique amongst the parties that were to participate in the Communists and Allies Group at Strasbourg, the SF can be seen from the outset as drawn towards the PCI's lack of dogmatism (and conversely repelled by the sectarianism of certain other communist parties), but inhibited by its ideological heritage and its support base from embracing the PCI's growing Europeanism.

Following its entrance into the European Parliament in 1973 – the SF did not actually participate in the formation of the Communists and Allies Group in 1973, but joined the group shortly afterwards – the party sought to thwart any further extension of the integration process through opposition to institutional development. Fully consistent with this orientation, the party opposed the revision of the Treaty of Rome in the direction of European political union and voted against ratification by the European Parliament of the Draft Treaty on European political union. SF members of the Danish Parliament were amongst the majority that rejected the Single European Act (SEA) in January 1986 and the party played a high-profile role in the referendum campaign that resulted despite its efforts to persuade people otherwise, in the approval of ratification of the Act by the Danish people on 26 February 1986.

During the 1987 Danish elections the SF fought on the basis of an economic and political programme that emphasised the need for Danish autonomy from EC 'interference' in fiscal and monetary matters and called for the declaration of Denmark as an unconditional nuclear weapons-free zone. The latter point also reflected the party's opposition to any common European defence policy, which, it was felt, would jeopardise Danish interests and run counter to the party's strong pacifist traditions.

Nevertheless, the late 1980s saw internal opposition emerge, particularly amongst younger party leaders, to the traditionally negative stance towards European unity. John Iversen, SF member of the European Parliament, who was increasingly influenced by thinking within the Italian Communist Party, played a key part. The decision, taken after the 1989 European election when Iversen alone was returned to the Strasbourg assembly for the SF, to join with the PCI and the PCE in the new Group for a Unitary European Left certainly reflected this, particularly as the founding programme of the Group declared it to be an alliance of leftwing forces working for a united Europe. (Alignment within the European Parliament would continue to be a problem for the SF. When the Group for a Unitary European Left disintegrated following the Italian PCI-PDS's defection to the Socialists, the SF briefly joined the Greens (1992–94). Later, it would join the GUE/NGL group, a decision made much easier by the arrival in Strasbourg of its Swedish and Finnish sister-parties.)

In the early 1990s SF disagreements over the process of European integration were to spill out into the open and threaten party unity. In actual fact, party policy had been undergoing a process of modification and change for some time. Christensen (1996, 530–2) argues that the political and constitutional situation in Denmark both gave the SF greater leeway for change than its Swedish and Norwegian sister-parties (the question of EU membership, and consequently the entire issue of European integration policy, was effectively off the agenda in those two countries until the start of the 1990s), and necessitated a greater degree of flexibility. The SF had wider scope for parliamentary action in the arena of European policy due to the (relative) weakness of the Danish social democrats, the instability of governments, and the constitutional provision for referenda on the European issue (which could be used to defuse party tensions); at the same time, the prize of potential inclusion in coalition governments if it 'played its cards right' and avoided alienating possible political allies meant that the leadership had an incentive to steer clear of policy cul-de-sacs.

Christensen argues that the evolution of the party's European policy falls into three phases. (The lines of demarcation between these, however, are sometimes blurred.) First, the period 1973–86 saw the party move from outright hostility towards EC membership, towards acceptance of the reality that 63 per cent of Danish voters had voted in favour of membership. It should be emphasised, however, that this was still, at this stage, a largely tactical shift; the party stopped campaigning for withdrawal from the EC, but undoubtedly still favoured such an outcome *in an ideal world*. Following its entry into the European Parliament the party had argued that its MEPs could only support proposals that would weaken European integration. However, by 1986, the party was arguing that although it still opposed the EC, 'we do not suffer from Euro-phobia when it comes to acting within EC institutions' (quoted in Christensen, 1996, 531).

The period 1986–88 saw a further modification of the party's position. In the February 1986 referendum on the SEA, 56.2 per cent of voters in Denmark voted in favour. The SF had campaigned against, citing four main reasons: that the SEA represented a step towards political union, that it increased the powers of the European Parliament, that it reduced the national veto, and that it began the process of moving towards a common foreign policy. Following the referendum defeat, changes to the party's strategy were discussed. The 1986 Party Congress decided that demands for EC withdrawal should not be a barrier to governmental participation, effectively signalling tactical acceptance of (but not support for) membership. A key party policy statement at this time argued that a shift in tone, from simply rejecting EC membership to asserting the need for an alternative, should characterise the party position. The party would argue that 'a workers' parties majority must examine possible alternatives to the EEC, that Danish legislation must be conducted irrespective of the EEC, that the resistance against the union and further integration must be maintained', and that the party should press hard for full utilisation of the various guarantees that pro-EC politicians had given the Danish people about the limited scope of the EC's ambitions and the agreement to preserve a national veto on key developments. The party resolved to press for full control by the national parliament over EC harmonisation directives, and to ensure that 'the progress which has been made in this country can be maintained and, if possible, transferred to other countries. We intend openly to reject any harmonisation which has a deteriorating effect or which prevents further improvements' (Socialist People's Party (SF), 1987, 3–4). The party also decided to focus on fighting for reform from within the EC, encouraging pro-integration party members to identify policy areas in which further and deeper integration might be seen to be fully compatible with the party's programme and objectives – such as stronger EC environmental policies.

Finally, Christensen traces a third phase in the evolution of policy – from 1988 until the time he conducted his research in the mid-1990s. He sees this phase as involving increased movement towards a pro-integration position, albeit a position that is highly critical of the present nature of the EU. Christensen perhaps overplays the degree of policy change during 1988–90: the key developments really take place from 1990 onwards; however, he is certainly right to emphasise the importance of pressure from the external political environment on the party leadership to avoid being locked into inflexible positions. The 1988 Party Congress adopted a policy statement, *With SF against the Common Market* (reproduced in Socialist People's Party (SF), 1988, 18–25), that contained much to reassure those members who might have been uneasy about too sudden a change in policy. The statement emphasised the party's political arguments against the EC, principally its detrimental impact on democratic institutions, its subservience to the interests of big business, and the fact that environmental, social and regional policies were so relatively weak. The party also pledged to work for a situation in which a majority of Danish voters might, by seeing that the EC acted as a brake on concrete progressive policy initiatives, come to the conclusion that membership should be reconsidered.

Nevertheless, the years following the 1988 Congress did see important changes in tactics and in rhetoric. The SF took its distance from the People's Movement Against the EC in Denmark, seeing this as Stalinist-dominated. The SF finally resigned from the People's Movement in 1991, preferring the rival June Movement which accepted Danish EC membership whilst opposing deeper integration. In 1989, the party campaigned for reform from within the EC under the slogan 'Rock the EC', and in 1990 it published its own alternative to the Treaty of Rome. This vitally important policy document advocated more EC democracy, supported open and accountable transnational co-operation, called for stronger environmental and social policies, and welcomed EC expansion and reform. The document (reproduced in Socialist People's Party (SF), 1991a, 7–10) drew an important distinction between two considerations. First, the party pledged itself to defend Danish sovereignty, 'because in our view there is a close interrelationship between democracy and national sovereignty'. Second, the party recognised that 'a number of problems can, nowadays, only be solved jointly by the States, in mutual obliging cooperation. But the common solving of such tasks must be based on democratic mechanisms.' The first consideration led the party to reject a supranational EC central bank and a single currency, the transfer to the EC of competences that would limit the Danish parliament's right to decide policy in budget, distribution, foreign and defence affairs, and the introduction of a common EC army or police force. The second consideration justified the proposed reforms to the EC outlined above, together with other measures such as a reform of the CAP to release monies for regional development within the EC as well as aid to developing countries, and common policies against tax evasion ('in the whole EC area there must be established a system of tax control at least corresponding to the Danish one, including obligation to open all accounts to the tax authorities').

In April 1991, the party signalled another significant shift in tactics and strategy. Whilst certain of the key themes in its critique of European integration were – and have continued to be – reaffirmed, for example, its rejection of a military role for the EC, its concern over the lack of democracy and the dominance of neoliberal technocratic thinking, and its rejection of a globally exploitative EC, other themes also emerged into prominence. These included: the argument that an EC composed of the rich states of Western Europe should give way to a much broader membership and that 'the EC is made accessible to all democratic States applying for membership', and the demand for institutional innovations within the EC such as the establishment of an EC ombudsman. The party also recognised that the Single Market 'has by now come so far that it is difficult to halt the process, both as a result of its inner dynamics and as a result of the European changes that have led to the victory of market economies all over Europe'. It also argued that 'the internationalisation of the class struggles has the effect that the new Europe, including the EC, becomes a decisive field of struggle for Socialists. This means that we (1) must strengthen our co-operation with other Left and Green forces in the EC countries to attain secure minimal norms for social rights and environmental protection in the whole area and fight against the EC policy of blind growth and (2) must strengthen our efforts at home to preserve an independent national field of operations for distribution of burdens, welfare, culture, environmental and economic policies' (Socialist People's Party (SF), 1991b, 18–19). This was a major development for a party that had hitherto tended to dismiss the possibilities of the EC as an arena for Left party co-operation on a strategic basis.

In December 1991, the party urged Danes to vote against the Maastricht Treaty, but it emphasised that this did not mean leaving the EC: 'a vote against the EC-Union [Treaty] is not a vote against the EC or against European co-operation. On the contrary, it is a vote for the kind of European co-operation which is based on openness and which is solving concrete problems instead of constructing a very closed giant state' (Socialist People's Party (SF), 1992a, 11). The SF again emphasised its alternative vision of EC development. The familiar themes featured once more: widening the EC to include Eastern Europe, giving economic concessions to the so-called Third World, and strengthening integration and cohesion in social policy, working conditions and the environment. In the subsequent Maastricht referendum (in June 1992) the Danes famously rejected the Treaty, albeit by the narrowest of margins (50.7 per cent to 49.3 per cent). The SF party statement acclaiming the referendum victory was careful to argue that:

> No was not a No to the EC as such. Opinion polls show that a large majority supports Danish membership and are strongly in favour of broad European cooperation, also based on mutual obligations between States. But not in favour of a federated Europe. This corresponds very much to the stand of the Socialist People's Party. In 1972, we were against Danish membership, and for many years it was our goal to get Denmark out of the EC. But we have, especially after 1989, accepted membership, and this is done explicitly in our new programme (1990). Instead, we work for change inside the EC, in favour of democracy and the safeguarding of political and social rights and the rights of the environment, but stressing that what we want to achieve is a Europe of cooperating peoples, maintaining their sovereign states in close and mutually obliging cooperation, based on solidarity and democracy, and not a European federation which will develop into a new power bloc, also in military respects, and be managed by a huge bureaucratic superstructure, far from the peoples. (Socialist People's Party (SF), 1992b)

Three points might be made about the significance of this statement. First, it marks an explicit acknowledgement of the shift from an EC-rejectionist stance towards a strategy of working to reform the EC from within. Such a strategy, of course, by no means implies that the SF had become a pro-integrationist party in the style of the PCI. Rather, it argued for a Europe of co-operating nation-states, resisting moves towards a federal political union, whilst also recognising the existence of areas in which EU-wide common policies might advance the cause of progressive politics. Second, the SF leadership recognised the political advantage of presenting the party as being in tune with Danish public opinion, principled yet pragmatic in its EU policy. This carried an implied criticism of the 'out of touch' Social Democratic leaders who had campaigned in favour of Maastricht, despite being unable to convince many of their own supporters; and it avoided the SF being tarred with the same brush as the hardline rejectionists in the People's Movement against the EC (that is, deemed unfit potential partners in government). Third, such a repositioning was bound to call forth internal party opposition.

In the wake of the 'No' victory in the first Danish Maastricht referendum, the SF was crucial to securing popular acceptance of the so-called 'national compromise', which was agreed at the Edinburgh EC summit in December 1992 and approved by Danish voters in May 1993. The national compromise involved the Danish opt-outs from Maastricht on the single currency, defence policy, EU citizenship and some police measures. The party's key role in drafting the compromise and securing popular acceptance heralded its arrival as an important 'inside' player within Danish politics and increased its legitimacy. But, as always, there was a political price to be paid. Paradoxically, an overwhelming majority of SF voters (84 per cent) still voted 'No' to Maastricht, national compromise notwithstanding, and tensions within the party grew. (The decision to recommend a 'Yes' vote on the national compromise had been reached by an extraordinary party congress with 223 votes in favour, 85 votes against and eight abstentions.)

During the period 1992–2002, a passionate debate took place within the SF about the party's European orientation. On the one hand, factors pushing for a less hostile attitude towards integration included the desire to escape from a political ghetto and become accepted as a party of government, the experience of working for change within the EU institutions, the satisfying experience of having had a profound influence on national policy when prepared to adopt a more flexible policy (i.e., over the national compromise), and the growing realisation that most Danes, though far from being euro-enthusiasts, were not prepared to countenance backsliding either. On the other hand, factors resisting pro-integrationism included a passionate belief on the part of many members that the nature and direction of the current integration process was hopelessly reactionary and not susceptible to minor amelioration, a desire to distinguish the party from the social democrats and to avoid assimilation by that party, and the need to compete electorally with the still powerful Danish anti-EC lobby (which, incidentally, includes the Danish Communist Party). Against perceived 'pro-integrationists' such as John Iversen (who lost his European Parliamentary seat in June 1994) were traditionalists within the party led by Holger Nielsen, who maintained a more hostile attitude towards the EU. Policy has continued to develop and modify but every such development tends to be a compromise between different strands, designed to maintain a maximum of party unity.

Thus, the party opposed ratification of the Amsterdam Treaty in 1998 (55 per cent of Danes voted in favour), arguing that it would lead to a 'Fortress Europe' and to political union, and that it had weak environmental commitments. This referendum campaign was in part an uncomfortable experience for the party. It had to distinguish itself from rightwing parties, campaigning on an overtly xenophobic platform; it also had to contend with the fact that a minority within the SF – including about one-third of delegates to the annual party conference, and around a half of the parliamentary group – supported ratification of Amsterdam and were permitted to campaign for a 'yes' vote. Although both wings made strenuous efforts to unite in the wake of the referendum, the party itself admits that votes at the 1998 Party Conference reflect the fact that 'there are differing opinions as to whether and to what extent a kind of [European] integration can be accepted' (Socialist People's Party (SF), 1998, 2). The 1999 European election manifesto again emphasised those aspects of EU policy that all SF members could agree upon – opposition to a federal United States of Europe, opposition to NATO expansion, calls for stronger environmental and social policies – but also offered concessions to the more pro-integrationist elements within the party. European co-operation was heralded as 'necessary' in dealing with many problems that defied national frontiers. The EU was recognised as 'the most important framework of future co-operation in Europe', and the party supported EU enlargement on the basis that the new member states should be admitted to the full rights of the existing member states (Socialist People's Party, 1998). Nielsen (1996 and 2001) has argued that the disappointing SF performance in the European Parliamentary elections of 1994 and 1999 (it polled 8.6 and 7.1 per cent, respectively, whereas the largely left-of-centre anti-EU popular movements polled 25.5 and 23.4 per cent respectively) reflect the damaging impact of party splits and loss of policy coherence. In 1994, the performance might have been even worse but for the charismatic candidature of Lilly Gyldenkilde who won the party's only seat. In 1999, the top two positions on the party's electoral list were divided between an anti-integrationist (who retained the only European Parliamentary seat) and a more pro-integrationist candidate (who lost).

In 2000, the SF campaigned against the single currency, arguing that the euro posed a threat to national sovereignty and to the Scandinavian welfare state model. It argued that the single currency project was 'built on non-solidarity principles, principles that will lead to less welfare and more inequality' (Socialist People's Party (SF), 2000, 2). However, rather than emphasising a positive alternative to the single currency, as was the case with the Swedish Left Party (see below), for example, the SF found itself arguing defensively. It emphasised that 'SF rejects a fight against the EMU that is based on nationalistic self-sufficiency' and that 'a rejection of the EMU is not a rejection of European co-operation' (Socialist People's Party (SF), 2000, 3). It also found itself arguing against the claim that a 'No' vote would leave Denmark isolated, even pointing to the agreement between Denmark and the EU to link the value of the Danish currency to that of the euro as proof that this would not be the case. On this occasion, SF was on the winning side; 53.3 per cent of voters rejected the euro (Buch and Hansen, 2002, 15; Qvortrup, 2001, 190–1).

The euro referendum campaign underlines one of the key paradoxes of the SF's slow evolution towards a most 'Euro-optimist' position (this expression was coined by Christensen, 1996), namely that such a position might not necessarily be a vote-winner for a small party. In actual fact, the party has had an electorally disappointing decade and a half since the late 1980s. Its share of the popular vote in the late 1980s was around 13 per cent. By the general election of 2001, this had fallen to a mere 6.4 per cent. The party that had been regarded as a model success story and a blueprint to follow by its Finnish and Swedish sister-parties at the beginning of their own transformations in the early 1990s, began the twenty-first century as the least successful of the three Nordic EU Left parties. Of course, Danish politics in general had moved to the right; Denmark alone of the three EU Nordic member states had a rightwing government at the time of writing. And there are other reasons for the poor showing of the SF than divisions over Europe. Nevertheless, such divisions – and the failure to capitalise on widespread discontent with the neo-liberal agenda associated with EU integration – have contributed to an apparent loss of direction and momentum. In actual fact, a more 'Euro-sceptical' approach might pay greater electoral dividends, in the short term at least. Writing of the single currency referendum campaign, Marcussen and Zolner (2001, 398) argue that 'on the No side, all spokespersons did extremely well. Both the Socialist People's Party (Holger K. Nielsen) and the Danish People's Party (Pia Kjaersgaard) would have gained extra seats in parliament if the referendum had been coupled with a general election.' Given the fact that most SF voters tend to be very wary of European integration, and that a Euro-sceptical approach may also be attractive to disillusioned social democrat voters, too rapid an evolution of party policy in the opposite direction might split the party, lose it votes, and undermine its identity vis-à-vis the social democrats.

3.7 The Finnish Left Alliance (VAS)

The Finnish VAS has its roots in the Finnish Communist Party (SKP), which fought every election held in Finland from the end of the Second World War until the start of the 1990s under the banner of its political alliance, the Finnish People's Democratic League (SKDL). The latter included a number of non-Communists, such as leftwing socialists, although it never succeeded in its aim of becoming a 'broad front' that included 'bourgeois democratic' elements committed to progressive change. In their 1980s study of the integration of the SKP into the political life of modern Finland, Borg and Paastela (1983) highlight several facts that are essential to bear in mind when considering the historical background to the emergence of the Left Alliance and the evolution of its policy on European integration. The first point concerns the nature of post-war Finland itself. The country was not merely neutral in military terms; it was almost unique among capitalist countries in consistently pursuing a policy of friendly relations with the USSR. Indeed, Western strategists coined the term 'Finlandisation' as a somewhat contemptuous description of the alleged process by which the USSR sought to detach democratic capitalist countries from the Western camp and convert them into part of a neutralised semi-buffer zone. This meant that anti-Soviet and anti-Communist rhetoric were never really an option for the bourgeois parties in post-1945 Finland, and indeed anti-Communism had all but been abandoned by the mid-1960s. The SKP was not really taunted about human rights abuses in the USSR and Eastern Europe as virtually no Finnish party took a stand on such issues. And the question of European integration did not really arise until the collapse of the USSR and allied regimes at the end of the 1980s forced a fundamental rethink of Finnish foreign policy.

A second point is that the Communists and their allies in the SKDL participated in coalition governments in Finland in 1944–48, 1966–71, 1975–76, and from 1977 onwards. As Borg and Paastela (1983, 105) point out, they were present in coalition governments more than all other Western European communist parties put together. Moreover, this participation was not confined to left-of-centre coalitions with the Social Democrats, but would also include participation in coalition with some of the bourgeois political parties. This partly reflected a conscious decision on the part of the Finnish political establishment to secure political stability through Communist integration into the political mainstream. It also reflected a decision on the part of a majority of the Finnish Communists to abandon 'maximalism' and seek acceptance as a fully legitimate party of government, even at the risk of becoming increasingly defensive and moderate in its tactics and demands. Thus, when Arter describes the Finnish Left Alliance as having become 'one of the least radical of all the West European post-communist parties' (Arter, 2002, 3), he is in fact describing a situation that has been a long time in the making.

A third important point to bear in mind is that the Finnish communist movement has long suffered from acute fragmentation. In the late 1960s, the party split into a majority and a minority faction. These have sometimes been characterised as 'Eurocommunist' (majority) and 'Stalinist' (minority), but the situation was always more complex than that. Differences between the two factions included arguments over what exactly should be the basis for communist participation in coalition government, how distinctive the communists should be from the Social Democrats and, later, how the movement should react to European integration. The split in the movement was quite serious – with each faction having its own congresses, recognised leaders, separate electoral lists, etc. Indeed, in the mid-1970s, Finnish communists achieved the unique position of being both in the coalition government and in the opposition at one and the same time. From 1986, the SKDL would act as an electoral umbrella for the Eurocommunist majority, with the hardline minority fielding their own candidates under the banner of the Democratic Alternative.

A final point that is relevant in the present context is that the Finnish Communist Party had been, along with the French and the Italian, one of the most significant of Western Communist parties in the post-war period. It was actually the largest party in Finland at the end of the 1950s and remained a party of more than 20 per cent of the vote until the beginning of the 1970s. During the 1970s it slipped to between 15 and 20 per cent and the rightwards drift of Finnish politics in the 1980s saw it slip further to between 10 and 15 per cent (for both factions together) by the end of that decade.

In other words, by the end of the 1980s, this was a party that was accepted as a part of the political establishment and a legitimate government partner, but which had precious few real achievements to show for its years in coalition governments. It was a party that did not suffer from the intense Cold War anti-communism that affected its sister-parties elsewhere in Western Europe, but did suffer from an acute crisis of ideological identity – specifically over the question of how, if at all, it differed from the Social Democrats. It was, moreover, an ageing party that had seen its electoral support halved within a generation and that was badly factionalised. Finally, in common with all other Finnish political parties, it saw the international realities that had governed Finland's foreign policy and its detachment from the processes of European integration changed utterly at the end of the 1980s. In short, it was a party that was anxious for a formula that would allow it to rejuvenate and renew itself – and which had not really participated in the sort of debates over European integration that had consumed the energies of other communist and left parties.

This was the background to the birth of the Left Alliance (VAS) as a new political party in which both wings of the fragmented Finnish communist movement, along with non-communists, could participate. VAS was founded in May 1990, was led for the first eight years of its existence by a non-communist (Claes Andersson), and has sought to carve out a distinctive niche for itself as a party of the non-social democratic left under the slogan 'Red Politics as a means to a Green and Just Future.' The extent of its success in clearly redefining its identity is, however, hotly contested. In Denmark and Norway, where Green parties have had very limited electoral success, the Left parties have successfully positioned themselves as 'red-green' parties of the post-materialist type, appealing to white-collar and educated voters. In both Finland and Sweden, however, electorally significant Green parties have challenged the Left parties for the so-called post-materialist vote. In southern Finland, especially, the Greens have been rather more successful than VAS at representing the 'new politics'. VAS remains, to a much greater extent than the Danish SF, for example, a blue-collar party, strong amongst the poorest and most marginalised, and divided over the question of class politics. Its attempts to position itself as a contender for the Green vote by opposing nuclear power stations, for example, has brought it into conflict with trade union supporters who are more concerned with job losses than with environmental questions. Moreover, the birth of the new party was somewhat spoiled by splits with hardliners. Nevertheless, the party leadership managed to convey clearly its desire to break with the past when it condemned the USSR over the spilling of blood in Lithuania in January 1991 and called for freedom for the Baltic States. Indeed, the Finnish President, mindful of traditional Finnish non-interference in Soviet affairs, actually advised the VAS leadership to tone down its language! (Arter, 1991b, 400) In parallel with developments elsewhere on the West European left during the 1980s and early 1990s – for example, within the PCI – the VAS leadership sought to redefine the nature of left politics. A party programme, adopted at the 1995 Party Congress, defined the party as belonging to a so-called 'third left'. The argument was that the 'first left' was essentially the bourgeois democratic left that had developed out of the French revolution and was concerned with political rights (e.g. universal suffrage); the 'second left' was the working-class movement (social democratic and communist) that developed out of the industrial revolution. The time was now appropriate, in the developed (post-)industrial countries, for a 'third left' that prioritised individual freedom, rooted in economic democracy, social solidarity, and a model of development that is 'humanely and environmentally sustainable' (Left Alliance (VAS), 1995a, 8).

Since 1995, VAS has joined Rainbow coalition governments in Finland with both social democrats and conservatives. Its electoral support has stabilised at around 10 per cent of the vote (10.9 per cent in 1999), but the party now struggles to point to any policy achievement that it can claim as its own, and it is moreover riddled with dissent over the policy compromises that have kept the government afloat. One potentially major cause of division within the new party is certainly policy towards European integration.

Finland applied to join the EU in March 1992. It did so at a time when both Sweden and Finland were experiencing the worst economic crisis in their post-war history, with rising unemployment, rising state debt and cuts in welfare spending. In the Finnish case, the collapse of the Soviet market for Finnish exports added to the country's problems and helped to convince many Finns that the only way out of their economic crisis was for the country to turn towards Western Europe. (Indeed, economic development in the late 1990s would be driven by exports of electro-technical goods, towards the EU market in large part). The Finnish application to join the EU saw VAS split over the issue. Initially, it has tried to 'fudge' the issue of EU membership. Its campaign programme for the 1991 elections had said little beyond promising a membership consultation, calling for a referendum on the question of Finland's membership of the EU, and stating rather vacuously that 'more facts and information, based on investigation, will be needed before final solutions can be made [*sic*]' (Left Alliance (VAS), 1990, 10). A June 1993 policy statement on the matter declared the party to be 'highly critical towards Finland's joining the EC'. At the same time, it declared that the party 'considers European integration as a positive phenomenon', and promised not to attempt to obstruct the membership negotiations but to try to help achieve 'the best possible result acceptable to the party and the majority of Finnish people'. Whilst repeating familiar and entirely sensible Nordic concerns about the threat to the Nordic welfare model and the lack of democracy within the EU, as well as the perceived threat to Finnish military neutrality, VAS continued to articulate a seemingly contradictory position, stating that 'on the one hand the Community needs more power to make decisions on minimum standards concerning for example environmental and social policy', and yet expressing reservations about granting the European Parliament greater powers (Left Alliance (VAS), 1993, 1–3). Two of its MPs demanded a clear rejection of the EU. However, the VAS party board decided in March 1994 against an anti-EU stand by twenty-seven votes to sixteen. The referendum on EU membership in October 1994 saw the party badly divided and when the Finnish Parliament voted on ratification of the EU accession treaty in November 1994, twelve VAS MPs voted in favour and seven voted against (Arter, 2002, 8).

Three points can be made at this stage. First, VAS did not carry quite the same legacy of strong opposition to EU integration as its sister-parties elsewhere in the Nordic region. That said, alone amongst Finnish parties a clear majority of its voters opposed EU membership, and a substantial section of the party felt that membership threatened to undermine democracy, welfare and social justice and to exacerbate social and regional imbalances. Second, the party leadership had a very pragmatic view of the membership question. Above all, the leadership was not prepared to allow an anti-EU stand to undermine the party's acceptability as a government partner or to confine it to a political ghetto. Party system factors thus played a large role in facilitating policy evolution on the EU issue. Third, careful management of the issue was essential to avoid party splits.

In March 1995 VAS formed a coalition government with social democrats, conservatives and Greens. The decision to enter the so-called Rainbow government was clearly a difficult one, and was taken by 47 votes to 25 at a joint meeting of the Party Council and the parliamentary group. The party openly admitted that:

> it wasn't easy for [VAS] to accept the common Governmental programme. The new government will freeze pensions (except the lowest), unemployment fees and subsidies for families with children as well as Finnish foreign development aid for year 1996. On the other hand the Government is cutting strong subsidies to the private companies and agriculture. The taxation on capital and ecological wasting will increase. (Left Alliance (VAS), 1995b, 5)

Many of the cuts were of course necessitated by the explicit commitment, contained in the Rainbow government programme, to prepare Finland for participation in the single currency (Government of Finland, 1995). Entry into the government effectively sealed the party majority's acceptance of 'an active role in the European Union based on the idea to develop the EU as a union between the member states. Finland will be a non-aligned country, outside military blocks and possible international military operations'. And the party bluntly gave its rationale for government participation: that it was better to try to steer the government from within towards more socially just policies, and that participation would make cooperation with the social democrats and trade union unity both easier (Left Alliance (VAS), 1995b, 5–6). In essence, the leadership argued that the party would be 'more critical than the others' in EU matters, seeking to get the best deal possible, whilst burying any rejectionist strategy. In November 1995, the Party Council adopted a new EU policy document that set out its priorities for the 1996 Intergovernmental Conference (IGC). Many of the measures proposed were widely shared across the left/right political divide: combating fraud, streamlining EU bureaucracy, making the EU more accountable, strengthening the role of the nation-state and retaining the national veto in foreign and security policy. Some proposals were couched in language that no social democratic party worthy of the name could object to: the need for the EU to promote greater gender equality, to fight racism and to protect the environment. Interestingly, now that VAS members sat in the European Parliament, the party seemingly moderated its stand on granting that body extra powers. It now urged that both the European Parliament and national parliaments should have the right to initiate EU legislation, and that the European Parliament should have increased powers vis-à-vis the European Commission. Whilst expressing concern about the likely effects of participation in the single currency on employment prospects, the party did not rule participation out; rather, it called for 'more information' (Left Alliance (VAS), 1996). The overriding goal was clearly to preserve party unity in the face of two seemingly contradictory facts: that the party was fully signed up to a government that was moving inexorably towards participation in the single currency, despite the fact that its performance on the employment front was deeply disappointing to VAS members and voters after one year in office; and that, as the party's international bulletin admitted, 'one quarter of [VAS] supporters is for [EU] membership, three quarters are against' (Left Alliance (VAS), 1996, 4).

In 1997 the VAS leadership skilfully linked the issue of participation in government to party approval of the single currency. Although this would be resented by opponents of the EU, such as the MEP Esko Seppänen (whose outstandingly good personal performance in the European Parliamentary elections proved that there was potential electoral mileage in an anti-integration stand), the tactic enabled the leadership to win a ballot of party members in December 1997: 52.4 per cent voted to accept the single currency. The VAS chairperson, Claes Andersson, personally opposed the single currency but was also on record as declaring that: 'I have become gradually more convinced that a political party that is not able or willing to bear the responsibilities of government slowly forfeits its credibility in the eyes of others, as well as losing its self-confidence and dynamism' (Arter, 2002, 8 and 16). This encapsulates the dilemma faced by the party. It was anxious to avoid being boxed into a political ghetto by adopting a hardline stand on an issue of paramount national importance. Yet, having turned its back on the option of seeking votes through becoming a vehicle for the anti-EU protest movement, and having reaffirmed its governmental vocation even at the risk of alienating a sizable section of its membership and electorate by fudging its EU policy, it would struggle to establish its identity. At the same time, there is no doubt that EU membership helped to revive the Finnish economy, which grew at around 5 per cent per annum from 1995 onwards.

In 1998 the young and popular Suvi-Anne Siimes, who would help to project a more modern, youthful and feminist image, succeeded Andersson as VAS leader (and as a cabinet minister). The outcome of the 1999 general election was slightly disappointing, however: the party failed to advance and actually lost two of its twenty-two seats, despite four years in government (the VAS share of the national vote fell marginally from 11.2 per cent to 10.9 per cent). The Finnish Greens polled their best result (7.3 per cent) since their foundation in 1987. However, the Greens in Finland, alone amongst Nordic Green parties, cannot be described as anti-EU. VAS may face pressure from the electoral competition to be more 'modern', feminist, environmentalist and radical in defence of the poor. Yet, despite the fact that almost half of its current parliamentary group might be described as former hardliners or anti-EU integrationists, it did not conclude that the lesson of the 1999 elections was that it should veer towards a more EU-critical stance. In fact, the party lost little time in renewing its commitment to a second Rainbow coalition government – by a much bigger majority (sixty-one members of the Party Council and parliamentary group voting in favour, only eight voting against) than in 1995. The party outlined its priorities in the new government as being to fight for full employment, to campaign against poverty and discrimination, and to argue for stronger regional policies.

Within a few months of the formation of the second Rainbow coalition, VAS suffered a disappointing result in the European Parliamentary elections. Its support dropped to 9.1 per cent and it lost one of its two MEPs. Significantly, the only remaining MEP was arch critic of European integration, Esko Seppänen. Raunio (2001a, 100) points out that turn-out in this election in Finland was a record low of just 31.4 per cent, and partly attributes this to the rhetoric of the politicians who downplayed the importance of the European Parliament. Given that VAS voters tend to be amongst the most critical in their appraisal of European integration, it is perhaps not unreasonable to conclude that many simply stayed at home on this occasion.

The dilemmas facing the party as it struggles to steer a coherent course and to define a clear political space for itself were well illustrated by a frank exchange of views that took place in the pages of its international bulletin, *Modern Left*, in April 2000 – on the tenth anniversary of the party's foundation. One contributor admitted that VAS 'still partly suffers from its past in the form of a national-populist opposition which it did not manage to keep outside the party. As a result of this inner division the party is not always able to formulate its line in ... extremely important matters, such as EU membership.' Another contributor, the Finnish academic Jan-Otto Andersson, admitted that membership of the Rainbow coalition government bound the party

> to a programme of continued cuts of the welfare state and to full integration into the EU, including the EMU. This increased the tensions within the party. The chance to take the lead of a more or less populistic offensive against the austerity and market-oriented policies was forfeited. [VAS] was not able to put its stamp on any particular government policy. The recovery of the economy succeeded relatively well, but mass unemployment lingered on and economic inequalities tended to grow despite the efforts of the party. Its role tended to be that of a minor partner to the Social Democrats.

Andersson then identified what he saw as the three main tendencies within the party: a 'populist' left that found support amongst the economically marginalised and those left behind by processes of globalisation and European integration; a 'modern' left that was supported by trade unionists and workers who had benefited from 'the remarkable strengthening of the international competitiveness of Finnish industry'; and a red/green and feminist 'third' left that has its supporters amongst women, young people and intellectuals. Obviously, the first constituency tends to be most hostile towards European integration the other two groups more open to policy change. As Andersson put it, 'how to accommodate these tendencies within the party has become a seemingly unending endeavour' (Left Alliance (VAS), 2000, 6–7).

Obviously, there are some aspects of European policy that unite all sections of the party. In particular, all can agree on the need: to defend Finnish neutrality and to work for a demilitarised EU; to oppose NATO membership, reduce Finland's defence budget and retain the national veto over foreign and security policy; for stronger solidarity between Europe and the developing countries; for strong environmental protection. However, in many other respects, the EU issue has the latent potential to wreak the sort of havoc internally as it has done with the British Conservative party, for example. The European debate will therefore require careful management by the party leadership in the years ahead. The points of divergence are well illustrated by a comparison of the official party position at the start of the twenty-first century with the analyses offered by its MEP.

Party General Secretary Ralf Sund spelled out the official position on the single currency in 1999, when he argued that the advent of the euro had been 'principally positive'. His reasoning was that under the old system of national currencies, the currency of a small open economy like Finland's was determined by the international capital market, and monetary and exchange rate policies were regulated by a Finnish central bank that was 'the most independent [i.e. outside democratic control] Central Bank in Europe'. Rather glossing over the realities of how the European Central Bank is set to operate, he argued that, with the euro, 'the essential thing is that [the] left has better starting points and possibilities to promote the objectives that are important for the ideas and politics of the left. Inside the old Finnish economic policy paradigm this was practically impossible' (Left Alliance (VAS), 1999, 5–7). The 2001 Party Congress adopted a platform for the 2001–04 period that lamented the indiscriminate pursuit of the neo-liberal mantra of competition and market forces within the EU, at the expense of social and ecological matters, and argued that 'bearing this in mind, we can conclude that a public discussion on a constitution for the European Union may not be such a bad idea after all'. Such a constitution should simplify and democratise decision-making procedures and move the EU from being a 'union of business alone' towards being above all a 'people's union' (Left Alliance (VAS), 2001, 27). This represents a remarkable step towards a reformist, though far from federalist or ardently integrationist, position. The document also called for greater powers for the European Parliament, and for a clear delineation of EU and national competencies. It endorsed enlargement of the EU to include Eastern and Central Europe as 'essential', adding that 'a successful enlargement entails an increase in security and economic stability, a reduction of differences in prosperity and greater responsibility for environmental issues and an increase in and enrichment of cultural interaction'. Given existing disparities, the party declared itself willing to accept a transitional phase during which the new member states would gradually adapt to realities such as the free movement of labour, and warned against the phenomenon of social dumping or the temptation of employers to use workers from the new member states to undercut the wages and social rights of workers in the existing member states.

Esko Seppänen MEP adopts an altogether more critical approach to European integration. VAS's sole representative in the 1999-2004 European Parliament declares himself convinced that the EU is 'a manifestation of global capitalism ... [which] has no social dimension whatsoever ... and is only following its own rational logic by converging towards highest profits and lowest taxes'. His own most important goal, he has written, is to fight for an 'anti-federalist Europe with full employment' (Seppänen, 2000a). Moreover, Seppänen is convinced that both the European Parliament and the constitutional Convention of the Future of Europe are 'unrepresentative' and that Finnish democratic standards are under threat from the European Parliament. Democracy, he believes, can only exist at the level of the nation-state; moreover, 'democracy should be [about] safeguarding the rights of minorities. Many nation states are minorities in the European Union and need democratic protection' (Seppänen, 2002).

In a speech in Estonia in October 2001, Seppänen completely rejected the positive evaluation of the single currency given by his own party general secretary. He decried the undemocratic nature of the European Central Bank, the imposition of monetary and economic policy on Finland 'from outside, by foreign decision-makers' and the negative effects on employment and welfare standards of the Stability Pact. Most significantly, he explicitly attacked the Rainbow government in which two ministers belonging to his own party sit, accusing it of political dishonestly in misleading the Finnish people about the nature of monetary union. That government and Prime Minister Lipponen were accused of leading 'Finland away from its former political neutrality ... Finland is prepared to give up its independence and become a state in a federation with supranational decision-making: political decisions are made depending on the size of the population of each state. EMU is a part of the federalist project of the European Social Democrats. [The] EU is being turned into a federal state. The NATO project is connected to it.' Moreover, 'the biggest problem from the point of view of a small country is the lack of democracy in the federal state and the weakening of democracy on a national level. That is what EMU represents' (Seppänen, 2001). Seppänen has also criticised the process of EU enlargement as potentially imposing huge costs on the peoples of the existing member states, involving the exploitation of workers from the new member states, and acting as a spur either to greater federalism or to a shift in decision-making power away from smaller states to the larger (Seppänen, 2000b).

Clearly, there are radically different attitudes towards European integration within VAS. These differences are rooted in the historic divisions within the Finnish communist movement that have been carried over into VAS, even if many of the members of the old party have not joined. The differences over EU policy are also bound up with many of the fundamental, indeed existential, questions that confront the party now – how to give expression to a radical left politics in an era of globalisation and loss of national economic control, how to participate in consensus politics and coalition government and yet maintain a distinctive identity, how to avoid assimilation to the larger social democratic party. It is entirely possible that European integration may be the terrain upon which decisive struggles over the party's future take place, especially in the light of the national and European elections that are scheduled for May 2003 and June 2004 respectively. It is likely that a fundamental reappraisal of party strategy will follow the Finnish electorate's verdict on the second Rainbow coalition government. The debate over Europe will be central to that reappraisal.

3.8 The Left Party of Sweden (V)

The Swedish V is less obviously a new left party of the post-communist variety than its Danish or Finnish counterparts, having grown 'organically' out of the old Swedish Communist Party. That has not prevented it from pursuing an effective adaptation strategy that has seen its electoral support rise beyond anything it gained previously. Central to its relative success has been its strong opposition to European integration and its determination to offer a voice to those Swedes, including leftwing social democrats, who see in European integration a threat to the Swedish model of welfare provision, social justice and democracy.

The Swedish Communist Party changed its name to the Left Party-Communists in 1967. Throughout the 1970s and 1980s the party achieved very modest electoral success, usually hovering just above the 4 per cent barrier that determines whether or not a party gains seats in the Swedish Parliament. On occasions, the party relied on the so-called 'comrade vote' of sympathetic social democrats to lift it above the 4 per cent hurdle, it being in the social democrats' interest to have a party in parliament that could provide external support to social democratic governments. Thus, it achieved representation in every parliament since 1970, although it was never formally accepted into coalition government. In May 1990, the party voted (by a narrow majority of 136 to 133 congress delegates) to change its name to the Left Party (V), having turned down a proposal to restyle itself as 'Left Socialists'. Although the collapse of the regimes in Eastern Europe naturally affected the Swedish communists, it is important to point out that the decision to change to a post-communist party was not seen as a sign of weakness. In fact, the party's 1988 election result (5.8 per cent and 21 seats in parliament) was its best in a decade, the party's membership was stable, and there was little sense of crisis or internal pressure for change. Rather, the party leadership perceived that an evolution into a post-communist, 'new left' type party offered the best chance of capitalising on a number of promising developments.

The party had long been committed to a reformist or Eurocommunist path. (Although many remained within V throughout the 1990s who still described themselves as communists, it would be extremely misleading to take this as a sign of nostalgia for the USSR or neo-Stalinism. More often than not, the 'communists' were young radicals who were anxious that an anti-capitalist perspective should not be lost, and that the new party should not become indistinguishable from the social democrats.) This reformist path also reflected the fact that the period since the 1970s had seen a transformation in the demographic profile of the party. From being a largely working-class party in the 1950s and 1960s, strong in the big cities and in the depressed ore-mining areas of the north, it had gone on to attract white-collar support in central and southern Swedish towns in the 1970s and 1980s. A huge growth in public sector workers in Sweden had also contributed to the change in the nature of the party; by 1990, it was largely a middle-class party whose average member was radical and leftist but unsentimental about Leninist ideological baggage (Berglund, 1989, 85, argues that it was largely middle class by the end of the 1960s). By 1990, the party leadership sensed that conditions were right for a period of potential expansion: the rightwards drift of the Swedish social democrats created a pool of disillusioned social democrat voters on that party's left flank; the opportunity existed to consolidate educated and white-collar support; and the decline in traditional working-class politics had been replaced by what Arter refers to as a 'pragmatic radical left' (Arter, 1991a, 61–4).

For decades, the party had portrayed itself as a necessary anchor to the left of the social democrats, dragging that party back from the right. In the 1990s, this argument, that a strong Left party was the surest way of guaranteeing that the social democrats continued to deliver social democracy, and not simply neo-liberalism, continued to be made. Of course, this raises the question of whether, as the social democrats become neo-liberals, the former communists are now simply becoming social democrats. It also poses the difficult strategic question of how V, supporting minority social democratic governments in return for certain concessions, can actually prevent a strategic embrace of neo-liberalism by the SAP (social democrats). The party certainly sees itself as very distinct from the social democrats. Officially it defines its identity as resting on 'four cornerstones': it is a 'socialist labour party' committed to the 'interests of the working class', a feminist party committed to fighting patriarchy, an environmental party that is opposed to nuclear energy and committed to renewable energy sources and sustainable development, and an international party that is working for 'a just economic world order' and to the fight for refugees' rights and against racism. Its internationalism also involved a rejection of Sweden's membership of the EU. 'Our goal is for Sweden to leave the EU. Instead we want to develop international cooperation between free and independent nations' (Left Party (V), 2002).

Indeed the last theme would become increasingly important, as the party tasted growing success in the 1990s. During that decade, the party hit upon what seemed to many to be a winning formula that distinguished it from the SAP, motivated many new voters to embrace it, and allowed it to contest neo-liberal economic policies of the SAP majority at both the strategic and ideological levels. This 'magic formula' was total opposition to European integration. (As in Finland, the end of the Cold War in 1990 has lifted the 'taboo' on discussing Swedish neutrality and stimulated a debate about the pros and cons of EU membership.)

From the outset, Left Party opposition to European integration was not couched in the old language of the communist movement – denouncing the EU as an anti-Soviet capitalist conspiracy or advocating national paths to socialism. Rather, the Left Party leadership, anxious to emulate the perceived success of their Danish counterparts in building a radical party of the post-materialist red/green left, emphasised defence of democracy, protection of the environment, and maintenance of the Nordic region's strong public sector and high levels of welfare provision. The strategy of presenting its arguments, not in the negative language of the so-called hardline communist parties but in the context of a softer and more caring image, was strengthened by the election of Gudrun Schyman as party leader in

1993. She gained a reputation as compassionate and likeable and in 1996 V defined itself as a feminist party. Its strategy seems to have appealed to women workers in the public sector in particular, and this section of the electorate also proved distrustful of the effects of EU membership.

As Christensen (1996, 533–7) argues, all Swedish parties lacked a clear policy on the EU issue until the late 1980s. When negotiations on the formation of a European Economic Area agreement started in June 1989, the Left Party argued for an open and democratic Europe where each nation kept its sovereignty. It supported economic co-operation but opposed EU membership and, above all, the Maastricht version of European integration, which it saw as enshrining a narrow neo-liberalism. In June 1991, the Swedish social democratic government announced its intention of applying for EU membership and the debate intensified considerably. In 1994, V campaigned energetically against Swedish membership of the EU in the country's referendum, as did the Swedish Greens. However, once the Swedish people (narrowly) voted in favour of membership, the party announced it would respect the result, vote for ratification of the Treaty in parliament, and work within the European Parliament. It thus sought to define a distinctive line that involved clear and decisive opposition to integrationism, without allowing the issue to assume the status of a dogma or to lead to its own isolation in parliament, where V continued to hope for a coalition government with the social democrats. Once again, as in Finland, party system factors are important in understanding the dynamics, direction and extent of policy change. Amongst the Nordic Left parties, the Norwegian Left Socialists would change least of all, the outcome of that country's referenda on EU membership having effectively removed the issue from the political agenda, whilst the Danish and Finnish parties would change most. The implication of this argument, formulated by Christensen (1996), is that V's EU policy might undergo further evolution and moderation were the party to formally join in a government coalition.

The strongly anti-EU policy of V has clearly paid electoral dividends. In 1994, it increased its support to 6.2 per cent, largely on the back of anti-EU campaigning. It emphasised three main themes in its call for Swedish voters to reject the EU: the threat to employment that the EU's neo-liberal policies posed, the threat to public spending and to the welfare state, and the question of democracy and accountability (Arter, 2002, 11–12). Some 90 per cent of V voters rejected EU membership in the November 1994 referendum. The Swedish people as a whole only approved membership by a narrow majority (52.3 per cent voted in favour) and, within a year, polls were suggesting that many of those who had voted Yes were having second thoughts. In the 1995 elections to the European Parliament in Sweden, V polled an impressive 12.9 per cent (the equally anti-EU Greens polling 17.2 per cent) and it retained 12 per cent in the 1998 general election. The party sought to tap into widespread voter concerns about the failure of promises of lower prices and lower unemployment to materialise, the introduction (by the Social Democrats in government) of budget cuts to reduce state debt, and the loosening of pollution controls. Given the strong levels of support for the Left Party amongst public sector workers, threatened cuts to the public sector that boosted job insecurity tended to increase the party's electoral standing.

The party's opposition to the single currency project was spelled out in a document that its MEP, Jonas Sjöstedt, presented at a New European Left Forum working group on the 1996 Intergovernmental Conference in April 1996 (Left Party (V), 1996 – from which all quotes are taken). Emphasising the political aspects of the single currency policy, he pointed out that the model of European Monetary Union pursued in the Maastricht Treaty (e.g., a Central Bank independent of democratic control) amounted to 'putting a detailed economic policy into a country's constitution'. He added that this 'is hardly done in any democratic state'. 'The model that the EMU creates which separates economy and politics is in itself a political model' – a model long pursued by the free market right. The single currency project, at least in the form it was actually taking, thus amounted to a triumph for rightwing ideology and a defeat for the left's insistence that democracy is not real democracy unless democratic control is extended to economic policy-making. Moreover, EMU was attacked as being 'socially unacceptable' in that it involved attacking social security systems and increasing unemployment. And of course its logical linkage to the project of political federalism, and an undermining of democratic control over politics, was underlined.

The V party position was further elaborated by highlighting the party's concerns that a central economic argument produced in favour of monetary union – that it would impose greater stability through forcing 'good economic policies on states' – reflected an elitist, technocratic approach to capitalism. This approach was in conflict with the rights of peoples to elect governments that had other priorities – such as social justice and full employment. The party also saw in monetary union a major shift in power away from nation states to the EU, a federalist development that it opposed.

These fundamental objections to monetary union did not prevent V from supporting some proposed changes to the Amsterdam Treaty that seemed to it to be desirable. Thus, it called for a strengthening of the social part of the Treaty in two respects. First, social dumping should be ended by bringing minimum standards for workers under the rubric of majority voting. In other words, there should be no opt-out for countries like the UK on social policy. Second, it should be left to individual countries to build on these minimum standards. In other words, the EU should not be permitted to 'level down' workers' rights to the standards of the weakest states.

V spelled out its alternative to the neo-liberal EMU project as involving at least five elements:

1 Increased democratic control over international capital and financial markets through global agreements on rules for multinational companies and measures against international speculation. These would be bolstered by 'minimum levels of capital income tax' and 'increased public control over private financial institutes'.

2 Harmonisation of contracyclical financial policies to reduce unemployment within and without the EU. It was argued that the EU's trade surplus made larger sums of support and loans to Eastern Europe and North Africa possible, especially if the CAP was gradually dismantled.
3 Common programmes for trade union rights and social minimum standards within the EU were urged. Future World Trade Organisation agreements should also include social and ecological principles for global trade.
4 Co-ordination between EU countries for a shorter working day, which was deemed desirable for social and gender equality reasons quite apart from jobs creation considerations.
5 Environmental taxation and development, setting the principle of sustainability above that of competition.

Such a programme amounted to a fundamental rejection of neo-liberalism and, if implemented, would obviously result in the EU becoming a very different sort of Union from the market-driven and market-dominated beast it is at present. This raises the question of whether the EU *could* be transformed from within into a genuine social Europe, or whether withdrawal from the present EU is the best way forward. As argued in Chapter One, this is often a tactical and strategic dispute rather than a matter of principle. It is not fundamentally contradictory for a party such as V to fight for an alternative vision of how the EU might develop whilst, in the face of overwhelming evidence that this prospect is difficult if not impossible to realise, to campaign for withdrawal. In practical terms, it is of course possible that, as Sweden adjusts more and more to EU membership and levels of hostility to membership abate (assuming this happens), V will itself increasingly adjust to fighting for its alternative vision of Europe from within the existing EU framework.

It is difficult to over-emphasise how important the electoral success of the party's opposition to neo-liberal European integration during the 1990s was to its strategic orientation. It had not only survived the transition to post-communism, but had attracted the highest share of electoral support in its history. It had achieved this by identifying with those (especially in the public sector) who felt most threatened by neo-liberalism.

During the period 1994–98 Sweden was governed by a minority Social Democratic government that had struck up an informal alliance with the bourgeois Centre Party. Although both these parties are divided over the issue of European integration – and the SAP in particular has a sizable anti-integrationist wing represented by, amongst others, Britt Theorin – this government presided over Sweden's entry into the EU and many of its leading figures were in favour of the monetary union project. In the aftermath of its 1998 electoral success, the Left party was optimistic that it could draw the SAP to the left, into a coalition government with itself and the Greens, and away from the neo-liberal policies it had been pursuing. The worst-case scenario would have been the formation of Grand Coalition between the SAP and the centre-right to pursue unashamedly pro-integrationist policies. In the event, the outcome was a minority social democratic government, supported by the Left party and the Greens in opposition. Within the party, there were many who felt that the time was not yet right for a formal coalition: that the party was too insecure, too unaccustomed to its new electoral strength, and that it needed maximum room for manoeuvre to exploit its anti-integrationist vote-winning stand. Equally, there were many within the SAP and within Swedish bourgeois circles who felt that a SAP–V–Green formal coalition would scupper any chance of Sweden participating in the single currency and be a disaster from the point of view of European integration, and who were opposed to such a formula for this reason.

From 1998 to September 2002 V remained in opposition and thus maintained its independence as an actor, whilst, as already stated, supporting a minority SAP government. This strategy was to deliver mixed results. Although V acted as an occasional brake on more pro-integrationist tendencies within SAP and, together with that party's own anti-integrationists, ensured that Prime Minister Goran Persson was forced to adopt a more cautious 'wait-and-see' approach to joining the single currency that he probably would have preferred, it would not be the chief beneficiary of the policies pursued during those years. The party could take pride in the fact that unemployment fell during the years when the government 'tilted to the left', and that measures were taken to rebuild the social security system, to stop privatisations. Ultimately, as we will see, the Social Democrats would reap the rewards of such policies to a greater extent than V.

In 1999, V achieved a stunning result in the European elections when it polled 15.8 per cent, making it (briefly) the third largest party. The performance was all the more impressive when one considers the low turn-out (38.8 per cent) and the fact that opponents of European integration clearly abstained in greater numbers than supporters did (Johansson, 2001, 205). V was one of the few parties to concentrate on EU issues and, at a time of NATO bombings over Yugoslavia, it ran a strongly anti-militarist and pro-neutrality campaign, emphasising the threat to Sweden's neutrality that further European integration allegedly posed. According to Johansson (2001, 205), exit polls showed that the issues that Swedish voters ranked as being of top importance were, in order of ranking: peace in Europe, democracy in the EU, employment, social welfare, the economy, the environment, national independence, equality between men and women, EU defence, EMU, conditions for enterprise, agriculture, refugees/immigration, and, finally, EU enlargement. It can be readily seen that V's campaign was fully in tune with public opinion.

The 2000 Party Congress adopted a platform that declared that 'opposition to the undemocratic policies of the EU has strengthened [our] profile'. The platform went on to unambiguously emphasise the socialist nature of the party, and to counterpose this to the nature and effects upon Swedish society of European integration:

> The working-class movement, and more especially the trade union movement, have a key role as the driving force behind progressive change in society. Other movements may be just as important, indeed even more so in their specific area of operation, but they can never fulfill the same role in society as the working-class movement.

> Distinctiveness as to positions taken, self-confidence with respect to class and clarity in ideology all help to strengthen the capacity of the working-class movement to influence the process of change in society.
>
> The Left Party is today the only nation-wide party to call for a socialist transformation of society. Currently this is also the most significant ideological difference between the Social Democratic party and us...
>
> In Sweden EU membership and policies adapting the country to EMU have strongly contributed to the growing power of capital. The deregulation of currency, trade and capital markets has underpinned the imbalance of power between national interests and those of capital. (Left Party (V), 2000)

The platform also rejected Sweden's membership of EMU and called for a transfer of power from the Bank of Sweden back to Parliament. Arguing that the EU 'is gradually assuming the constitution of a state with a common currency, co-ordinated foreign and refugee policies, a common army and increasingly harmonised fiscal policies', the platform pledged the Left Party to maintain 'its EU-critical position and its objective is that Sweden leaves the EU'. It also called for a referendum on EMU (which polls, at this stage, indicated would be rejected by a clear majority of voters). Indeed, in a speech to the Danish Socialist People's Party Congress in May 2000, Jonas Sjöstedt, Left Party MEP, accused the rightwing forces of running scared of a referendum on the single currency which, he argued, was faring so badly that 'even the Polish zloty and Ugandan shilling now seem hard currencies compared to the Euro'. In a highly significant passage he accused social democratic leaders such as Persson and Denmark's Nyrup Rasmussen or doing nothing to challenge or alter the neo-liberal nature of the single currency project. Going to the heart of the Left Party's disagreement with the social democrats he argued that:

> In the social democratic rhetoric for EMU, the single currency is often talked about as if it were created as a counter power to a more and more powerful capital, as a way to be able politically to handle the effects of internationalisation. But nothing could be more wrong. EMU's core is, instead, freedom for capital, the absence of political governance and permanent precedence of monetary goals over social aims. This is to capitulate to market liberalism, not to govern it. When the right in the EU unites with the social democrats around the monetarism of EMU this means that the social democrats have given up their fundamental ideas on an economic policy that differs from the predominant market liberalism. This is a capitulation that has nothing to do with internationalism. (Sjöstedt, 2000)

And yet, one of the ironies of politics is that the main beneficiary of the 'tilt to the left' in Sweden after 1998 was to be the very social democrats that Sjöstedt criticised. The run-up to the September 2002 general elections in Sweden was dominated by the spectre of a Europe-wide 'turn to the right'. After defeat of centre-left governments in France, Italy and Portugal, near-defeat in Germany, and the continuing rightwards drift of Blair's 'New Labour' government in the UK, commentators speculated that Sweden might be next in line. The elections saw the

SAP mount a vigorous defence of the Swedish welfare model against the bourgeois parties, especially the Conservative Moderate (M) party that campaigned for tax (and by implication spending) cuts. SAP also benefited from the fall in unemployment to just 4.3 per cent, one of the lowest rates in the EU. The September 2002 elections saw the left triumph over the right, but the big winner was the SAP, which took 40 per cent of the vote – its best performance in recent years. V's share of the vote fell to 8.3 per cent. That would have been a highly impressive performance at any point before 1998, but was a bitter disappointment after the electoral highs of 1998–99, and after the experience of supporting SAP in government since 1998. (The party suffered a further blow in early 2003 when, following media coverage of an apparent irregularity in her income tax returns, Gudrun Schyman resigned as leader. She was replaced by a three-woman collective leadership.)

In the aftermath of September 2002, Goran Persson ruled out offering V actual seats in cabinet, on the basis of the party's anti-Euro stance, but called for a renewal of the existing partnership 'with deeper co-operation'. That, in essence, was the only realistic course open to the Left Party. As 2002 drew to a close speculation was mounting that Persson would push for a referendum on the single currency in 2003/04 and strongly campaign to win his own party supporters around to a 'Yes' vote. V, together with the Greens, will of course lead the 'No' campaign. In the short, and perhaps medium, term, it is unlikely that there will be any major change in the party's general approach to European integration. The party's hostility towards the neo-liberalism that is at the heart of the EU reflects serious analysis and deep conviction; it is shared by the great majority of members and supporters; it had given the party a coherent political profile and a clear niche in the 'electoral market-place', bringing an increased share of the vote and some political influence. Should Swedes vote to reject the euro, the party's position may even be strengthened. Should they approve the euro by a small majority, there will still be many Swedish voters who are alienated from and suspicious of the federalist and integrationist project. A sudden abandonment of position, or a drift towards more incoherent policies (along Finnish VAS lines) does not necessarily make any sense. In the longer term, however, if Sweden joins the euro, V may well have to adjust to new realities and fight its battles for an alternative vision of Europe from within the EU, abandoning its pro-withdrawal rhetoric. It has already shown an ability to adjust to a changing political environment, and an unwillingness to box itself into a corner in a way that might impede its ability to adapt and survive, indeed thrive[1].

---

1 On 14 September 2003 Swedish voters rejected the euro by a decisive margin of 56.3% to 41.5% (with 2.2% abstaining by casting blank ballots). The Left Party had played a leading role in the campaign for a 'No' vote.

4
COMPARATIVE PERSPECTIVES

In the preceding chapters I have sought to provide a comprehensive picture of the evolution of the European policies of the Left parties, bearing in mind both the range of organisational, ideological, electoral and party system factors that have influenced policy formation and the wide range of analyses and prognoses that these parties have produced. In the next chapter I will return to this question of diversity and divergence, considering the future prospects for the Left parties on the European plane. In this chapter I wish to consider whether the Left parties' approaches to European integration (and the related question of globalisation of both economy and politics) are in any sense unique, or whether there is room for convergence with either of the other two main 'families' of parties that might be considered to be on the 'left of centre' in European politics, namely the Greens and the Social Democrats.

Of course, some – including some Green parties – argue that to be Green is to be neither left nor right, but beyond such divisions. Nevertheless, those European Green parties that have tended to be electorally successful have tended to be those that appealed to a left-of-centre electorate and assumed a left-of-centre profile; very often Green parties compete for both members and voters with the Left parties we have examined; and when Green parties have entered the governments of EU member states (e.g., Italy, France, Finland, Germany) or supported such governments from the opposition benches (e.g., Sweden), this has almost invariably been as part of some broad left-of-centre alliance or arrangement. For these reasons, I feel justified in considering the Green analyses of European integration in this context.

As regards the Social Democrats, well, some might argue that some such parties have abandoned any real claim on a left-of-centre identity and embraced the policies of neo-liberalism too uncritically. However, this is rarely the official position of any of the Left parties I have examined, almost all of which have at one time or another been involved in tactical or strategic alliances with their social democratic counterparts. Indeed, arguably the key existential question that Left parties face is how best to try to establish themselves as credible alternatives to the left of social democracy, attractive to disillusioned social democratic voters – by seeking to be the left conscience of social democracy in the context of broad alliances, or by declaring all-out political struggle against the'betrayal' perpetrated by the Social Democrats. Given that the former option risks loss of policy coherence and political identity and the latter risks political isolation and seeming irrelevance, it is useful to examine the broad thrust of Social Democratic policy on European integration as part of the present study.

Naturally, I do not have time or space to elaborate in any great detail on the evolution of Green or Social Democratic policy on European integration. However, even a brief summary of the main points of argument may help establish points of convergence and divergence with the Left parties.

The Greens and the European Union

As Bomberg comprehensively shows, the Greens have been to the fore of those political forces in Europe that have offered a highly critical analysis of the nature of the current process of European construction (Bomberg, 1998 – upon which the following summary draws heavily). That is not to say that all Green parties are opposed to European integration; but all are certainly critical of the forms which integration has taken in recent decades. In particular, they are critical of the centralised, bureaucratic and technocratic approaches that have characterised the process of European construction and of the prevalence of market forces in economic thinking. Bomberg points out that Green parties have drawn on five 'overlapping tenets' of Green thought in mapping their alternative vision of Europe: decentralisation, ecological sustainability, community/grassroots democracy, the 'global local nexus' and diversity.

It is perhaps not surprising that Greens should wholeheartedly embrace concepts of *decentralisation* and subsidiarity. The Green parties have drawn extensively on the European federalist tradition, seeing the post-war European nation-states as an aberration which did not accord with the diverse identities of the peoples of Europe and which led to cultural and political paralysis. Indeed, this intellectual inheritance has allowed something of a rapprochement between Green parties and some of the more progressive or centre-left regionalist and micro-nationalist parties, such as Plaid Cymru, the Scottish National Party and some Basque nationalists, culminating in the joint group they formed together in the European Parliament after the 1999 European elections. Greens have argued since the 1970s for enhanced participation in smaller political units. In a similar vein, the Young European Federalists have called since the 1970s for a federation of European regions as a way of enhancing democracy and the quality of life; this emphasis on democracy and empowerment has distinguished the young European federalists from both economic functionalists and elitists who sought to build the European Union from the top-down. Under Petra Kelly in Germany, the Green party adopted these federalist ideas in 1980.

The idealism of the European federalist movement, which grew out of the anti-fascist resistance movement in many countries – and was associated with thinkers such as the Italian Altiero Spinelli – ties in well with Green philosophy. Both European federalist idealists and Greens argued that industrialised states were overly centralised and too bureaucratic; both advocated simplification of public administration and initiatives to enhance accountability and citizenship. French Greens attributed disastrous environmental decisions to the elitist and centralised nature of policy-making which allowed a small, unrepresentative French elite – trained in the technocratic thinking of the top schools and colleges – to embark on a major programme of nuclear power-station construction or nuclear testing in the South Pacific without having to justify or be accountable for their actions. German Greens argued that the modern nation-state was inherently dangerous because its power is inevitably used for economic competition, exploitation of nature and arms races and warmongering.

In general, Greens have argued that smaller and more participatory units of organisation would result in a safer world. They have criticised advocates of a United States of Europe or a European Superpower as falling victim to the deadly logic of power politics, which always results in exploitation and arms races. Instead, they call for European unity to be built on the basis of a loose confederation of culturally diverse regions – a regional network. This decentralised 'Europe of the regions' is categorically not the same as the nationalist Eurosceptics' vision of a Gaullist or Thatcherite Europe of strong nation-states.

Such a vision obviously ties in well with the policies of parties such as the PCE/IU and the Greek Synaspismos. However, equally obvious is the fact that Left parties that defend the potentially progressive role of the nation-state might have problems with the Green tendency to berate it. Moreover, there is considerable diversity amongst Green parties as to how to reach the desired end-goal of a Europe based on decision-making at the lowest possible level. Some parties – for example, the Swedish and the Irish Greens – are openly hostile to the EU, believing that such a Europe is best built outside the EU framework. Other Greens – above all, the Green party in Germany under the leadership of Joschka Fischer – have clearly embraced the EU as the (potential) motor force of a new federal Europe.

The concern with *ecological sustainability* leads the Greens to mount a critique of a European Union founded on the endless accumulation of material things, determined to out-do the USA and Japan in becoming a capitalist superpower capable of exploiting new markets in the search for profits – i.e., exploiting poorer countries. The argument that we need European unity and a single currency in order to compete ever more fiercely on the world stage in the endless search for economic growth is not one which Greens would ever entertain. Instead, they argue that the EU's current priorities such as control of inflation and pursuit of growth should take a back seat to sustainability and that job-sharing, social redistribution and new environmentally friendly ways of generating energy and recycling resources are the appropriate answer to mass unemployment. For example, Greens argue that eco-taxes should be levied on non-renewable energy and that social and environmental costs should be included in calculating the market price of goods. The most trenchant criticism of EU policies has been reserved for the CAP, which is described as a disaster that encourages intensive chemical-based farming which causes pollution, destruction of land and waste of food. Greens argue for the CAP to be replaced with an agricultural policy that involves less machinery, more employment of human labour, and more emphasis on ecological renewal. They also call for EU initiatives against animal experimentation, genetic engineering of food, and use of dangerous chemicals such as organo-phosphates. There is much in all of this with which the Left parties would be in total agreement. The fundamental critique of the EU as, in its present form, an exploitative capitalist power is shared by most Left parties.

As regards *community and grassroots democracy*, Green parties have called for strong local communities that would instil a sense of local loyalty and identification. There are problems with this vision of a Europe based on strong self-reliant communities. Critics of the Greens have drawn parallels with earlier romantic movements based on 'blood and soil' including some associated with the far right. The Greens reject this and emphasise their attachment to egalitarianism and grassroots democracy, claiming that an extreme rightwing variant of their version of radical democracy would be a contradiction in terms because it would involve hierarchy and repression. But problems remain. What protection would there be for minorities in such communities? And, above all, what body would regulate relations between them and guarantee freedom of movement and travel. Left parties tend to emphasise either a strong role for the nation-state (if they are anti-integrationist) or a strong role for a European Parliament and European government, upholding a concept of European citizenship (if they are pro-integrationist).

Greens call for a new global order to deal with problems of peace, the environment, and exploitation of the southern hemisphere by the northern. They tend to see the nation-state as both too large and too small: too large to facilitate grass-roots participation in politics and real democratic control over politicians, police, armies and civil servants – and too small to do anything effective about environmental catastrophes or the multinational corporations which, in contemporary capitalism, exploit both the global environment and the poor of the world. Thus, Green parties have developed the (rather vague) notion of a new *global–local nexus*. Greens differ markedly from pro-integrationist Left parties in that they have until now rejected the idea of a strong European Government as a way forward for dealing with problems that lie beyond the control of the nation-state. They fear the power that would be concentrated in such a body. Their emphasis on a global–local nexus locates the initiative firmly in local communities and individuals. They call for people to 'think globally and act locally', gradually constructing a new global order on the basis of a diverse multitude of local and regional initiatives. Green parties have also called for a complete reorientation of EU aid policy. They demand that aid to developing and underdeveloped countries should be linked to ecologically sustainable projects and not to economic projects that meet the demands of the global market or the demands of the World Bank or the IMF for the speedy repayment of 'third-world' debt. They support an immediate cancellation of all third world debt. These policies would meet with the general approval of all Left parties.

Greens regard their celebration of *diversity* as distinguishing them from other political traditions, which celebrate the cultural uniformity typical of both the nation-state and the market place, and also from the extreme right, which believes in the authoritarian imposition of monoculturalism. For many European Green parties, respect for individual rights and the rights of cultural, racial, religious and sexual minorities is a cornerstone of the sort of holistic multicultural society that the platform of the Green Group in the European Parliament calls for. In reality, Left parties have moved a very long way in recent years towards an embrace of other political traditions, such as feminism and environmentalism. Undoubtedly, the post-communist and 'new left' parties, such as the Nordic parties and Synaspismos, have moved most towards the embrace of diversity. Several others – above all the KKE and the PCP (despite its electoral alliance with a Portuguese Green party that many other European Greens regard as little more than a communist front) – remain grounded in a workerist and statist tradition. Many Greens share the suspicion that even those Left parties that claim to have changed are motivated by electoral opportunism or panic over the loss of their old identity. Many on the Left doubt the sincerity or reality of the Greens' anti-capitalism.

These five tenets of Green thought taken together amount to a quite trenchant critique of the present EU – wherby it is seen as being centralised, non-ecological, alienated from its peoples, democratically very weak, and actually encouraging the growth of an extreme right. For Greens, a decentralised Europe of the Regions would transcend nation-state boundaries which are seen as artificial and repressive, Thus, there is no reason why Basques now living on both sides of the Franco-Spanish border should not form a self-governing community if that is what they want. Regions would be 'culturally defined and historically developed'. This vision is no doubt attractive to a variety of people who are unhappy with the bureaucratic nature of the EU at present, the cultural repression of minorities within nation-states, or the pursuit of wasteful economic policies.

There is obviously much that Green parties and Left parties share, in terms of their critique of how European integration has developed to date, and how an alternative Europe might look in the future. The big difference and possible stumbling block to joint co-operation lies in Left parties' attachment to the role of the state, be it the nation-state or a potential new European state (depending on the degree of anti- or pro-integrationism). Although some Green parties, especially the German, seem to behave more and more in traditional social democratic terms, Greens have traditionally distrusted the state. The lack of attention given to an analysis of state power can, in turn, makes Green visions of how Europe might develop seem rather vague and idealistic.

Finally, Green parties share with the Left parties a range of practical problems when it comes to organising and operating at the transnational level. As Bomberg (1998) points out, the EU is neither local nor global but something in between. As such, a vision which emphasises the global–local nexus often plays down the EU itself as a political actor or a forum in which Green parties should seek to organise in transnational terms. Second, Greens frequently disagree over priorities – such as the threat posed by the nationalist forces, or the extent to which the socialist left is a potential friend or an enemy along with capitalism. Third, Green parties differ in their assessment of whether the EU can be transformed from within into a more democratic, decentralised, federation of regions – this is essentially the position of Italian, French and German Greens who certainly do not advocate their countries' withdrawal from the EU but rather want action to change its political and economic direction; or whether the EU is a monster beyond redemption and a confederation of regions of Europe can best be built by scrapping the EU altogether and starting again – this tends to be the position of the British and Swedish Greens, for example. This can lead to very serious divisions – for example, over the key, practical as well as ideological, issue of whether the nation-state or the EU is the best starting-point from which to launch the Green project. When German and Italian Greens campaign for stronger EU legislation to protect the EU's immigrants or bring about greater gender equality, they implicitly accept that a stronger EU can be a force for some good. When Swedish Greens campaign against their country's membership altogether on the grounds that it threatens Sweden's welfare state, they implicitly accept that the nation-state is worth defending against the EU. In other words, ideological differences notwithstanding, when it comes to the practical questions of how best to organise and advance, Greens and Left parties often display remarkably similar tactical and strategic problems and inter-party disagreements.

There is little doubt that the 1990s was a decade in which many Green parties in Europe underwent substantial change. Green parties have long been riven by disputes between so-called fundamentalist and realist wings. The former tend towards 'pure' Green or 'deep' Green positions, dismissing left and right as equally unpalatable and refusing to compromise their ideological beliefs in the interests of power politics. The latter tend towards a pragmatic approach that emphasises the need to make concrete policy gains. This predisposes them towards alliance strategies – usually with parties of the left or centre-left. By the end of the 1990s, Green parties that participated in coalition governments (in France, Italy, Germany and Finland) were dominated by their realist wings. And although these disputes and divisions have not gone away – the German Greens in particular remain heavily factionalised – the acceptance of compromise and prioritising of alliance strategies was deep-rooted. It is precisely these parties that had come to be the most amenable to the idea that the EU could be reformed from within. Daniel Cohn-Bendit, who headed the French Green electoral list for the European Parliament in 1999, described the EU as 'an adventure to be lived with passion' (*Guardian*, 17 May 2000). Joschka Fischer of the German Greens called for the EU to become a federal state with a directly elected president and a strong legislature. Paul Rosenmöller of the Dutch Green Left told the Council of the European Federation of Green Parties in June 2001 that his party had 'learnt to appreciate the European Union', was now 'the most European party in the Netherlands' and was 'not afraid of the F [federalism] word' (Rosenmöller, 2001). Yet Swedish Greens remained resolutely opposed to both EU membership and the single currency, and wary of going any further than critical support for a minority social democratic government, lest their policies become watered down (Burchell, 2001a), and UK Greens campaigned in 1999 against the single currency and in favour of the pound (Green Party, 1998). The common manifesto that Green parties signed for the 1999 European Parliamentary elections involved a delicate balance, emphasising the critique of neo-liberalism that all parties could agree upon but avoiding any direct mention of either federalism or the single currency (European Federation of Green Parties, 1999).

These strategic and ideological differences have frequently frustrated attempts to forge a transnational strategy for Green parties within the EU. These differences have sometimes involved both the degree of emphasis that should be given to issues of social justice and the question of whether Greens should co-operate with the Left and Socialist groups inside the European Parliament. However, it has primarily been strong disagreement between advocates of dismantling the EU and advocates of working to develop and reform it from within that has (as with the Left parties) frustrated attempts at joint action. These problems were brutally illustrated in the splits between Green MEPs over the Maastricht Treaty in the run-up to 1993.

All Greens were critical of Maastricht. In particular, they shared with many Left parties four main concerns: that Maastricht was driven by a free market, neo-liberal logic; that it said nothing about ecological sustainability; that it was undemocratic, taking powers away from national parliaments without transferring them to either the European Parliament or regional parliaments; and that it contained provision on defence and security which could see a European army emerge. But Greens could not agree a common strategy on how to oppose Maastricht, or even if they should oppose it outright or campaign for changes to the Treaty. Some Greens – such as the French and the Italian – argued that a common foreign policy was acceptable in principle provided the institutions of the EU were democratised. In this respect, they converged with pro-integrationist Left parties. Others, such as the Germans, were more concerned about Europe becoming a superpower. Some Green parties argued that Maastricht should be rejected outright; others argued that to do so would encourage the growth of xenophobic and racist sentiment. The debate highlighted that while Greens could agree upon a critique of what was wrong with the world, once again when they were forced to make hard choices about what practical improvements they could hope for, they were as divided as the Left parties.

In 1993, a European Federation of Green Parties was launched and included representatives from non-EU Green parties, although its core is located in the European Parliament. Its platform represents a very modest set of proposals agreed upon by diverse Green parties. It is not binding upon Green MEPs. Since the 1999 European Parliamentary elections, Green MEPs have been divided into a number of European Parliamentary groupings. Most have joined with Scottish, Basque and Welsh nationalists in a new predominantly Green group called the Greens/European Free Alliance. The Group has attempted to streamline its operations and move away from extreme rotation of posts and towards greater parliamentary effectiveness. Yet, to some extent it is hampered by its extreme heterogeneity. In particular, schisms may resurface between those in favour of deepening federalism within the EU as it presently exists and those opposed to membership of the EU altogether. In essence, both the Group of the Greens/European Free Alliance and the Confederal Group of the European Unitary Left/Nordic Green Left within the European Parliament contain such a range of views and positions that movement towards stronger transnational party co-operation is rendered difficult. By the same token, whilst many

Greens and many Left parties converge on various issues, future co-operation is likely to be on an issue-by-issue basis and in a way that will see some Greens and Left parties lining up on one side of the European integration debate, and other Greens and Left parties lining up on the opposite side.

The Social Democrats and the European Union

As we saw in Chapter 1, social democrats tended to be hostile towards European integration in the early years, when Christian Democrats and other centre-right parties made much of the running. The social democrats tended to see European integration as benefiting big monopoly capital and as a threat to the ability of centre-left governments to implement real reforms at the national level (a perspective which still informs the thinking of anti-integrationist Left parties). The 1980s, however, was a decade that profoundly changed social democratic thinking on the EU. The rise of the Thatcherite-Reaganite 'New Right', with its neo-liberal assault on the whole social democratic project (above all, trade union rights, 'social partnership' and welfare spending), encouraged many social democrats in the belief that social democracy was best defended and relaunched at the pan-European level. The German Social Democrats became enthusiastic advocates of deeper European integration as did the French Socialists, after Mitterrand's famous European U-turn in response to the thwarting of his first administration's experiment in 'reflation in one country'. The British Labour Party, too, which had campaigned for the UK's withdrawal from the EC in 1983, came to see in European integration a possible means of reversing some of the seemingly relentless assaults on workers' rights that had characterised the long years of Conservative rule. By the end of the 1980s, Featherstone could write that the socialist and social democratic parties 'have gradually moved towards a common acceptance of participation in the EC integration process; the question of EC membership looks increasingly like a concern of the past' (Featherstone, 1988, 303). Many of the social democratic parties continue to contain within them substantial bodies of opinion that are suspicious of, or downright hostile to, further integration. This is above all true of the Nordic social democrats, but also to some extent the British Labour Party and the French Socialists (though the defection of J.-P. Chevènement's Citizens' Movement from the latter has provided an alternative home for French centre-left 'Eurosceptics'). However, the conviction that aspects of the EU needed to be strengthened in order to realise party goals that seemed to be thwarted at the national level was widespread among social democratic parties by the 1990s (Ladrech, 2000, 3-4).

These goals have included the defence of the welfare state, of workers' rights and of the European social model in general. Indeed, some of the southern European social democratic parties, such as the Portuguese and the Italians, have looked to the EU as a solution to problems that they feel are insolvable at the national level (Ladrech, 2000, 73). Second, there has been a belief that European union might allow governments to exercise some influence over international trade and commerce and that monetary union might help to curb currency speculation.

Third, social democrats have often argued that European integration will act as a spur to employment creation. Fourth, they argue that integration, if accompanied by measures designed to overcome the notorious 'democratic deficit' within the EU, would allow the reconquest of a 'political space' – in other words, would help to make politics relevant again in the face of the seemingly ever-growing impotence of states. Finally, that a united Europe would be better placed to find its own voice internationally, to promote a more just international order, and to be less subservient to the USA. On this last point, it should be noted that most social democrats have been keen to emphasise that they are supportive of NATO and that Europe should work in partnership with the USA, but there are clear difference between the ardent pro-Atlanticists of, for example, Blair's 'New Labour', on the one hand, and the French and German Social Democrats, on the other.

Some parties have gone further in articulating their hopes, aspirations and plans for European integration. The French Socialists have called for: 'European-level measures resembling an activist and interventionist state, for example, a high-tech industrial policy'; new European-level regulations governing the public sector; stronger European social policy measures, including a minimum salary, and minimum standards regarding labour rights; taxes on polluting forms of energy; and more fiscal harmonisation. (Ladrech, 2000, 72; Jospin, 2002). The Italian PDS, in 1995, published an ambitious list of nearly 230 proposals for action (Democratic Party of the Left, 1995). These included: abolition of unanimous voting in the Council of Ministers for all measures except revision of the Treaties and admission of new member states; raising of funds to finance a major programme of jobs creation; upgrading of employment creation (in the Treaties) to the principal objective of monetary union; protecting the European social model by inserting into the Treaties guarantees of fundamental rights of social welfare provision; institutionalising permanent dialogue with trade unions about employment, industrial and social policy; balancing monetary union by 'assigning priority to policies of economic and social cohesion, in order to guarantee harmonious development of the Union'; and strengthening the existing structural funds and harnessing these to a new common industrial policy. The German Social Democrats, in opposition, called for an 'alliance for jobs' to be launched alongside the single currency, and for the harmonisation of employment, economic and financial policies to be bindingly enshrined in the proposed revision of the Maastricht Treaty (which actually produced the Amsterdam Treaty). The SPD also called for uniform immigration and labour market legislation throughout the EU and declared that 'the same wages for the same work' should be a governing principle across the EU. The party also called for higher investment and energy taxes. Some regional SPD party organisations – for example, in Baden-Württemberg – ran on an anti-euro platform, warning of the dire implications for employment of the Maastricht criteria governing the single currency, and some French Socialist leaders called for guarantees of a strong employment creation policy to be made an irreversible condition of French support for the Euro (*Guardian*, 5 March 1996).

There is much in the above that the Left parties we have examined – or at least many of them – could support. The social democrats may not be committed to transcending, or going beyond, capitalism. But clearly many of their stated policy ambitions involve controlling capitalism (to a significant extent) and challenging the dominance of neo-liberal free market philosophy. A general movement to the left at the European level in the latter half of the 1990s might well have created conditions for a strategic realignment of the Left and social democratic parties. Undoubtedly, such hopes lay behind the electoral and government alliances between these families of parties that were indeed formed in a number of key EU states. The Italian PDS entered government (as part of a coalition that included the PRC) in 1996; the French Socialists (with Communists and Greens) and the British Labour Party achieved office in 1997; and the German SPD (with the Greens) won power in 1998. By the end of 1998, for the first time in the history of post-war Western Europe the 'big four' countries – Germany, France, the UK and Italy – were all led by centre-left governments. By the time of the 1999 European Parliamentary elections, thirteen of the fifteen member states had governments that were led by, or included, social democratic parties. The social democrats dominated the process that produced both major revisions to the Maastricht Treaty – the Amsterdam and Nice Treaties. Moreover, the launch of the Party of European Socialists in 1992 had enabled the social democrats to exercise considerable influence. The PES has been much more successful than either the Green or Left transnational party groups in the European Parliament in achieving effective unity of purpose and in making its presence felt as a political actor. The presence of Jacques Delors at many PES meetings and the ability of the PES to feed agreed social democratic proposals on employment creation (for example) to the social democratic members of the Council of Ministers were all good portents for future action. An unprecedented opportunity seemingly existed to replace neo-liberal hegemony with a renewed social democratic hegemony at the EU level. It did not happen.

Already by 2003, the disappointment was very widespread. The centre-left coalitions had lost power in Italy and France. The social democrats were also out of office in Portugal, Austria, Ireland and Holland. In Germany, the SPD–Green coalition was clinging to power by its fingertips. In the UK, New Labour seemed more Atlanticist and in thrall to neo-liberal thinking than ever.

From the point of view of the Left parties (and many leftwing social democrats would no doubt share this view), the problem is that there has been a clear discrepancy between the stated ambitions of the social democratic parties and the actual behaviour of social democrats in power. This goes beyond the difficulties in adapting the complicated machinery of EU decision-making to social democratic goals or the problems of transnational policy co-ordination. It concerns the existence or otherwise of a political will to turn the EU in a new direction.

The fact is that social democratic parties continue to be divided, both between themselves and internally, about European integration. However, these divisions are not so much about the desirability or otherwise of integration; they are rather about the degree to which it is possible or feasible to defy the neo-liberal trends of the past two decades. Despite the policy plans in opposition, once in office, social democratic-led governments pursued participation in the single currency with enthusiasm, coming to terms with the need to meet the Maastricht criteria even when this meant cutting welfare spending, accepting growing unemployment, and effecting programmes of wholesale privatisation. The Stability Pact was not explicitly repudiated (although the German government earned a reprimand from the EU Commission in late 2002 for violating it). The neo-liberal thinking that seemed to dominate aspects of the UK Labour government's economic thinking led that government to veto plans to raise the necessary EU funds to finance a large-scale jobs creation programme. The Blair government instead insisted on 'labour market flexibility', which many social democrats saw as a euphemism for making it easier for employers to sack workers. Social and economic cohesion funds did not receive the huge boost promised in opposition; the EU still lags behind in terms of common industrial policy; the promised reform of the CAP remained mired in controversy.

Of course, the social democrat-led governments can take the credit for some undoubted advances at Amsterdam. That Treaty did mark a certain 'move to the left', in so far as it highlighted the importance of employment creation as a policy goal. Yet, how meaningful this is, in the absence of the necessary funds to finance such programmes and in the light of the failure of attempts to force the European Central Bank to pay as much attention to fighting unemployment, as it is required to pay to monetary stability and low inflation, is questionable. A typical example of the disillusionment felt by many left social democrats by the end of the 1990s is the denunciation of the failures of social democracy in office by the former German SPD Finance Minister Oskar Lafontaine. In office, Lafontaine had argued for democratic control over the European Central Bank, for the upgrading in priority of employment creation policies, and for measures designed to counter the power of the multinationals. He was forced out of office when his Chancellor, Gerhard Schroeder, failed to support him. In his memoirs of that period, Lafontaine recalled the President of the European Central Bank, Wim Duisenberg, saying that 'it is normal for politicians to express their opinions from time to time on the interest rates policies of those charged with defending the status of the currency. But it is equally normal for us not to listen.' Lafontaine concludes that 'if the value of the currency is regarded as a more important issue than employment, the banks will become more important than democratically elected governments. If a 'stability culture' of this kind becomes established, the unemployed in Europe will have a hard and long road ahead of them' (Lafontaine, 2000, 142). This, of course, is what Left parties have argued all along.

Amsterdam also enshrined a commitment to fighting racism and sexual inequality. But, once again, critics accused the EU of failing to strengthen the rights of immigrant workers and refugees and of evolving in the direction of 'Fortress Europe'.

The disappointments on the economic growth and social justice fronts are matched by a failure by the centre-left governments (at Amsterdam and Nice) to agree upon a comprehensive institutional reform of the EU that decisively addressed the democratic deficit. Such reforms that emerged – for example, reducing the automatic right of the smaller member states to a European Commissioner – whilst arguably sensible on grounds of efficiency could also be seen as strengthening the big states at the expense of the smaller. The European Parliament is not yet a fully empowered legislature. Some centre-left governments – notably, Blair's Labour government – seem likely to use the Convention that is charged with drafting a new Constitution for Europe by 2004 to attempt to limit rather than deepen the powers and competences of the EU. These failures and disagreements on the part of the social democrats on both the economic and social fronts have not in any way reduced the growing disillusionment with politics in general and the EU in particular that is now evident in many European countries and which is fuelling support for far-right and populist parties.

In yet other respects, the record of the social democrats in office at a time when they had an unprecedented opportunity to challenge neo-liberal hegemony is disappointing. The EU seemed paralysed in terms of formulating an effective common foreign and defence policy response to the crisis in Kosovo in the late 1990s, when NATO took the lead. As war between the USA and Iraq loomed in early 2003, the EU was again marginalised; the Blair government seemed to lean more towards Washington than towards any common EU policy response. The apparent subservience to the USA and reliance upon NATO is not only anathema to the Left parties, but also to many within the European social democratic and Green parties – and indeed to many European federalists in general.

Conclusion

This brief summary has, I hope, established that divisions over the key challenges of European integration exist within and between Green and social democratic parties, as they do within and between Left parties. In the case of the Left parties, they are united in contesting neo-liberalism and, in that sense, in aspiring to transcend the presently dominant free-market model of capitalism, and in seeking a Europe that is no longer subservient to the USA in foreign and security policy. However, they are divided in their strategic assessment of whether those goals are best realised through deepening EU integration or in contesting and perhaps rejecting the current model of European construction altogether. In the case of the Greens, very similar divisions exist, although Green and Left parties are divided in their historical approaches to questions of state power and economic growth, and in their assessment of one anothers's tactical and strategic intentions. In the case of the social democrats, they are divided on the question of how desirable and feasible it is to contest the main thrust of neo-liberalism. Although, in opposition, social democratic parties identified many of the weaknesses involved in the process of European construction as it had developed during the 1970s and 1980s, in government during the late 1990s, they were not so successful at finding either the political will or the strategic co-ordination needed to steer Europe in a fundamentally new direction. The result has been a loss of electoral support as centre-left voters became disillusioned with the performance of their parties in office, the waste of an opportunity to establish a new social democratic hegemony at the EU level (at least for now), the breakdown of political alliances between the social democrats and Left parties in several countries (Italy, France and Spain, for example), and the appearance given by several social democratic parties (UK, Greece and Spain, for example) that they believe their electoral appeal can be based on pursuing quintessentially neo-liberal policies of privatisation and 'labour market reform' with greater enthusiasm than their centre-right competitors.

Although Left parties' critiques of the current direction of European construction are shared by many left-wing social democrats, the immediate future prospects for co-operation between Left and social democratic parties cannot be said to be good. Left parties are well aware that it is precisely on the terrain of contesting neo-liberalism, and offering a clear alternative to the negative economic and social consequences of market-led globalisation and European integration that they must distinguish themselves from the social democrats and establish their *raison d'être*. A failure to do this may mean internal disarray and voter desertion as many question what exactly the Left parties continue to stand for. This has already happened in France and Spain, for example. The Left parties' best hope may be to position themselves sufficiently to the left of, and critical of, the social democratic parties as to attract those social democratic voters who are disillusioned by the apparent 'sell-out' to neo-liberalism, whilst avoiding any relapse into the maximalist rhetoric of the communist or Marxist past, which may repel such potential supporters.

Clearly there are many areas in which the critiques of current processes of European integration that Green and Left parties have formulated converge, as do their policy prescriptions. There would appear to be a sound basis for political co-operation between these families of parties. In several EU member states, they have already co-operated together, either in opposition or indeed in government (with the social democrats). Problems for future co-operation exist, however. These sometimes centre on the fact that in several countries Left and Green parties appeal to a very similar demographic group and are in direct electoral competition. This is true of all the Nordic countries where, in addition, the adoption of 'Red/Green' slogans and labels by the Left parties can provoke the suspicion and ire of Greens. In France, the success of the Greens in eating into the support of the PCF leaves that party suspicious of co-operation. In Germany, the growing moderation of the Greens (in government with the SPD from September 1998) led several prominent members to defect to the left-wing PDS; Green electoral success in the 2002 general elections, coupled with the failure of the PDS to supersede the five per cent barrier necessary to gain full representation in parliament, may have temporarily tipped the balance here in the Greens' favour; however, disillusionment with the SPD/Green government could again encourage the PDS to position itself as an alternative to (rather than potential ally of) the Greens. In many southern European countries, Green parties are either absent or are very weak. Despite the policy convergences, then, there are many electoral and party system factors that seemingly work against Left and Green party strategic co-operation.

5

CONCLUSION: EUROPE AND THE FUTURE OF THE LEFT PARTIES

Having examined the evolution of the policies of the Left parties towards European integration by way of a number of case studies, and attempted to contextualise this evolution both historically and theoretically; and having compared the Left parties' positions with those of parties from the Green and social democratic traditions and commented on the prospects for relations between these parties; we are now in a position to summarise the present state of the Left parties and the prospects for future co-operation between them. The present study has sought throughout to stress that policy evolution cannot be understood without taking into account a wide range of factors – historical, ideological and organisational, national and international, electoral and party system-related – that affect different parties differently. Ten issues in particular have emerged as central to the European orientation of the Left parties.

First, all the parties I examined in Chapter 3 share a strong critique of free market capitalism, a marked rejection of neo-liberalism. In this respect, they are indeed transformatory parties – they aspire towards a transcendence of the currently dominant neo-liberal model of capitalism. The old divide between 'revolution' and 'reform' may be less than useful here; the PCP may be happier at describing itself as 'revolutionary' than the Danish SF, for example; but all the parties I have examined are hostile to the relentless and ruthless rise of corporate power, which they see as anti-democratic and anti-popular. All of these parties, therefore, share a strong disapproval of the neo-liberal aspects of the Maastricht Treaty, embodied in the convergence criteria that governed the introduction of the single currency and further enshrined in the Stability Pact. They reject the agenda of jobs cutting, privatisations, welfare spending cuts, erosion of workers' rights (under the guise of labour market flexibility), erosion of social protection, and attacks on trade unions. However, they are divided on whether the very project of monetary union itself is to blame, or whether it is potentially a progressive one: whether Maastricht and the euro should be rejected outright, or whether, for all their weaknesses and failings, they can yet be an instrument in the creation of a more progressive Europe capable of guaranteeing an alternative to US-style capitalism. Thus, Synaspismos, the PCE/IU, the Finnish Left Alliance and the PdCI adopt one approach; the PCP, KKE and (for somewhat different reasons) the Swedish Left Party adopt another. The Danish SF, the PCF and the PRC fall somewhere in between.

Second, all of the Left parties have argued that genuine European unity requires real economic and social cohesion. They are agreed that such cohesion is made more, not less, difficult by the neo-liberal nature of the present integration process. They have argued that capitalism creates disequilibria and then attempts to exploit imbalances in order to erode workers' rights and wages and reap greater profits. They are agreed that relations of solidarity between European states and regions should be harnessed to a model of economic development that involves redistribution and a concerted drive to tackle relations of dependency between core and periphery. They are less in agreement as to whether the EU can be reformed in such a way as to promote this – through a profound strengthening of the economic and social and structural funds, the introduction of a strong common industrial policy, the radical and progressive reform of the CAP, etc. – or whether the EU acts as a barrier to genuine cohesion.

Third, all of the Left parties in this study – with the possible exception of the KKE, which finds it difficult to say anything positive about the EU – believe that the EU should play a much more positive role in protecting the environment, promoting sustainable development, and penalising polluters. Even those that are in general hostile to deeper integration concede that certain problems, above all, environmental, transcend national boundaries and require transnational solutions.

Fourth, all Left parties (again, with the possible exception of the KKE) are open to the development of stronger regional policies. This is above all a priority for the Finnish, Spanish and Italian parties.

Fifth, the Left parties strongly condemn the relative lack of priority given to the question of immigrant workers' rights and the rights of refugees and asylum seekers. They are amongst the foremost critics of 'Fortress Europe'. They call for stronger measures to tackle racism and to guarantee an 'open Europe', which seeks to fully integrate immigrants.

Sixth, all of the Left parties without exception see the EU as it has developed to date as profoundly undemocratic. They share a common critique of the elitist, top-down, bureaucratic and technocratic model of European integration that predominates. They see such as model as intrinsically linked to corporate capitalism – as reflecting the interests of the big multinationals who rely upon an exclusion of the mass of citizens from the process of European construction, a weakening of European civil society and an erosion of democratic control and accountability in order to evade scrutiny. The Left parties reject the notion that economic power should be concentrated in the hands of bankers and technocrats; they strongly object to the notion of a supposedly 'independent' European Central Bank. They are less united on how European democracy can be reinvigorated. The anti-integrationists amongst them look to a defence of the nation-state and of the powers of national parliaments, making a clear connection between democracy and national sovereignty. The pro-integrationists argue for full powers to the European Parliament, democratic control by a European Government over the European Central Bank, and a Constitution for the EU that greatly strengthens citizens' rights as well as guaranteeing the power of a European Government to formulate and implement policies for which it has a democratic mandate, in the face of multinational opposition. Some Left parties are clearly in a position of transition between these two positions, at present unsure as to how to best achieve the shared goal of a strengthening of popular control and a weakening of corporate power. In general, the anti-integrationists and defenders of national sovereignty also adhere to a rather outdated model, rooted in the recent European past, that sees EU integration as masking German dominance and a German threat to the sovereignty of their countries. The pro-integrationists reject such sentiments along with nationalism in general.

Seventh, most of the Left parties support EU expansion to the countries of Eastern and central Europe, accepting this as the will of the majority of the peoples there. The exceptions to this are the KKE and, to a lesser extent, the PCP, which seem trapped in a vision of the world that is rooted in the East/West conflict of the Cold War period. The KKE speaks of EU expansion as an 'imperialist' takeover of the 'former socialist' countries. All of the other Left parties, whilst supporting expansion, are anxious that this be accomplished without (1) a weakening of the rights of workers and citizens in the new member states, effectively drawing those countries into dependence on the EU core and casting them in the role of permanent second-class citizenship, and (2) without capital being in a position to use expansion in order to force down wages and further erode workers' rights in the existing member states. In addition, the Left parties in southern Europe fear the loss of EU spending in southern Europe after expansion will impact most on the poor there.

Eighth, all of the Left parties share a marked anti-militarism, at times bordering on pacifism, especially where the Nordic 'new left' parties are concerned. All strongly oppose European subservience to NATO and would like to see the breakup of NATO. All are strongly opposed to the EU developing as a major militarised superpower or a major manufacturer of arms. Some are willing to support in principle common European security, defence and foreign policies but only on condition that these develop outside of the constraints of NATO. Indeed, they see such policies as enabling Europe to break free from its subservience to the USA. Others object in principle to such policies, which they believe will almost inevitably assume an imperialist hue.

Ninth, the Left parties all object vociferously to what they see as the 'new imperialism'. This is manifest both in the swaggering arrogance of the USA on the world stage, determined to enforce its political, military and economic dominance, with a sometimes reluctant but rarely outrightly critical EU following behind in tow; and in the exploitative trade and commercial relations that the EU has developed with many 'third-world' or lesser developed countries.

Finally, the Left parties clearly have very different views on the overriding issue of supranationality – to which, in a way, policy responses to all the other issues are linked. If there has been a trend on the Left over the past twenty years or so, then that trend has clearly been away from purely national 'roads to socialism' and towards acceptance of at least some aspects of supranationality. This is true not only of the enthusiastic pro-integrationists (such as Synaspismos), but also of the Nordic parties and even the PCF. Only the KKE remains resolutely opposed to supranationality. The differing approaches to supranationality bring us to the final issue we must examine, which is the prospects for effective co-ordination of policy-making and of strategic planning on the part of the Left parties in the face of the ever-growing challenges of European integration and globalisation.

We have seen that the PES has developed as a transnational political actor on the European stage, as has the Christian Democratic European People's Party (EPP). Indeed, co-operation between these two has effectively dominated the work of the European Parliament for many years. Left parties lag behind. The Confederal Group of the European United (or Unitary) Left (GUE) came into existence in July 1994, on the initiative of the PCE/IU and Synaspismos, soon joined by PCF, PCP and KKE MEPs. The adhesion of Swedish, Finnish and Danish MEPs in 1995 led to the group adding the suffix 'Nordic Green Left' to its title. The founding declaration describes the group as 'firmly committed to European integration, although in a different form from the existing model' and 'notwithstanding the different approaches that its various components may choose to follow' (Confederal Group of the European United Left/Nordic Green Left (GUE/NGL), 1994). In actuality, the wide disparity between the approaches to supranationality of the various components has prevented the group from developing into anything remotely like as effective an actor on the EU political stage as the PES. As its title suggests, it remains 'confederal'. After the 1999 elections, the German PDS joined the group as did a Greek left-social democrat grouping, DIKKI. Five French Trotskyists from the Workers' Struggle/ Revolutionary Communist League (LO/LCR) also became members, as did one MEP from the Netherlands Socialist Party, a small staunchly anti-EU party of Maoist origins. The Cypriot AKEL and the Norwegian Socialist Left Party are associate members. Needless to say, such broad diversity has strengthened the group numerically within the EP, but has further weakened its internal cohesion. Between 1999 and 2003, the group gained further adherents: in 2001, Ilka Schroeder, a German Green, defected to the group, as did Freddy Blak, a Danish Social Democrat; in 2002, two anti-EU Danish MEPs – Jens Okking of the June Movement and Ole Krarup of the People's Movement Against the EU – transferred to the group, as did four French MEPs who had belonged to the PES – Sami Nair of the anti-EU Citizen's Movement, Gérard Caudron of the PS, and Michel Scarbonchi and Michel Dary of the Left Radicals. Increasingly, the Group was becoming a home for leftists of various shades who were unhappy with their existing alignment within the European Parliament. Thus, at the time of writing, the GUE/NGL is the fourth largest European Parliamentary grouping with fifty MEPs, but is less capable than ever of formulating a coherent political line or strategy.

Not surprisingly, many (especially the more pro-integrationist) within the Left parties would like to address this problem. The New European Left Forum (NELF), launched in 1991 to promote dialogue and policy ideas exchange between Left parties across Europe (and not just the EU), and the GUE/NGL Group have often worked together, organising meetings and exchanges. (The NELF is also significant in that its membership includes the Dutch Green Left, which sits in the European Parliament as part of the Greens European Free Alliance (EFA) Group and is thus well placed to act as an interlocutor between the Left and Green parties.) But several parties have expressed the view that the gathering challenges of integration and globalisation require a more concerted response. As we have already seen, the Spanish party has argued for the creation of stronger mechanisms for co-operation. The German PDS and Synaspismos issued a joint statement in April 2001 arguing that 'European political parties, as have been established by other political forces, constitute an EU institution, provided for by the Treaty of Nice. It is high time to include in the political agenda the creation of a political subject of the European left, open to the new social and ecological movements, safeguarding the autonomy of the forces from each country that will comprise it' (Synaspismos, 2001). Italy's PRC has also called for closer co-ordination of the European Left parties, seeking to use gatherings of the anti-capitalist European Social Forum to promote discussion and dialogue. In an interview in June 2002, PRC programme officer Marco Berlinguer, acknowledging that some Left parties disputed the need for 'a strong European force', nevertheless insisted that 'the European left needs to unite if it wants to make any difference to society' and cited a common programme for the 2004 European Parliamentary elections as 'the main task for us' (Weekly Worker, 2002). It is possible, therefore, that the more pro-integrationist amongst the Left parties will move forward in the not-too-distant future towards the creation of a European party of the 'radical, democratic Left', but it is unlikely that the GUE/NGL in its present form would simply become the European Parliamentary group of that party.

BIBLIOGRAPHY

Archive collections and interviews

Altiero Spinelli papers – Historical Archives of the European Union, European University Institute, Florence.
Interview with Luciano Bolis, Florence, September 1989.

Web sites

Confederal Group of the European Unitary Left/Nordic Green Left
  www.europarl.eu.int/gue/tree/parties/en/default.htm
European Federation of Green Parties www.europeangreens.org/
Green/European Free Alliance Group in the European Parliament
  www.greens-efa.org/
Party of European Socialists www.int/pes/en/default.htm
(Danish) Socialist People's Party www.valg.sf.dk/english/set_english.htm
(Finnish) Left Alliance www.vasemmistoliitto.fi
French Communist Party www.pcf.fr/
French Communist Party in the European Parliament www.bouge-leurope.org/
(Greek) Coalition of Left and Progress www.syn-gr/index/en/enmainframe.htm
Greek Communist Party www.kke.gr?kke.en.html
(Italian) Left Democrats www.dsonline.int/index_de.asp
(Italian) Left Democrats in the European Parliament www.dspe.net
(Italian) Communist Refoundation Party www.rifondazione.it/internazionale/
(Italian) Party of Italian Communists www.gue-ngl-pdci.com/
Portuguese Communist Party www.pcp.pt/english/english.html
Spanish Communist Party www.pce.es/
(Spanish) United Left www.izquierda_unida.es/home.html
(Swedish) Left Party www.vansterpartiet.se

Books and articles

Aaronovitch, S. and J. Grahl (1997), 'Building on Maastricht', in P. Gowan, and P. Anderson (eds), *The Question of Europe*, London, Verso.
Abse, T. (1986), 'The PCI Congress', *New Left Review*, 158, 91–7.
Abse, T. (1994), 'Italy: a New Agenda', in P. Anderson, and P. Camiller (eds), *Mapping the West European Left*, London, Verso.
Altvater, E. (1982), 'Crisi di un modello: la socialdemocrazia tedesca', *Critica Marxista*, March–April, 41–59.
Amodia, J. (1987), 'Izquierda Unida: Second Test, Second Failure', *Journal of Communist Studies*, 3:4, 170–3.

Anckar, D. (1997), 'The Finnish European Election of 1996', *Electoral Studies*, 16:2, 262–6.
Anderson, P. and P. Camiller (eds) (1994), *Mapping the West European Left*, London, Verso.
Anderson, P. (1997), 'The Europe to Come', in P. Gowan, and P. Anderson (eds), *The Question of Europe*, London, Verso.
Andriani, S. (1983), 'Riforme Sme: una sfida per la sinistra europea', *Politica ed Economia*, April, 3–4.
Anguita, J. (1996a), 'Changing things in Europe', unpublished document.
Anguita, J. (1996b), 'Ante la Unión Europea', *Europa*, April, 14–19.
Ansart, G. (1980), 'Le sens et la portée de l'action des élus du PCF à l'assemblée européenne', *Cahiers du Communisme*, June, 92–9.
Antunes, M. (1985), 'La Sinistra Portoghese e la Comunità europea', *Problemi del Socialismo*, November–December, 171–9.
Arter, D. (1991a), 'The Swedish Leftist Party', *Parliamentary Affairs*, 44:1, 60–78.
Arter, D. (1991b), 'The Finnish Leftish Alliance: "A Defensive Victory"?', *Journal of Communist Studies*, 7:3, 398–404.
Arter, D. (2000), 'The Finnish Election of 21 March 1999: Towards a Distinctive Model of Government?', *West European Politics*, 23:1, 180–6.
Arter, D. (2002), '"Communists We No Longer Are, Social Democrats We Can Never Be": the Evolution of the Leftist Parties in Finland and Sweden', *Journal of Communist Studies and Transition Politics*, 18:3, 1–28.
Asor Rosa, A. (1990), *Viaggio nel cuore del PCI: Inchiesta sugli orientamenti e sugli umori del popolo comunista*, Roma, Editori Riuniti.
Aviv, I. (1979), 'The French Communist Party from 1958 to 1978: Crisis and Endurance', *West European Politics*, 2:2, 178–97.
Aylott, N. (1997), 'Between Europe and Unity: the Case of the Swedish Social Democrats', *West European Politics*, 20:2, 119–36.
Aylott, N. (2002), 'Let's Discuss this Later: Party Responses to European Divisions in Scandinavia', *Party Politics*, 8:4, 441–61.
Baker, J. A. (1986), 'PCI Weighs Soviet Foreign Policy', *Problems of Communism*, May–June, 79–84.
Barbarella, C. (1989), 'La sinistra europea di fronte alla sfida del '92', *Critica Marxista*, January–April, 127–37.
Bardi, L. (1994), 'Transnational Party Federations, European Parliamentary Party Groups, and the Building of Europarties', in R. S. Katz and P. Mair (eds), *How Parties Organise: Adaptation and Change in Party Organization in Western Democracies*, London, Sage.
Bas, J.-C. (1985), 'Les communistes et la construction européenne en 1985', *Est et Ouest*, 22, September, 3–4.
Basso, L. (1979), 'Le prospettive della sinistra europea', *Problemi del Socialismo*, January–March, 11–8.
Baudouin, J. (1980), 'Le PCF: retour à l'archaisme?', *Revue Politique et Parlementaire*, November–December, 30–40.
Bell, D. (1992), 'The French Communist Party in the 1992 Departmental and Regional Elections', *Journal of Communist Studies*, 8:3, 135–40.
Bell, D. (1996a), 'Western communist parties and the European Union', in J. Gaffney (ed.), *Political Parties and the European Union*, London, Routledge.
Bell, D. (1996b), 'Post-Communism in Western Europe', *Journal of Communist Studies and Transition Politics*, 12:2, 247–52.

Bell, D. (1998), 'The French Communist Party in the 1990s', *Journal of Communist Studies and Transition Politics*, 14:3, 126–33.
Bell, D. (2000), *Parties and Democracy in France*, Aldershot, Ashgate.
Bell, D. and C. Lord (1998), *Transnational Parties in the European Union*, Aldershot, Ashgate.
Berglund, S. (1989), 'The Decline and Fall of Swedish Communism?', *Journal of Communist Studies*, 5:1, 83–8.
Bergström, H. (1991), 'Sweden's Politics and Party System at the Crossroads', *West European Politics*, 14:3, 8–30.
Berlinguer, E. (1982), *After Poland: Towards a New Internationalism*, Nottingham, Spokesman Books.
Berlinguer, E. (1984), 'L'Europa, la pace, lo sviluppo', *Critica Marxista*, January–April, 5–19.
Bibes, G., and J. Ranger (1986), 'Les Partis Communistes Italien et Français dans le Scrutin Europeen de 1984: Plus Differentes que Jamais', in *Les Élections Européennes de Juin 1984*, Paris, Publications de la Sorbonne, 109–57.
Billard, C. (1989), 'Pour le Progrès social en France et en Europe: le Vote Communiste', *Cahiers du Communisme*, May, 24–30.
Billard, C. (1992), 'Europe des multinationales ou Europe des travailleurs', *Cahiers du Communisme*, June, 55–62.
Boffa, G. (1981), 'L'internazionalismo del Pci', *Critica Marxista*, January–February, 5–19.
Bolloten, B. (1985), 'Hegemony and the PCE', *Survey*, 29:3, 64–72.
Bomberg, E. (1998), *Green Parties and Politics in the European Union*, London, Routledge.
Bomberg, E. (2002), 'The Europeanisation of Green Parties: Exploring the EU's Impact', *West European Politics*, 25:3, 29–50.
Borg, O. and J. Paastela (1983), 'Communist Participation in Governmental Coalitions: the Case of Finland', *Quaderni Fondazione Feltinelli*, 26, 105–28.
Bosco, A. (2000), *Comunisti: trasformazioni di partito in Italia, Spagna e Portogallo*, Bologna, il Mulino.
Brito, C. (1989), 'A new response to the Challenge of the Times', *World Marxist Review*, April, 49–53.
Brunell, A. (1986), 'Parliaments and Eurocommunism: the Italian case', *Parliamentary Affairs*, 39:3, 368–85.
Buch, R. and K. M. Hansen (2002), 'The Danes and Europe: From EC 1972 to Euro 2000 – Elections, Referendums and Attitudes', *Scandinavian Political Studies*, 25:1, 1–26.
Budgen, S. (2002), 'The French Fiasco', *New Left Review*, 17, 31–50.
Bull, M. (1989), 'Perestroika is Catching: the Italian Communist Party Elects a New Leader', *Journal of Communist Studies*, 5:1, 79–83.
Bull, M. and P. Daniels (1990), 'The "New Beginning": The Italian Communist Party under the leadership of Achille Occhetto', *Journal of Communist Studies*, 6:3, 22–43.
Burchell, J. (2000), 'Here Come the Greens (Again): the Green Party in Britain during the 1990s', *Environmental Politics*, 9:3, 145–50.
Burchell, J. (2001a), '"Small Steps" or "Great Leaps": How the Swedish Greens are Learning the Lessons of Government Participation', *Scandinavian Political Studies*, 24:3, 239–54.
Burchell, J. (2001b), 'Evolving and Conforming: Assessing Organisational Reform within European Green Parties', *West European Politics*, 24:3, 113–34.

Burklin, W. P. (1987), 'Governing Left Parties Frustrating the Radical Non-established Left: the Rise and Inevitable Decline of the Greens', *European Sociological Review*, 3, 109–26.
Butler, A. (1995), *Transformative Politics: the Future of Socialism in Western Europe*, London, St. Martin's Press.
Callinicos, A. (2001), *Against the Third Way*, Oxford, Polity.
Callot, E.-F. (1988), 'The French Communist Party and Europe: the idea and its Implementation (1945–1985)', *European Journal of Political Research*, 13:6, 301–16.
Camiller, P. (1989), 'Beyond 1992: the Left and Europe', *New Left Review*, 175, 5–17.
Camiller, P. (1994), 'Spain: the Survivor of Socialism?', in P. Anderson and P. Camiller (eds), *Mapping the West European Left*, London, Verso.
Carchedi, G. (2001), *For Another Europe: A Class Analysis of European Integration*, Oxford, Polity.
Carnevali, G. (1982), 'Pci e Comunità europa. Le contraddizioni di una necessità organizzativa', *Il Mulino*, March–April, 228–42.
Carrillo, S. (1977), '*Eurocommunism*' *and the State*, London, Lawrence and Wishart.
Carroll, R. (2000), 'Italy's Former Communists Win Blair's Blessing', *Guardian*, 14 January.
Carvalhas, C. (1996), *Statement on the Opening of the Intergovernmental Conference to Review the Treaty on European Union*, Lisbon, Portuguese Communist Party.
Carvalhas, C. (1999), 'Um bom resultada da CDU é uma Vitória para Portugal', *Avante!*, 2 June.
Carvalhas, C. (2000), 'Speech to the 16th Congress of the PCP', www.pcp.pt/english/sg20001208.html.
Carvalhas, C. (2002a), 'Declaration on the Election Results', www.pcp.pt/english/sg20020317.html.
Carvalhas, C. (2002b), 'Speech at the 26th Avante! Festival's closing rally', www.pcp.pt/english/sg20020908.htm.
Casanova, A. (1992) 'Pour que la France soit elle-même en Europe et dans le monde', *Cahiers du Communisme*, June, 13–26.
Castellina, L. (1988), 'The European Community: Opportunity or Negative Conditioning? The Impact of the Integration Process on the Left', *Socialism in the World*, 66, 26–33.
Castoriadis, C. (1979), 'The French Communist Party: a Critical Anatomy', *Dissent*, Summer, 315–25.
Cervetti, G. (1986), 'Note dul Congresso della socialdemocrazia tedesca', *Critica Marxista*, September–October, 45–52.
Chiarante, G. (1981), 'Francia e Italia: i problemi dell'alternativa', *Critica Marxista*, July–August, 5–54.
Christensen, D. A. (1996), 'The Left-Wing Opposition in Denmark, Norway and Sweden: Cases of Euro-phobia?', *West European Politics*, 19:3, 525–46.
Christensen, D. A. (1998), 'Foreign Policy Objectives: Left Socialist Opposition in Denmark, Norway and Sweden', *Scandinavian Political Studies*, 21:1, 51–70.
Christiansen, N. F. (1992), 'The Danish No to Maastricht', *New Left Review*, 195, 97–101.
Christiansen, N. F. (1994), 'Denmark: End of an Idyll?', in P. Anderson and P. Camiller (eds), *Mapping the West European Left*, London, Verso.
Cirera, D. (1992), 'Maastricht: défense commune contre sécurité commune', *Cahiers du Communisme*, June, 89–98.
Cirera, D. (1997), 'L'enjeu européen', *Cahiers du Communisme*, May, 12–13.
Clift, B. (2001), 'The Jospin Way', *Political Quarterly*, 72:2, 170–9.

Coalition of Left and Progress (Synaspismos) (1996), 'Proposals for a radical re-orientation of Greek foreign policy', Athens, Coalition of Left and Progress.
Coalition of Left and Progress (Synaspismos) (1997), 'Statement by Synaspismos President Nicos Constantopoulos on the decisions of the Amsterdam Intergovernmental Conference', www.syn.gr/en/int/pres_statement_18jn.htm.
Coalition of Left and Progress (Synaspismos) (1998), 'Synaspismos and the Amsterdam Treaty', www.syn.gr/en/kpe/diarkes9804.htm.
Coalition of Left and Progress (Synaspismos) (1999), 'To Stop the War, To Change Europe, To Change Greece', Athens, Coalition of Left and Progress.
Coalition of Left and Progress (Synaspismos) (2000a), '19th Meeting of the New Left Forum', www.syn.gr/en/intl/nelf0011_rome.htm.
Coalition of Left and Progress (Synaspismos) (2000b), 'Synaspismos CPC on Nice Intergovernmental Summit', www.syn.gr/en/kpe/kpe0011.htm.
Coalition of Left and Progress (Synaspismos) (2001), 'Joint statement by the Presidents of Synaspismos and PDS', www.syn.gr/en/intl/0104_pds.htm.
Coalition of Left and Progress (Synaspismos) (2002), 'What is Synaspismos?', www.syn.gr/en/profile.htm.
Cole, A. (1999), 'French Socialists in Office: Lessons from Mitterrand and Jospin', *Modern and Contemporary France*, 7:1, 71–87.
Cole, A. (2001), 'National and Partisan Contexts of Europeanization', *Journal of Common Market Studies*, 39:1, 15–36.
Communist Party of Greece (KKE) (1995), 'Les Theses du CC du Parti Communiste de Grece sur la revision en 1996 du Trait de Maastricht', Athens, Communist Party of Greece.
Communist Party of Greece (KKE) (2000), '16th Congress resolutions and speeches', www.kke.gr/cpg/2000/16thCongress/resolutioneng.html.
Communist Party of Greece-Interior (KKE-es) (1981), 'Proposals on the Consequences of Greece's Accession to the European Economic Community', reproduced in *Communist Affairs: Documents and Analysis*, 1, 1, 320–2.
Communist Party of Spain (PCE) (2002), *Documentos Aprobados en el XVI Congresso del Partido Comunista de España*, www.pce.es/xvicongresso/construc_europea.htm
Confederal Group of the United European Left/Nordic Green Left (GUE/NGL) (1994), *The GUE/NGL Constituent Declaration*, www.europarl.eu.int/gue/tree/en/declar.htm.
Confederal Group of the United European Left/Nordic Green Left (GUE/NGL) (1996), 'Reforming Maastricht: Economic Aspects', unpublished document with statements by leaders of the Spanish Communist Party/IU, the French Communist Party and the Greek Communist Party.
Corbett, R., F. Jacobs, and M. Shackleton (2000) *The European Parliament*, 4th edn, London, John Harper.
Corbett, R. (2001), 'The European Parliament's Progress 1994–1999', in J. Lodge (ed.), *The 1999 Elections to the European Parliament*, Basingstoke, Palgrave.
Courtois, S. (1992), 'The French Communist Party's Reactions to the Collapse of the CPSU', *Journal of Communist Studies*, 8:1, 187–95.
Cumming, G. (1999), 'Jospin Steers France towards "Euroland": a Political Review of the year 1998', *Modern and Contemporary France*, 7:2, 235–8.
Cunha, C. (1993), 'L'opposition du parti communiste portugais à l'adhésion à la CEE', in P. Delwit and J.–M. De Waele (eds), *La Gauche Face aux Mutations en Europe*, Bruxelles, Université de Bruxelles Presse.

Cunha, C. A. (2000), 'The Portuguese Communist Party and the European Union', *Portuguese Studies Review*, 8:2, 96–109.
Cunhal, A. (1988), 'Reality Calls for a High Sense of Responsibility', *World Marxist Review*, March, 7–8.
Curi, U. (1986), 'Nuovi dilemmi e opportunità per la sinistra europea', *Democrazia e Diritto*, 6, November, 83–118.
D'Alema, M. (1990), 'Formulas for Progress', *World Marxist Review*, January, 52–5.
D'Angelillo, M. (1983), 'Politica economica e dimensione internazionale: sulla crisi di identità della socialdemocrazia tedesca', *Il Mulino*, November–December, 888–915.
Daniels, P. (1987), 'The Italian Communist Party: Good-bye to Eurcommunism', *The World Today*, 139–42.
Daniels, P. (1985), '"In the Middle of the Ford": the Italian Communist Party in the mid-1980s', *Journal of Communist Studies*, 1:2, 194–207.
Daniels, P. (1989), 'The Impasse of Italian Communism', *Journal of Communist Studies*, 5:2, 228–33.
Daniels, P. (1992), 'The Democratic Party of the Left and the 1992 Italian General Election', *Journal of Communist Studies*, 8:3, 129–35.
Daniels, P. (1996), 'Italy', in Lodge, J. (ed.), *The 1994 Elections to the European Parliament*, London, Pinter.
Daniels, P. (1998), 'From Hostility to Constructive Engagement: the Europeanisation of Labour', *West European Politics*, 21:1, 72–96.
Daniels, P. (2001), 'Italy', in Lodge, J. (ed.), *The 1999 Elections to the European Parliament*, Basingstoke, Palgrave.
Debatisse, D. and S. Dreyfus (1979), 'Non à l'élargissement, non au déclin de la France', *Cahiers du Communisme*, January, 16–29.
Deleage, J-P. (1997), 'The Fragile Victory of the French Ecologists', *Environmental Politics*, 6: 4, 159–64.
Delwit, P., J. Gotovitch and J.-M. de Waele (1992), *Europe des Communistes*, Brussels, Editions Complexe.
Delwit, P. and J.-M. de Waele (1993), *La Gauche Face aux Mutations en Europe*, Brussels, Editions de l'Université de Bruxelles.
Democratic Party of the Left (1995), *Idee Programmatiche per L'Europa*, Rome, Sapere 2000 srl.
Derycke, C. (1987), 'Il se passe quelque chose dans les pays capitalistes d'europe', *Cahiers du Communisme*, May, 86–93.
Derycke, C. (1988), 'Europe 1992: il est possible d'en conjurer les périls', *Cahiers du Communisme*, September, 76–84.
Diaz Lopez, C.-E. (1979), 'The Eurocommunist Alternative in Spain', *Political Quarterly*, 50:3, 349–57.
Dietz, T-M. (2000), 'Similar but Different? The European Greens Compared to Other Transnational Party Federations in Europe', *Party Politics*, 6:2, 199–210.
Diliberto, O. (2001), 'Opening Speech by PdCI National Secretary Oliviero Diliberto at GUE/NGL meeting', www.gue-ngl-pdci.com/dili%20speech.doc.
Dimicoli, Y. (1987), 'Le grand marché: une agression contre les peuples', *Cahiers du Communisme*, November, 108–15.
Doukas, G. (1991),'The Thirteenth Congress of the KKE: Defeat of the Renovators', *Journal of Communist Studies*, 7:3, 393–8.

Drake, H. and S. Milner (1999), 'Change and Resistance to Change: the Political Management of Europeanisation in France', *Modern and Contemporary France*, 7:2, 165–78.
Dunphy, R. (1990), 'Divided We Stand: the Communists in the European Parliament', *Making Sense: Ireland's Political and Cultural Review*, 14, 8–15.
Elander, I. (2000), 'The Green Party in Sweden since the 1998 Parliamentary Elections/Towards a Green Welfare Economy?', *Environmental Politics*, 9:3, 137–44.
European Federation of Green Parties (1999), *Green Manifesto for the European Elections 1999*, n.p., European Federation of Green Parties.
Farakos, G. (1990), 'The Challenge and the Dream', *World Marxist Review*, 5:6, 20–2.
Fath, J.-L. (1979), 'Et Maintenant?', *Cahiers du Communisme*, September, 68–77.
Fath, J.-L. (1980), 'Adaptations pour une europe à géométrie variable', *Cahiers du Communisme*, December, 104–10.
Featherstone, K. (1988), *Socialist Parties and European Integration: a Comparative History*, Manchester, Manchester University Press.
Featherstone, K. and G. Kazamias (2001), 'Greece', in J. Lodge (ed.), *The 1999 Elections to the European Parliament*, Basingstoke, Palgrave.
Featherstone, K. and D. Katsoudas (1987), *Political Change in Greece: Before and After the Colonels*, London, Croom Helm.
Feld, W. (1968), 'The French and Italian Communists and the Common Market: the Requests for Representation in the Community Institutions', *Journal of Common Market Studies*, 6:3, 250–66.
Fiszbin, H. (1985), 'Il y a encore des communistes à gauche', *Revue Politique et Parlementaire*, 914, 50–6.
French Communist Party (PCF) (1979), 'Élections européennes: première analyse des résultats', *Cahiers du Communisme*, August–September, 157–9.
French Communist Party (PCF) (1992), 'Le Parti communiste s'adresse aux Français', *Cahiers du Communisme*, July–August, 13–16.
Friend, J. W. (1980), 'The Roots of Autonomy in West European Communism', *Problems of Communism*, September–October, 28–43.
Gaffney, J. (1996a), 'France', in Lodge, J. (ed.), *The 1994 Elections to the European Parliament*, London, Pinter.
Gaffney, J. (ed.) (1996b), *Political Parties and the European Union*, London, Routledge.
Galante, S. (1988), *Il Partito comunista italiano e l'integrazione europea: il decennio del rifiuto: 1947–1957*, Padova, Liviana Editrice.
Gallagher, T. (1979), 'The Portuguese Communist Party and Eurocommunism', *Political Quarterly*, 50:2, 205–18.
Gallagher, T. (1988), 'Twilight Draws Closer for Portugal's Communists: the General Election of 19 July 1987', *Journal of Communist Studies*, 4:1, 90–6.
Garzia, A. (ed.) (1985), *Un nuovo europeismo: sinistra italiana e Spd a confronto*, Roma, CRS.
Gaspar, C. (1990), 'Portuguese Communism Since 1976: Limited Decline', in *Problems of Communism*, January–February, 45–63.
Gibbons, J. (2001), 'Spain', in Lodge, J. (ed.), *The 1999 Elections to the European Parliament*, Basingstoke, Palgrave.
Giddens, A. (ed.) (2001), *The Global Third Way Debate*, Oxford, Polity.
Gilbert, M. (1998), 'In Search of Normality: the Political Strategy of Massimo d'Alema', *Journal of Modern Italian Studies*, 3: 3, 307–17.

Gillespie, R. (1990), 'Realignment on the Spanish Left', *Journal of Communist Studies*, 6:3, 119–25.
Gillespie, R. (1992a), 'Thirteenth Congress of the PCE: the Long Goodbye', *Journal of Communist Studies*, 8:2, 165–72.
Gillespie, R. (1992b), 'Spain: Centrifugal Forces in the United Left', *Journal of Communist Studies*, 8:4, 306–11.
Giolitti, A. (1985), 'Sinistra europea e unità del vecchio continente', *Problemi del Socialismo*, September–December, 178–88.
Glotz, P. (1985), *La Socialdemocrazia Tedesca a una Svolta*, Rome, Editori Riuniti.
Glotz, P. (1986), 'Forward to a New Europe: a Declaration for a New European Left', *Dissent*, 3: Summer, 327–39.
Goldey, D. B. (1997), 'The Portuguese general election of October 1995 and Presidential election of January 1996', *Electoral Studies*, 16:2, 245–54.
Government of Finland (1995), *Programme of the Government of Prime Minister Paavo Lipponen*, Helsinki, Ministry for Foreign Affairs.
Gowan, P. (1997), *The Debate on Europe*, London, Verso.
Gowan, P., and P. Anderson (eds) (1997), *The Question of Europe*, London, Verso.
Gray, L. (1979), 'Eurocommunism: a Brief Political-Historical Portrait', *Res Publica*, 21:1, 79–98.
Graziano, L. (1983), 'Compromesso storico e "Unità nazionale": su alcuni dilemmi dell'eurocomunismo', *Quaderni Fondazione Feltrinelli*, 26, 129–46.
Green Party (1998), *Act Local, Act Global: Greening the Europe Union – a Challenge to Globalisation*, n.p., Green Party (England and Wales).
Gremetz, M. (1981), 'Une France forte, indépandante et active dans le monde', *Cahiers du Communisme*, March, 27–31.
Gremetz, M. (1985), 'Le Role de la France dans le Monde', *Cahiers du Communisme*, July–August, 74–87.
Gremetz, M. (1986), 'Quelques aspects récents de la situation internationale', *Cahiers du Communisme*, June, 70–6.
Gremetz, M. (1987), 'Tendances actuelles de la situation internationale et luttes pour une nouvelle politique extérieure de la France', *Cahiers du Communisme*, March, 86–98.
Gremetz, M. (1987), 'Acte unique européen: une grave menace pour la France et son peuple', *Cahiers du Communisme*, September, 94–102.
Gremetz, M. (1989a), '1992: un grand marché capitaliste ou de véritables coopérations dans l'intéret des peuples?', *Cahiers du Communisme*, January, 38–46.
Gremetz, M. (1989b), 'Le vote pour se défendre, pour que ca change en France et en Europe', *Cahiers du Communisme*, May, 4–13.
Gremetz, M. (1992), 'Référendum: la portée du non', *Cahiers du Communisme*, July–August, 5–11.
Grunberg, G. (1983), 'The Crisis in the French Communist Party: a Review of Recent Literature', *European Journal of Political Research*, 11, 99–108.
Gruppi, L. (1987), 'Il Pci e la socialdemocrazia', *Critica Marxista*, September–October, 117–29.
Guerra, A. (1985), 'Le PCF dans le Miroir du PCI', *Revue Politique et Parlementaire*, 914, 63–71.
Gundle, S. (1987), 'On the brink of decline? The The PCI and the Italian elections of June 1987', *Journal of Communist Studies*, 3:4, 159–66.

Guyomarch, A. (1995), 'The European Elections of 1994', *West European Politics*, 18:1, 173–87.
Guyomarch, A., H. Machin and E. Ritchie (eds) (1998), *France in the European Union*, Basingstoke, Macmillan.
Guyomarch, A. (2000), 'The June 1999 European Parliament Elections', *West European Politics*, 23:1, 161–74.
Haahr, H. H. (1993), *Looking to Europe: the EC Policies of the British Labour Party and the Danish Social Democrats*, Aarhus, Aarhus University Press.
Habermas, J. (1998), 'There are Alternatives', *New Left Review*, 231, 3–23.
Habermas, J. (1999), 'The European Nation-State and the Pressures of Globalization', *New Left Review*, 235, 46–59.
Habermas, J. (2001), 'A Constitution for Europe?', *New Left Review*, 11 (new series), 5–26.
Hassner, P. (1980–81), 'Eurocommunism in the Aftermath of Kabul', *Atlantic Community Quarterly*, 18: Winter, 453–63.
Hassner, P. (1983), 'Eurocommunism and the EuroLeft: the Search for an International Framework', *Quaderni Fondazione Feltrinelli*, 26, 9–27.
Hassner, P. (1986), 'Europe Between the United States and the Soviet Union', *Government and Opposition*, 21:1, 17–35.
Hellman, S. (1978), 'The Italian CP: Stumbling on the Threshold?', *Problems of Communism*, November–December, 31–48.
Herzog, P. (1989), *Europe 92: Construire Autrement et Autre Chose*, Paris, Editions Sociales.
Hix, S. (1993), 'The Emerging EC Party System? The European Party Federations in the Intergovernmental Conferences', *Politics*, 13: 2, 38–46.
Hix S. (1996), 'The Transnational Party Federations', in J. Gaffney (ed.), *Political Parties and the European Union*, London, Routledge.
Hix, S. (1999), 'Dimensions and Alignments in EU Politics: Cognitive Constraints and Partisan Responses', *European Journal of Political Research*, 35: 1, 69–106.
Hix, S. (2001), 'Legislative Behaviour and Party Competition in the European Parliament', *Journal of Common Market Studies*, 39:4, 663–88.
Hix, S. and C. Lord (1997), *Political Parties in the European Union*, Basingstoke, Macmillan.
Heffernan, R. (2001), 'Beyond Euroscepticism: Exploring the Europeanisation of the Labour Party since 1983', *Political Quarterly*, 72:2, 180–9.
Hobsbawm, E. (2000), *The New Century*, London, Little, Brown.
Hoffman, J. (1999), 'From a Party of Young Voters to an Ageing Generation Party? Alliance '90/The Greens after the 1998 Federal Elections', *Environmental Politics*, 8:3, 140–6.
Holden, R. (1999), 'Labour's Transformation: the European Dynamic', *Politics*, 19:2, 103–8.
Hopkins, S. (1990), Dissension in the French Communist Party: a Review in the wake of events in the USSR & Eastern Europe, unpublished paper.
Hosli, M. (1997), 'Voting Strength in the European Parliament: the Influence of National and of Partisan Actors', *European Journal of Political Research*, 31: 3, 351–66.
Howarth, D. (2001), France', in J. Lodge (ed.), *The 1999 Elections to the European Parliament*, Basingstoke, Palgrave.
Iivonen, J. (1988), 'The Twenty-First Congresses of the Finnish Communist Parties' *Journal of Communist Studies*, 4:1, 88–90.
Ingrao, P. (1986), 'The European Left and the Problems of a New Internationalism', *Socialism in the World*, 53, 54–72.
Ingrao, P. (1990), *Interventi Sul Campo*, Napoli, CUEN.

Initiative for Catalonia (IC) (1992), *Iniciativa i Maastricht: Una aportació al coneixement, la reflexió i el debat*, Barcelona, IC.
Initiative for Catalonia (IC) (1996), *Intergovernmental Conference*, unpublished document.
Irving, R. E. M. (1977), 'The European Policy of the French and Italian Communists', *International Affairs*, 53: 3, 405–21.
Italian Communist Party (PCI) (1977–1989), *The Italian Communists*, a bimonthly international bulletin, Roma, PCI.
Italian Communist Party (PCI) (1989a), *The PCI's Programme for Europe*, Roma, PCI.
Italian Communist Party (PCI) (1989b), *18 Congresso del Partito comunista italiano – documenti dell'Ufficio stampa*, Roma, PCI.
Jahn, D. and A.-S. Storsved (1995), 'Legitimacy Through Referendum? The Nearly Successful Domino-Strategy of the EU Referendums in Austria, Finland, Sweden and Norway', *West European Politics*, 18:4, 18–37.
Jenson, J. and G. Ross (1983), 'The Rise and Fall of French Eurocommunism', *Quaderni Fondazione Feltrinelli*, 26, 57–77.
Johansson, K. (2001), 'Sweden', in Lodge, J. (ed.), *The 1999 Elections to the European Parliament*, Basingstoke, Palgrave.
Johansson, K. and T. Raunio (2001), 'Partisan Responses to Europe: Comparing Finnish and Swedish Political Parties', *European Journal of Political Research*, 39:2, 225–49.
Jospin, Lionel (2002), *My Vision of Europe and Globalisation*, Cambridge, Polity.
Jové, S. and A. Mansilla (1995), 'La Reforma del Tratado de Maastricht: Aspectos Económicos', *Europa*, July, 16–21.
Judge, D. (1993), *A Green Dimension for the European Community* (Edinburgh, Edinburgh University Press.
Kapetanyannis, B. (1979), 'The Making of Greek Eurocommunism', *Political Quarterly*, 50:4, 445–60.
Kapetanyannis, B. (1987), 'The Communists', in K. Featherstone and D. Katsoudas (eds), *Political Change in Greece: Before and After the Colonels*, London, Croom Helm.
Kesselman, M. (1983), 'The Economic Analysis and Programme of the French Communist Party: Consistency Underlying Change', in P. G. Cerny and M. A. Schain (eds), *French Politics and Public Policy*, London, Pinter.
Kitschelt, H. (1988), 'The Life Expectancy of Left-Libertarian Parties: Does Structural Transformation or Economic Decline explain Green Party Innovation? A Response to Wilhelm P. Burklin', *European Sociological Review*, 4, 155–60.
Kitschelt, H. (1989), *The Logics of Party Formation: Ecological Politics in Belgium and West Germany*, London, Cornell University Press.
Klein, N. (2002), *Fences and Windows: Dispatches from the Front Lines of the Globalization Debate*, London: Flamingo.
Kourvetaris, Y. A., and B. Dobratz (1987), *A Profile of Modern Greece in Search of Identity*. Oxford, Oxford University Press.
'L.L.' (1980), 'Il voto del Parlamento europeo sull'intervento militare Sovietico in Afghanistan', *Il Federalista*, 49–52.
Ladrech, R. (1996), 'Political Parties in the European Parliament', in J. Gaffney (ed.), *Political Parties and the European Union*, London, Routledge.
Ladrech, R. (2000), *Social Democracy and the Challenge of European Union*, London, Lynne Rienner.
Ladrech, R. (2002), 'Europeanisation and Political Parties: Towards a Framework for Analysis', *Party Politics*, 8:4, 389–403.

Ladrech, R. and P. Marliere (eds) (1999), *Social Democratic Parties in the European Union*, Basingstoke, Macmillan.

Lafontaine, O. (1998), 'How to Defeat Social Dumping: the Future of German Social Democracy', *New Left Review*, 227, 72–87.

Lafontaine, O. (2000), *The Heart Beats on the Left*, Oxford, Polity.

Laprat, G. (1979), 'Institutions communautaires: instruments de la supranationalité ou expression de la démocratie?', *Cahiers du Communisme*, February, 90–101.

Laprat, G. (1983), 'Une activité constructive conforme aux intérets de la France', *Cahiers du Communisme*, June, 80–7.

Laprat, G. (1984), 'Après l'échec du sommet d'athènes', *Cahiers du Communisme*, January, 68–75.

Laprat, G. (1985a), 'Le Groupe Communiste et Apparentés du Parlement Européen: Unité et Reconnaissance du Fait National', *Revue d'Intégration Européenne*, 1: Autumn, 81–105.

Laprat, G. (1985b), 'Les Groupes Politiques au Parlement Européen: la Dialectique de l'Unité et de la Diversité', *Revue du Marché Commun*, 286, 220–30.

Laprat, G. (1987), 'Le "grand marché" européen: 1992 ... et après', *Cahiers du Communisme*, July–August, 78–83.

Laroche, P. (1979), 'CEE: Italie', *Cahiers du Communisme*, March, 1979, 87–96.

Laroche, P. (1986a), 'Politiques pour le profit ou luttes pour sortir de la crise', *Cahiers du Communisme*, February, 82–91.

Laroche, P. (1986b), 'La situation italienne: enjeux, perspectives, questions', *Cahiers du Communisme*, July–August, 72–83.

Lazar, M. (1988), 'Communism in Western Europe in the 1980s', *Journal of Communist Studies*, 4:3, 243–57.

Lazard, F. (1989), 'Le quotidien, l'Europe et le rassemblement', *Cahiers du Communisme*, June, 16–22.

Le Digabel, J. (1992), 'Les communistes dans la campagne pour le non', *Cahiers du Communisme*, July–August, 20–5.

Le Duigou, J.-C. (1989), 'Pour les droits des travailleurs dans l'enterprise en europe', *Cahiers du Communisme*, June, 24–30.

Le Guen, R. (1992), 'Un France fort pour des coopérations sans domination', *Cahiers du Communisme*, June, 64–71.

Le Marec, J.-P. (1992), 'L'étau de la monnaie unique', *Cahiers du Communisme*, June, 72–8.

Lécureuil, C. (1996), 'Prospects for a European Party System after the 1994 European Elections', in J. Lodge (ed.), *The 1994 Elections to the European Parliament*, London, Pinter.

Left Alliance (VAS) (1990), *Campaign Program for Parliamentary Election 1991*, Helsinki, Left Alliance.

Left Alliance (VAS) (1993), *The Left-Wing Alliance and the European Community*, unpublished memo.

Left Alliance (VAS) (1995), *Left-Wing Alliance and the Development of the European Union*, Helsinki, Left Alliance.

Left Alliance (VAS) (1995a), *Left-Wing Alliance Party Programme Theses*, Helsinki, Left Alliance.

Left Alliance (VAS) (1995b), *Modern Left*, Helsinki, Left Alliance.

Left Alliance (VAS) (1996), *The Left-Wing Alliance in Government*, Helsinki, Left Alliance.

Left Alliance (VAS) (1999), *Modern Left: Special Edition*, Autumn, Helsinki, Left Alliance.

Left Alliance (VAS) (2000), *Modern Left: Ten Years of the Left Alliance*, Helsinki, Left Alliance.
Left Alliance (VAS) (2001), *More Freedom and Democracy: Policies for the Party Congress, 2001–2004*, Helsinki, Left Alliance.
Left Party (V) (1996), 'EMU, Employment and Social Rights', unpublished document.
Left Party (V) (2000), *A Socialist Offensive: Statement from the Left Party Congress, June 2000*, www.vansterpartiet.se/PUB_Material/3839.cs.
Left Party (V) (2002), *Our Four Cornerstones*, www.vansterpartiet.se/PUB_Material/3836.cs.
Leich, J. F. (1971), 'The Italian Communists and the European Parliament', *Journal of Common Market Studies*, 9:4, 271–81.
Levi, L. and S. Pistone (1990), 'L'Elezione del Parlamento europeo e i programmi dei partiti', *l'Italia e l'Europa*, 14, March, 11–162.
Lodge, J. (1984), 'European Union and the First Elected European Parliament: the Spinelli Initiative', *Journal of Common Market Studies*, 22:4, 377–402.
Lodge, J. (1996), *The 1994 Elections to the European Parliament*, London, Pinter.
Lodge, J. (2001), 'Invisible, Irrelevant but Insistent? Euro-elections and the European Parliament', in J. Lodge (ed.), *The 1999 Elections to the European Parliament*, Basingstoke, Palgrave.
Lodge, J. (ed.) (2001), *The 1999 Elections to the European Parliament*, Basingstoke, Palgrave.
Loeb-Mayer, N. (1983), 'Prospects for Relations between Communist and Socialist Parties in the European Parliament', *Quaderni Fondazione Feltrinelli*, 26, 31–54.
Loulis, J. C. (1986), 'The KKE at the Crossroads', *Journal of Communist Studies*, 2:2, 200–4.
Lucardie, P., J. van der Knoop, W. van Schuur and G. Voerman (1995), 'Greening the Reds or Reddening the Greens? The Case of the Green Left in the Netherlands', in W. Rudig (ed.), *Green Politics Three*, Edinburgh, Edinburgh University Press.
"l.v.m." (1976), 'Il XXII Congresso del Partito comunista francese', *Il Federalista*, 20–5.
McGiffen, S. P. (2001), *The European Union: a Critical Guide*, London, Pluto.
Macleod, A. (1980), 'The PCI's Relations with the PCF in the Age of Eurocommunism, May 1973–June 1979', *Studies in Comparative Communism*, 13:23, 168–96.
Macleod, A. (1983), 'The French and Italian Communist Parties and the Portuguese Revolution', in L. S. Graham and D. L. Wheeler (eds), *In Search of Modern Portugal: the Revolution and its Consequences*, Wisconsin, University of Wisconsin Press.
Maestro, Á (2002), *On the PCE Congress*, www.3bh.org.uk/IV/main/IV%20Archive/IV340/IV340%2016.htm.
Magone, J. (1996), 'Portugal', in J. Lodge (ed.), *The 1994 Elections to the European Parliament*, London, Pinter.
Magone, J. (2001), 'Portugal', in Lodge, J. (ed.), *The 1999 Elections to the European Parliament*, Basingstoke, Palgrave.
Manaille, M. (1996), 'Les raisons de combattre le projet de monnaie unique', *Cahiers du Communisme*, March, 25–7.
Marchais, G. (1982), 'Rapport du Comité Central au 24 Congrès du PCF', *Cahiers du Communisme*, February–March, 58–62.
Marcou, L. (1985), 'Le parti communiste Français et le mouvement communiste international', *Revue Politique et Parlementaire*, 914, 57–62.
Marcou, L. (1987), 'The Impossible Ally: a Survey of Western Communism in the 1980s', *Journal of Communist Studies*, 3:1, 71–80.

Marcussen, M. and M. Zolner (2001), 'The Danish EMU Referendum; Business as Usual', *Government and Opposition*, 36:3, 379–401.
Marijnissen, J. (1996), *Enough! A Socialist Bites Back*, The Netherland: Socialistische Partij.
Marquand, D. (1995), 'Reinventing Federalism: Europe and the Left', in D. Miliband (ed.), *Reinventing the Left*, Oxford, Polity.
Martell, L. (2001), *Social Democracy: Global and National Perspectives*, Basingstoke, Palgrave.
Marx, B. (1989a), 'What 1992 has in store for Europe', *World Marxist Review*, January, 79–84.
Marx, B. (1989b), 'Régression commune ou luttes et rapprochements des peuples pour le progrès', *Cahiers du Communisme*, April, 46–57.
Masson, G. (1989), 'Identité et souveraineté nationales, bases de véritables coopérations entre les peuples', *Cahiers du Communisme*, June, 32–7.
Masson, G. (1992), 'Maastricht ou la souveraineté nationale', *Cahiers du Communisme*, June, 27–33.
Mather, J. (2001), 'The European Parliament – a Model of Representative Democracy', *West European Politics*, 24: 1, 181–201.
Maxwell, K. (1980), 'The Communists and the Portuguese Revolution', *Dissent*, Spring, 194–206.
Menichini, S. (1991), 'Nuovo vecchio Pci: Dal Brancaccio, nel nome di Berlinguer, parte Rifondazione comunista', *Il Manifesto*, 12 February.
Merkel, W. (2001), 'The Third Ways of Social Democracy', in A. Giddens (ed.), *The Global Third Way Debate*, Oxford, Polity.
Miles, L., and A. Kintis (1996), 'The New Members: Sweden, Austria and Finland', in J. Lodge (ed.), *The 1994 Elections to the European Parliament*, London, Pinter.
Miliband, D. (ed.) (1995) *Reinventing the Left*, Oxford, Polity.
Miliband, R. (1994), *Socialism for a Sceptical Age*, Cambridge, Polity.
Milward, A. (1996), 'Approaching Reality: Euro-Money and the Left', *New Left Review*, 216, 55–65.
Minucci, A. (1989), *I Comunisti e l'Ultimo Capitalismo*, Roma, Newton Compton Editori.
Monbiot, G. (2003), 'The Bottom Dollar', *Guardian*, April 22.
Montani, G. (1986), 'Active Participation in the European Left is the only Alternative to the Decline of the Italian Communist Party (PCI)', *The Federalist*, 1, 39–43.
Mujal-León, E. (1983), *Communism and Political Change in Spain*, Bloomington, Indiana University Press.
Mujal-León, E. (1986), 'Decline and Fall of Spanish Communism', *Problems of Communism*, March–April, 1–27.
Murray, P. (1996), 'Nationalist or Internationalist? Socialists and European Unity', in Murray, P., and P. Rich (eds), *Visions of European Unity*, Boulder, Colorado, Westview Press.
Mussi, F. (1989), 'The Ideological Objectives of the Renewal', *World Marxist Review*, August, 43–7.
Napolitano, G. (1983), 'Governare da sinistra un arduo periodo di transizione', *Critica Marxista*, January–February, 61–72.
Napolitano, G. (1987), 'Due esperienze a confronto', *Critica Marxista*, September–October, 5–9.
Napolitano, G. (1989), *Oltre i Vecchi Confini: il Futuro della Sinistra e l'Europa*, Milano, Mondadori Editore.

Natta, A. (1989), *I Tre Tempi del Presente,* Milano, Edizioni Paoline.
Neunreither, K. (2001), 'The European Union in Nice', *Government and Opposition,* 36:2, 184–208.
Newell, J. L. (2000), *Parties and Democracy in Italy,* Aldershot, Ashgate.
Nielson, H. J. (1996), 'Denmark', in J. Lodge (ed.), *The 1994 Elections to the European Parliament,* London, Pinter.
Nielson, H. J. (2001), 'Denmark', in J. Lodge (ed.), *The 1999 Elections to the European Parliament,* Basingstoke, Palgrave.
O'Neill, M. (1997), 'New Politics, Old Predicaments: the Case of the European Greens', *Political Quarterly,* 68:1, 50–67.
Paavonen, T. (2001), 'From Isolation to the Core: Finland's Position Towards European Integration, 1960–1995', *Journal of European Integration History,* 7:1, 53–75.
Paggi, L. (1982), 'I comunisti italiani e l'esperienza delle società occidentali', *Critica Marxista,* July–August, 95–111.
Paggi, L. and M. d'Angelillo (1989), *I Comunisti Italiani e il Riformismo: Un Confronto con le Socialdemocrazie Europee,* Torino, Einaudi.
Party of Communist Refoundation (PRC) (1999), 'Un'alternativa per l'Europa. Pace, lavoro, democrazia. Il Programma di Rifondazione per le elezioni europee del 13 Giugno 1999', Roma, PRC.
Party of Communist Refoundation (PRC) (2000), *Document on International Policy,* www.rifondazione.it/internazionale/doc/doce/dir20000629eng.html.
Party of European Socialists (1999), 'Manifesto for the 1999 European Elections', www.pes.org/upload/publications/39EN14_en.pdf.
Party of Italian Communists (PdCI) (1999), 'Più Europa per tutti: un governo federale europeo per una Europa solidale e di pace', www.gue-ngl-pdci.com/iniziative.
Pasquino, G. (1979), 'Eurocommunism: Challenge to West and East', *Problems of Communism,* September–December, 85–91.
Pasquino, G. (1987), *Una Certa Idea della Sinistra,* Milano, Saggi Tascabili Laterza.
Patricio, M. T. (1990) , 'Orthodoxy and Dissent in the Portuguese Communist Party', *Journal of Communist Studies,* 6:4, 204–8.
Perlmutter, T. (1990), 'The PCI: from Historic Compromise to Reconstitution', *Problems of Communism,* September–October, 93–8.
Pharakos, G., and G. Cervetti, G. (1988), 'Communists in Western Europe: Retreat or Build-up of Forces? Two Views of the Problem', *World Marxist Review,* October, 82–5.
Pieralli, P. (1985), 'Il Pci e la politica estera dell'Italia (1975–1985)', *La Politica,* 3–4, December.
Piquet, R. (1990), 'The quest for unity', *Making Sense,* 14, January–February, 16–7.
Polillo, G. and P. Valenza (eds) (1990), *Noi Reformisti: Per Una Cultura di Governo della Sinistra,* Napoli, CUEN.
Pontusson, J. (1994), 'Sweden: After the Golden Age', in P. Anderson and P. Camiller (eds), *Mapping the West European Left,* London, Verso.
Portelli, H. (1980), 'La "politique étrangère" de la gauche Française', *Projet,* 146, June, 715–8.
Portuguese Communist Party (PCP) (1992), *Sur le Traité de Maastricht,* Lisbon, Portuguese Communist Party.
Portuguese Communist Party (1994a), *The PCP and the European Parliament Elections: resolution of the Central Committee,* Lisbon, Portuguese Communist Party.

Portuguese Communist Party (PCP) (1994b), *The Economic, Social and Political Situation in Community Europe*, Lisbon, Portuguese Communist Party.
Portuguese Communist Party (PCP) (1995), *The PCP's Position on the 1996 Inter-Government Conferences for the revision of the Treaty of European Union*, Lisbon, Portuguese Communist Party.
Portuguese Communist Party (PCP) (1999a), *Eleições para o Parlamento Europeu 13 de Junho de 1999 – Declaração Programática*, Lisbon, Portuguese Communist Party.
Portuguese Communist Party (PCP) (1999b), *União Europeia e Portugal*, Lisbon, Portuguese Communist Party.
Portuguese Communist Party (PCP) (2000), 'Theses of the 16th Party Congress', www.pcp.pt/english/xvi-congress/teses1.html
Portuguese Communist Party (PCP) (2001), 'A vitória do Não na Irlanda', www.pcp.pt/actpol/temas/uniao-eu/no20010608.html.
Prevost, G. (1981), 'Eurocommunism and the Spanish Communists', *West European Politics*, 4:1, 69–83.
Prospero, M. (1990), *Il Nuovo Inizio: dal PCI di Berlinguer al Partitio Democratico della Sinistra*, Chieti, Métis.
Qvortrup, M. (2001), 'How to Lose a Referendum: the Danish Plebiscite on the Euro', *Political Quarterly*, 72:1, 190–6.
Qvortrup, M. (2002), 'The Danish Referendum on Euro Entry, September 2000', *Electoral Studies*, 21:3, 493–8.
Raby, D. (1989), 'The Twelfth Congress of the Portuguese Communist Party', Journal of Communist Studies, 5:2, 220–2.
Ranger, J. (1986), 'Le Déclin du P.C.F.', *Revue Française de Science Politique*, 36:1, 46–63.
Raunio, T. (1999), 'Facing the European Challenge: Finnish Parties Adjust to the Integration Process', *West European Politics*, 22:1, 138–59.
Raunio, T. (2001a), 'Finland', in J. Lodge (ed.), *The 1999 Elections to the European Parliament*, Basingstoke, Palgrave.
Raunio, T. (2001b), 'The Party System of the European Parliament after the 1999 Elections', in J. Lodge (ed.), *The 1999 Elections to the European Parliament*, Basingstoke, Palgrave.
Raunio, T. (2002), 'Why European Integration Increases Leadership Autonomy within Political Parties', *Party Politics*, 8:4, 405–22.
Richardson, D. and C. Rootes (eds) (1995), *The Green Challenge: the Development of Green Parties in Europe*, London, Routledge.
Roberts, G. (1999), 'Developments in the German Green Party, 1995–1999', *Environmental Politics*, 8:3, 147–52.
Roca, J. M. (1992), 'Changes in the Ranks of Spanish Communism, 1991–92', *Journal of Communist Studies*, 8:3, 140–4.
Rosenmöller, P. (2001), 'The Future of Europe is Now', speech to the Council of the European Federation of Green Parties, unpublished.
Ross, G. (1992), 'Confronting the New Europe', *New Left Review*, 191, 49–68.
Ross, G., and J. Jenson (1994), 'France: Triumph and Tragedy', in P. Anderson and P. Camiller (eds), *Mapping the West European Left*, London, Verso.
Rossanda, R. (1979), 'Troppe sinistre, nessuna sinistra per l'Europa', *Problemi del Socialismo*, January–March, 119–31.
Rubbi, A. (1989), 'The "New Internationalism": a Drama with a Happy Ending?', *World Marxist Review*, April, 61–5.

Rudig, W. (1996), 'Green Parties and the European Union', in J. Gaffney (ed.), *Political Parties and the European Union*, London, Routledge.
Ruscoe, J. (1982), *The Italian Communist Party, 1976–81*, Basingstoke: Macmillan.
Sacco, G. (1979), 'PCI e PCF di fronte al contesto economico internazionale', *Nord e Sud*, 5, January–March, 99–124.
Sainteny, G. (1995), 'French Communism: the Challenge of Environmentalism and Ecologism', *West European Politics*, 18:4, 110–29.
Sassoon, D. (1976), 'The Italian Communist Party's European Strategy', *Political Quarterly*, 47:3, 253–75.
Sassoon, D. (1979), 'Eurocommunism, the Labour Party and the EEC', *Political Quarterly*, 50:1, 86–99.
Sassoon, D. (1981), *The Strategy of the Italian Communist Party*, New York, Pinter.
Sassoon, D. (1996a), *Social Democracy at the Heart of Europe*, London, Institute of Public Policy Research.
Sassoon, D. (1996b), *One Hundred Years of Socialism: the Western European Left in the Twentieth Century*, London, Fontana.
Schiavone, A. (1989), *La Sinistra del Terzo Capitalismo*, Bari, Saggi Tascabili Laterza.
Sechi, S. (1982), 'Il Pcf: partito di governo o partito al governo?', *Il Mulino*, January–February, 52–82.
Segre, S. (1983), 'Europa comunitaria: fermi non si può stare', *Politica ed Economia*, January, 5–6.
Seppänen, E. (2000a), *Esko Seppänen profile*, www.kaapeli.fi/Seppanen/English/ CV2000.htm.
Seppänen, E. (2000b), *The Enlargement of the European Union*,www.kaapeli.fi/Seppanen/English/enlarge htm.
Seppänen, E. (2001), *The Effects of EMU on Finland*, www.kaapeli.fi/Seppanen/English/speachintallinn.htm.
Seppänen, E. (2002), *What is Democracy?*, www.kaapeli.fi/Seppanen/English/whatisdemocracy.htm.
Serfaty, S. (1977), 'The Italian Communist Party and Europe: Historically Compromised?', *Atlantic Community Quarterly*, 15, autumn, 275–87.
Setien, J. (2002), *Neither Half Full nor Half Empty*, www.3bh.org/IV/main/IV%20Archive/IV340/IV340%2017.htm.
Sitter, N. (2001), 'The Politics of Opposition and European Integration in Scandinavia', *West European Politics*, 24:4, 22–39.
Siune, K. (1993), 'The Danes Say No to the Maastricht Treaty: the Danish EC referendum of June 1992', *Scandinavian Political Studies*, 16:1, 93–103.
Sjöstedt, J. (2000), 'Speech at Danish Socialist People's Party Congress', unpublished document.
Social Democratic Party of Germany (SPD) (1986), *I Programmi della Socialdemocrazia Tedesca*, Roma, Editori Riuniti.
Socialist People's Party (SF) (1987), *International Bulletin*, 2, Copenhagen, Socialist People's Party.
Socialist People's Party (SF) (1988), *International Bulletin*, 1, Copenhagen, Socialist People's Party.
Socialist People's Party (SF) (1991a), *International Bulletin*, 1, Copenhagen, Socialist People's Party.
Socialist People's Party (SF) (1991b), *International Bulletin*, 2, Copenhagen, Socialist People's Party.

Socialist People's Party (SF) 1992a), *International Bulletin*, 1, Copenhagen, Socialist People's Party.
Socialist People's Party (SF) (1992b), *The Danes Say No to Maastricht!* Copenhagen, Socialist People's Party.
Socialist People's Party (SF) (1995), *The Proposals of the Socialist People's Party Denmark for the 1996 Intergovernmental Conference*, Copenhagen, Socialist Peoples Party.
Socialist People's Party (SF) (1998), *International Bulletin*, 2, Copenhagen, Socialist People's Party.
Socialist People's Party (SF) (2000), *SF's Statement on the EMU adopted by the national congress in Vordingborg May 19th–21st 2000*, Copenhagen, Socialist People's Party.
Sodara, M. J. (1984), 'Whatever Happened to Eurocommunism', *Problems of Communism*, November–December, 59–65.
Spinelli, A. (1975), 'La nostra battaglia per l'Unione europa', *l'Italia e l'Europa*, 7–8, 39–55.
Spinelli, A. (1983), 'Verso l'Unione europea', *Il Federalista*, 115–30.
Spinelli, A. (1986), *Discorsi al Parlamento Europeo*, Bologna, il Mulino.
Steinkühler, M. (1982), 'Eurocommunism After the Polish Repression', *Aussenpolitik*, 33:4, 323–47.
Steinkühler, M. (1985), 'Eurocommunism – a Strategy that Failed?', *Aussenpolitik*, 36:4, 376–87.
Stephens, P. (2001), 'The Blair Government and Europe', *Political Quarterly*, 72:1, 67–75.
Svasand, L. and U. Lindström (1996), 'Scandinavian Political Parties and the European Union', in J. Gaffney (ed.), *Political Parties and the European Union*, London, Routledge.
Svensson, P. (1994), 'The Danish Yes to Maastricht and Edinburgh: the EC referendum of May 1993', *Scandinavian Political Studies*, 17:1, 69–82.
Swidler, L. and E. Grace (eds) (1988), *Catholic-Communist Collaboration in Italy*, London: University Press of America.
Szajkowski, B. (ed.) (1980), *Documents in Communist Affairs, 1980*, Basingstoke, Macmillan.
Szajkowski, B. (ed.) (1983), *Documents in Communist Affairs, 1983*, Basingstoke, Macmillan.
Taggart, P. (1998), 'A Touchstone of Dissent: Euroscepticism in Contemporary Western European Party Systems', *European Journal of Political Research*, 33: 3, 363–88.
Teasdale, A. (2000), 'The Politics of the 1999 European Elections', *Government and Opposition*, 34:4, 433–55.
Tegyey, G. (1978), 'Partis et Groupe Politiques du PE: Communistes et Appartentés', *Objectif Europe*, December, 37–8.
Teló, M. (1985), 'Some of the Conditions Needed for the Peace Policy of the West European Left', *Socialism in the World*, 47–8.
Teló, M. (1985), 'Il Pci dall'eurocomunismo all'eurosinistra', *Problemi del Socialismo*, 6, September–December, 216–25.
Therborn, G. (1997), 'Europe in the Twenty-First Century', in P. Gowan and P. Anderson (eds), *The Question of Europe*, London, Verso.
Tiersky, R. (1988), 'Declining Fortunes of the French Communist Party', *Problems of Communism*, September–October, 1–22.
Timmermann, H. (1979), 'The Eurocommunists and the West', *Problems of Communism*, May–June, 31–54.
Timmermann, H. (1989), 'The Communist Party of the Soviet Union's Reassessment of International Social Democracy: Dimensions and Trends', *Journal of Communist Studies*, 5:2, 173–84.
Trivelli, R. (1989), 'The PCI's Decline is not Inevitable', *World Marxist Review*, March, 38–40.

United Democratic Coalition (1994), *Encontro Nacional sobre as Eleiçoes Para o Parlamento Europeu*, Lisbon, CDU.
United Left (1993), 'A New Europe in a New World,' unpublished document.
United Left (1996), 'Reforming Maastricht: Economic Aspects', unpublished document.
United Left (IU) (1997), *La Revisión del Tratado de la Unión Europea. Documento Estrasburgo III*, unpublished document.
Urban, G. (1978), 'Have They Really Changed?: a Conversation with Altiero Spinelli', *Encounter*, 50:1, 7–27.
Urban, J. B. (1986), *Moscow and the Italian Communist Party: From Togliatti to Berlinguer*, London, I. B. Tauris.
Valentini, C. (1997), *Berlinguer: L'eredità difficile*, Roma, Editori Riuniti.
Verney, S. (1987), 'The Spring of the Greek Left: Two Party Congresses', *Journal of Communist Studies*, 3:4, 166–70.
Verney, S. (1988), 'The New Red Book of the KKE: The Renewal That Never Was', *Journal of Communist Studies*, 4:3, 170–3.
Verney, S. (1996), 'The Greek Socialists', in J. Gaffney (ed.), *Political Parties and the European Union*, London, Routledge.
Verney, S. and K. Featherstone (1996), 'Greece', in J. Lodge (ed.), *The 1994 Elections to the European Parliament*, London, Pinter.
Vinci, L. (1995), 'I tratti portanti di politica economica dell'attuale costruzione europea', unpublished speech.
Vinci, L. (1996a), 'Intervento sulle questioni e sull'itinerario della ricostruzione dell'antagonismo politico organizzato in Europa occidentale', unpublished speech.
Vinci, L. (1996b), 'Come Rifondazione Comunista lotta, nelle nuove condizioni politiche italiane, contro l'Europa di Maastricht', unpublished draft article.
Vinci, L. (1996c), 'Intervento al 3 congresso nazionale di PRC', unpublished paper.
Waller, M. (1988), 'West European Communism – Red for "Stop", Green for "Go"', *The World Today*, March, 43–6.
Waller, M. (1989a), 'The Radical Sources of the Crisis in West European Communist Parties', *Political Studies*, 38, 39–61.
Waller, M. (1989b), 'Les Partis Communistes Ouest-Européens à l'Heure Gorbatchev', special issue of *Problémes Politiques et Sociaux*, 608, 1–63.
Waller, M. and M. Fennema (eds) (1988), *Communist Parties in Western Europe: Decline or Adaptation*, Oxford, Oxford University Press.
Webb, C. (1979), 'Eurocommunism and the European Communities', *Journal of Common Market Studies*, 17:3, 236–58.
Webster, P. (1992), 'French Left Finds Ammunition to Fire up Listless Campaign', *Guardian*, 16 September.
Weekly Worker (2002), *Anti-Capitalism: Slow Progress for ESF*, www.cpgb.org.uk/worker/436/progress.html.
Wilde, L. (1994), *Modern European Socialism*, Aldershot, Dartmouth.
Wilson, F. L. (1985), 'French Communism on the Defensive', *Problems of Communism*, November–December, 77–84.
Wilson, F. L. (1992), 'Communism at the Crossroads: Changing Roles in Western Democracies', *Problems of Communism*, May–June, 95–106.
Wurtz, F. (1992), 'Un nouveau project Européen', *Cahiers du Communisme*, June, 5–11.
Wurtz, F. (1996), 'Changer l'Europe', Paris, French Communist Party.

Yergin, A. S. (1979), 'West Germany's Sudpolitik: Social Democrats and Eurocommunism', *Orbis*, 23, 51–71.
Zilliaius, K. (2001), '"New Politics" in Finland: the Greens and the Left-Wing in the 1990s', *West European Politics*, 24:1, 21–54.

Index

Note: page numbers in **bold** refer to main entries.

Aaronovitch, Sam 13–15
Afghanistan, Soviet invasion of 40, 57
Almunia, Joaquin 129
Amendola, Giorgio 53, 54–5, 75, 77
Amsterdam Treaty 18
Andersson, Claes 141, 144
Andersson, Jan-Otto 145
Anguita, Julio 68, 126–7, 129
Azcárate, Manuel 122

Berlinguer, Enrico 37, 43, 45–8 *passim*,
    54–5, 57, 63, 81, 82, 87
    on new internationalism 44
Berlinguer, Marco 87, 173
Bertoli, Giovanni 75
Bolis, Luciano 67
British Labour Party 163
Brito, Carlos 115
Butler, A. 11

Callinicos, Alex 15–16
Camiller, Patrick 8
CAP *see* Common Agricultural Policy
Carchedi, G. 16–18
Carrillo, Santiago 25, 33, 33–4, 124–5
Carvalhas, Carlos 118, 121
    and Marxism-Leninism 119
Castellina, Luciana, on EEC, opposition
    to 3–4
centre-left governments 16, 22, 166–7
    see also social democratic parties
Cervetti, Gianni 83
Chevènement, Jean-Pierre, Citizens'
    Movement 100, 163
Choliere, Yves
    and North Atlantic Treaty Organisation
    98

Christensen, N. F. 133–4
Cohn-Bendit, Daniel 102, 161
Common Agricultural Policy 12, 17
Communist and Allies Group, 53, **54–69**
    and Community enlargement 59–61
    and Community institutional
        development 61–5
    and economic and social policy 57–8
    function and role of 65–9
    and Mediterranean policy 59–60
    see also Group for a Unitary European
        Left; Left Unity Group
communist parties 1, 23
Communist Party of Greece 36, **103–8**
    and Communist and Allies Group 60
    and defections 106–7
    and electoral support 105, 107–8
    and EU, Greek membership of 108
    and Greek independence 104
    and Left Coalition 106
    and PASOK 104–5
    and single currency 107
    and Single Market 105–6
Communist Party of Greece – Interior 29,
    34–5, 42, **108–9**
    and Communist and Allies Group 60
    and EC, Greek membership of 109
    and electoral support 109
    see also Greek Left; Synaspismos
Communist Party of Spain 25, 30, 36–7, 42,
    51, **121–31**
    and Communist and Allies Group 59–60
    and dissension 130
    and European commitment 121–2
    and Italian Communist Party 123
    and Leninism 32–3
    and Maastricht Treaty 124

and Portuguese events (1974–76) 38, 39
and Spanish Socialist Workers' Party 39
see also Eurocommunism; Izquierda Unida
Confederal Group of the European United Left / Nordic Green Left 6, 172, 173
Convention on the Future of Europe 167
Cossutta, Armando 90
Crocodile Club 63
Cunhal, Alvaro 114–15, 117, 119

d'Alema, Massimo 85
Damanaki, Maria 110
Danish Socialist People's Party 51, 62, 65, 69, **131–9**
 and Amsterdam Treaty 137
 and Danish autonomy 132
 and EEC, alternatives to 133–4
 electoral support 138
 European election programme (1999) 137–8
 and euro referendum 138
 and Group for a Unitary European Left 132–3
 ideological heritage 131–2
 and Maastricht Treaty referendums 135–6, 136–7
 orientation, debate on 137
 and Single European Act 132, 133
 and Treaty of Rome 134–5
Delors, Jacques 2, 165
democratic centralism 34–5
Democratic Party of the Left (Italy) 37, 52, 82, 164
Diaz Lopez, C.-E. 32–3
Digabel, Jacques Le 100
Draft Treaty on European Union 3, 63–4
Dubcek, Alexander 61
Duisenberg, Wim 166
Dutch Green Left 173

economic and social cohesion 170
El Socialism del Futuro 52
environment, the 170
ETA 128
EU expansion 171
Eurocommunism 24–40 *passim*, 48, 52
 demise of 39–40
 and Leninist tradition 32
 and Portuguese events (1974–76) 38, 39
 as a transitional platform 27
Eurocommunist parties **24–40**
 and Afghanistan, Soviet invasion of 40
 and democracy 37
 and Moscow, interference from 28
 and Poland, martial law in 40–1
 and socialism, vision of 26
 summit meetings 26
'Euro-left' 40, 43–7 *passim*, 52
European Central Bank 12
European Communist and Workers' Parties
 Berlin conference (1976) 26
 Paris conference (1980) 41–3 *passim*
European constitution 11–12
European democracy 170–1
European Federation of Green Parties 162
'Euroscepticism' 7

Fanti, Guido 63
Featherstone, K. 19
Finland 142
Finnish Communist Party **139–41**
 electoral support 140
 in government 139–40
 see also Finnish Left Alliance
Finnish Left Alliance **141–7**
 electoral support 144
 and EU constitution 146
 and European Parliament 146
 in government 143
 and Intergovernmental Conference (1996) 143
 and single currency 146, 147
 tendencies within 145
 and 'third left' 141
Fischer, Joschka 158, 161
Florakis, Harilaos 104, 106, 108
 on PASOK 104–5
Folena, Pietro 52
'Fortress Europe' 170
French Communist Party 19, 21, 25–7 *passim*, 36, 54, 75, **91–103**
 and Communist and Allies Group 54, 56–7, 66–7, 68
 and democracy 37

dissidents 52
and electoral support 26–7, 99–101 *passim*, 102–3
and European election manifesto (1979) 93–5
and European Parliament 58, 92–3
and Italian Communist Party 30–2, 54, 58, 59–62 *passim*, 64, 65–8, 92, 94, 96–7
and Left Unity Group 68, 70
and Maastricht referendum 100
and *Mouvement des Rénovateurs Communistes* 31
and nationalist rhetoric 95
and NATO 98
and Portuguese events (1974–76) 38
and *rassemblement des forces de la gauche* 36
retrenchment of 41–2, 43
and Single European Act 96, 97–8
and Socialist Party 100–1
and Spinelli 66–7
and Union of the Left 36
see also Eurocommunism
Frutos, Francisco 129, 130

globalisation 14
Glotz, Peter, on social democracy 49
Gorbachev, Mikhail 45, 107
Grahl, John 13–15
Greece 122
Greek Left 35, 51, 52, 106
Greens **157–63**, 167–8
and Confederal Group of the European United Left / Nordic Green Left 162–3
and diversity 159–60
and ecological sustainability 158–9
European 156
and Europe of the Regions 160
and federalist ideas 157–8
Finnish 144
French 102
German 158, 168
and global-local nexus 159
and grassroots democracy 159
and the Left 160, 161, 168
and Maastricht Treaty 162
Swedish 161
UK 161
Greens / European Free Alliance 162
Gremetz, Maxime, on France's international role 95
Group for a Unitary European Left 48, 50, 61, 68, **68–70**
GUE / NGL *see* Confederal Group of the European United Left / Nordic Green Left

Habermas, Jurgen 13
on 'third way' 9–11
Herzog, Philippe 99
Hobsbawm, Eric, on federalism 12–13
Hue, Robert 36, 99, 101, 102–3

Iglesias, Gerardo 125
Ingrao, Pietro 78–9
Iraq war (2003) 9, 167
Irish Workers' Party 70
Italian Communist Party 6, 26–7, 30, 33, 34, 37, 39–40, 42, 52–3, **72–87**
and Communist and Allies Group 54–6, 58, 59–62 *passim*, 64, 65–8
electoral support 26–7
and Eurocommunist partners 51–2
and 'Euro-left' 40, 43–7
and European election programmes (1979) 7985–6
European role of 47–8
and federalism 82–4
and French Communist Party 30–2, 54, 58, 59–62 *passim*, 64, 65–8
and 'historic compromise' 25, 55
and national sovereignty 75
and NATO 81–2
and 'new internationalism' 38–9, 44, 45–6
and Portuguese events (1974–76) 38, 39
and social democracy 84
and social democratic parties 49–50
and Socialist Group 48, 51
and Soviet assessment of Community 74
and Spanish Socialist Workers' Party 52

and Spinelli 25, 77–8, 80
and third way 46
in transition 48–51
see also Democratic Party of the Left;
Eurocommunism; Party of
Communist Refoundation
Italy, and Europe, place in 76–7
IU *see* Izquierda Unida
Iversen, John 132, 137
Izquierda Unida 34, 52, 124, 124–30 *passim*
electoral support 125, 129
and ETA 128
and Kosovo war 128–9
and Maastricht Treaty 125–6
and Spanish Communist Party 127–8

Jospin, Lionel 101, 102
Jotti, Nilde 67, 76

Kapetanyannis, B. 34–5
KKE *see* Communist Party of Greece
KKE-es *see* Communist Party of Greece – Interior

Lafontaine, Oskar 12, 15–16, 166
Laprat, Gérard
on Communist and Allies Group 67
on Single Market 97
Larsen, Aksel 131, 132
Left intellectuals 18–19
Left Party of Sweden **148–55**
electoral support 150–1, 153, 155
and EMU 151–2, 154
reformist path 148–9
and single currency 151, 154
and Social Democratic government 152–3, 155
socialist nature of 153–4
Left Unity Group 61, 70
Lizarra, Pact of 128
Llamazares, Gaspar 129, 130
Longo, Luigi 74
l'Humanité 66
l'Unità 34

Maastricht Treaty 8–9, 13–15, 169
convergence criteria 17–18
McGiffen, S.P. 17, 18

Maestro, Angeles 130–1
Marchais, Georges 25, 34, 43, 104
Marquand, David 8
Marx, Bernard 98, 99
Masson, Gilles 100
Miliband, Ralph, *Socialism for a Sceptical Age* 15
Mitterrand government 2
Monbiot, George 9
Moscovici, Pierre 102

Napolitano, Giorgio 37, 69, 70, 83
NATO *see* North Atlantic Treaty Organisation
Natta, Alessandro 34, 48
New European Left Forum 21, 172–3
'new internationalism' 38–9, 44, 45–6
New Right, neo–liberalism 2
Nice Treaty 12
North Atlantic Treaty Organisation 81–2, 98, 102, 171

Occhetto, Achille 34, 68, 69–70, 82

Palero, Francisco 124
Pancaldi, Augusto 31
Papariga, Aleka 106
Party of Communist Refoundation **87–90**, 90–1, 173
and Maastricht Treaty 88–9
and split 90
see also Party of Italian Communists
Party of Democratic Socialism (Germany) 168, 173
Party of European Socialists 165
see also social democratic parties
party federations 21
Party of Italian Communists 90
PASOK 104, 104–5
PCE *see* Communist Party of Spain
PCF *see* French Communist Party
PCI *see* Italian Communist Party
PCP *see* Portuguese Communist Party
PdCI *see* Party of Italian Communists
PDS (Germany) *see* Party of Democratic Socialism
PDS (Italy) *see* Democratic Party of the Left

Persson, Goran 153, 155
Pharakos, Grigoris 106
Piquet, René 68
Poland, martial law 40–1
political parties, policy formation 19–21
Portugal 122
Portuguese Communist Party 36, 42, 113–21
    and CDU (United Democratic Coalition) 116, 117
    and Communist and Allies Group 60
    dissenters 116
    electoral support 114, 116, 117, 118–19
    European election programmes (1989) 116; (1994) 116–17; (1999) 119–20
    and French Communist Party 114
    and international situation 120
    and Maastricht Treaty 116–17
    and national-communism 113–14
    and 1974–76 events 38
    and single currency 118
    and Single European Act 115
PRC *see* Party of Communist Refoundation
protectionism 10
PS *see* Socialist Party

regional policies 170
Rhineland capitalism 16
Rochet, Waldeck 92
Rosenmöller, Paul 161
Rubbi, Antonio 45
Rumsfeld, Donald 9

SAP *see* Social Democratic Workers' Party (Sweden)
Sassoon, Donald 1, 44
Schyman, Gudrun 149–50, 155
Seabra, Zita 115
Seppänen, Esko 144, 146–7
Setien, Julio 130
SF *see* Danish Socialist People's Party
Siimes, Suvi-Anne 144
Single European Act 64, 84, 96, 97–8
Sjöstedt, Jonas 151
    on single currency 154
social democracy
    Glotz's vision of 49
    Italian Communist Party's case for 84

social democratic parties 1, 49–50, **163–7**
    and Amsterdam Treaty 166
    divided 165–6
    in government alliances 165
    and Maastricht Treaty revisions 165
    record in office 167
Social Democratic Party of Germany 49, 163, 164
Social Democratic Workers' Party (Sweden) 154–5
Social Democrats 156, 167–8 *passim*
    and 'New Right' 163
    see also social democratic parties
Socialist Party (France) 100–1, 163, 164
Spain 122
Spanish Socialist Workers' Party 39, 52
SPD *see* Social Democratic Party of Germany
Spinelli, Altiero 25, 28, 42, 59, 61, 63–5 *passim*, 80
    and Communist and Allies Group 55–6
    and Crocodile Club 63
    on French Communist Party 54, 66–7
    on Italian Communist Party 62, 77–8
Stability Pact 102, 169
Stalinist regimes, collapse of 22–3
Straw, Jack 12
Sund, Ralf 146
supranationality 171–2
Swedish Communist Party, Left Party-Communists, renamed 148
    see also Left Party of Sweden
Synaspismos **110–12**, 173
    and Amsterdam Treaty 111–12
    electoral support 110
    and European election programme (1999) 112
    and Greek Communist Party 111
    and Greek foreign policy 110–11

Taggart, P., on 'Euroscepticism' 7
third way 9–11, 46
    changed meaning of 47
Third Way governments 16
Tindemans, Leo, Report on European Union 61

Treaty of Rome 4, 18
Trentin, Bruno 72–3
Trotskyist parties 102, 103, 173

Union of the Left (France) 92
Union of Soviet Socialist Republics,
    collapse of 3
United States of America 9, 167, 171
USA *see* United States of America
USSR *see* Union of Soviet Socialist
    Republics

V *see* Left Party of Sweden
vanguardism 35–7
VAS *see* Finnish Left Alliance
Vinci, Luigi 88–9
Voight, Karsten 50

Wilde, L. 8–9